PROBLEMS and CONFLICTS BETWEEN LAW and MORALITY in a FREE SOCIETY

PROBLEMS AND CONFLICTS BETWEEN

Law and Morality

IN A FREE SOCIETY

JAMES E. WOOD, JR. & DEREK DAVIS, Editors

J.M. DAWSON INSTITUTE OF CHURCH-STATE STUDIES

Baylor University • Waco, Texas 76798-7308

Published by the J.M. Dawson Institute of Church-State Studies
Baylor University
Waco, Texas 76798-7308
USA

PROBLEMS AND CONFLICTS
BETWEEN LAW AND MORALITY
IN A FREE SOCIETY

Address correspondence to
J.M. Dawson Institute of Church-State Studies
P.O. Box 97308, Baylor University, Waco, Texas 76798 USA

FIRST EDITION 1994

Library of Congress Cataloging-in-Publication Data
Preassigned Catalog Card Number: 93-07295

International Standard Book Numbers:
ISBN 0-929182-19-7(CLOTH)   ISBN 0-929182-20-0(PAPER)

Prepared camera ready by the publications staff of J.M. Dawson Institute of
Church-State Studies using Mass-11 TM Version 8.0© Microsystems Engineering
Corporation on Vax 8700 minicomputer by Digital Equipment Corporation
printing to Varityper VT600W using Palatino typeface. The latter is trademarked
by Allied Corporation. Software licensed to Baylor University.

Contents

PREFACE

The relevance of the subject of this volume, "Problems and Conflicts Between Law and Morality in a Free Society," to contemporary American society and, indeed, to the very maintenance of a free and pluralistic society, can hardly be overstated. During the past several decades, problems and conflicts between law and morality have been greatly exacerbated in the United States, and throughout much of the world, by the forces of a continuing social revolution and the resurgence of a highly politicized religious ethos that is bent upon turning moral absolutes, based upon one's religion, into public law.

Admittedly, many thorny constitutional and legal questions arise in a free society in addressing questions bearing on law and morality, both for lawmakers and lawbreakers. There are those inevitable tensions, and even conflicts, which arise between the claims of morality— which for many is based on religious morality— and law. What is lawful for many may not be moral, and what is moral for some may not be lawful. Such conflicts arise when the individual, because of conscience, has to choose whether or not to obey the law and when those persons who make and uphold the law have to decide whether or not to treat someone with a moral claim to disobey the law differently from other persons who violate the same law(s). This volume seeks to address a wide range of the conflicts and problems between law and morality in a free and secular state where there are constitutional guarantees forbidding "an establishment of religion" and "prohibiting the free exercise of religion." This volume is the last of a three-volume series planned for publication by the J. M. Dawson Institute of Church-State Studies. The two earlier volumes, *The Role of Religion in the Making of Public Policy* (1991) and *The Role of Government in Monitoring and Regulating Religion in Public Life* (1993) addressed the prior questions relating to the role of religion in public affairs and the role of government in religious affairs. This volume is concerned with a third dimension in church-state relations, one that revolves around law and morality— the latter with its close association with religion— and the problems and conflicts that arise between them in the enactment and enforcement of law.

As in the two previous volumes of this series, the essays in this volume were expressly prepared for presentation at a symposium held at Baylor University under the auspices of the J. M. Dawson Institute of Church-State Studies. The essays in this volume, although they were originally written for publication in this volume, were initially presented at the symposium on "Problems and Conflicts Between Law and Morality in a Free Society," held at Baylor University, 5-6 April 1993. All of the essays in this volume have been to some degree revised and expanded for publication in this volume.

As in the two previous symposia, registrants for this symposium included persons from a number of colleges and universities, representing a wide range of academic disciplines. The well over one hundred registrants included a variety of religious traditions — Protestant, Catholic and Jewish— in addition to Baylor faculty and students. Organizations represented included the National Association of Independent Colleges and Universities, the Association of Catholic Colleges and Universities, Americans United, and numerous Protestant denominations.

Special acknowledgment is made here, first of all, to the authors for their original essays, which were first presented at the symposium and expressly prepared for inclusion in this volume. The seriousness and creativity of the authors are reflected in the essays themselves. In addition, appreciation is expressed here to our colleagues who, in a variety of ways, are directly involved in the programs of the Institute, for their contribution to and support of the symposium: Robert M. Baird, Rosalie Beck, James A. Curry, David W. Hendon, Glenn O. Hilburn, David L. Longfellow, Robert T. Miller, Harold W. Osborne, Bob E. Patterson, Stuart Rosenbaum, Bradley J. B. Toben, and Charles M. Tolbert; to Wanda Gilbert and Janice Losak for their contributions in the planning, promotion, and registration for the symposium; and to Brian A. Marcus and Zhao-qi Zhang for their preparation of the index for this volume. As in the case of the two previous volumes of this series, a very special word of acknowledgment belongs to Patricia Cornett for her able and tireless editorial assistance and for creating the camera-ready copy for publication of this volume.

Finally, we are pleased to express a special word of gratitude to The Pew Charitable Trusts for their grant to assist the J. M. Dawson Institute of Church-State Studies at Baylor University in convening the third symposium in this series and in supporting the publication of this third volume; their generous support of the work of the Institute in this endeavor is deeply appreciated.

James E. Wood, Jr.
Derek Davis

1

Religion, Morality, and Law

JAMES E. WOOD, JR.

The importance of the theme of this volume, "Problems and Conflicts Between Law and Morality," to contemporary American society and, indeed, to the very maintenance of a free and pluralistic society, can hardly be overstated. During the past several decades, problems and conflicts between law and morality have been greatly exacerbated in the United States, as well as throughout much of the world, by widespread social dislocation and social revolution and the resurgence of highly politicized religion that is bent upon turning moral absolutes into political absolutes.

I

By way of an introduction to the subject of this volume, it should be noted that this essay is directed beyond morality and law to *religion*, morality, and law. In view of the inextricably close connection that is generally made between religion and morality, in addressing the theme of this volume some preliminary consideration needs to be given to the relationship of religion and morality. For the relationship of religion and morality is one that has long engaged the attention of major thinkers throughout the centuries, and has consequently been the subject of considerable analysis and debate.[1]

In spite of centuries-old philosophical thought in which differentiation has been made between religion and morality, a widespread popular notion persists that religion and morality are conterminous and, therefore, inseparable. Even when the distinction is made that religion has primarily to do with one's relations to the divine and that morality has primarily to do with relations between persons,[2] it is widely assumed that religion provides the foundation of morality. It must also be acknowledged that human behavior in any given religion may include both obligations to be observed with respect to the object of one's religious faith as well as those obligations imposed on the adherent in his or her relations with other persons. Even these fairly traditional distinctions, however, that religion has primarily to do with one's relations to the object of one's faith and that morality has primarily to do with relations between persons, are less likely to be held at the more popular level of belief. Similarly, many citizens are even further inclined to make little differentiation between religion, morality, and politics, at least at the practical level. Almost a decade ago, at a prayer breakfast in Dallas, Texas, former President Ronald Reagan, a champion at that time of the New Religious Right, shared a sentiment held by many Americans when he declared, "The truth is, politics and morality are inseparable. And as morality's foundation is religion, religion and politics are necessarily related."[3] In responding to these remarks of the president, Milton Konvitz suggested that the logic could be stated to mean that "religion is basic to morality; morality is basic to politics; therefore religion is basic to politics."[4]

Such a sweeping claim that religion is the foundation of morality, a popular view not only expressed by politicians but by many citizens at large, should not go unchallenged. Is it valid to claim that religion is the foundation of morality? In the purview of the phenomenology of religion, such a claim raises serious questions. In the first place, there are those religions, even in American society, which place belief and dogma at the core of their tradition, not ethics or morality. That is to say, identification with these religious traditions has primarily to do with one's acceptance or adherence to a particular belief system and not a code of moral behavior. In the light of the phenomenology of religion, therefore, it is possible for religion to exist without morality and thereby to make the claim that morality is not essential to religion as such. Second, the harsh reality is that from a descriptive analysis of empirical data presently available, there appears to be virtually no correlation existentially in American society between religion and morality among the general populace. By almost any statistical measurement of human behavior— marital infidelity, spousal abuse, divorce, pregnancies of unmarried women, abused children, dysfunctional families, racial and sexual discrimination, political corruption, tax evasion, or dishonesty in financial dealings, to name a few— there appears to be little, if any, indication that a professed religious identity or an affiliation with some form of organized religion results in any pattern of moral behavior different from the populace at large.[5]

Likewise there is no empirical evidence to suggest that those who claim some religious identity possess any more moral acuity than those citizens who do not. Some would even argue that this may well apply to members of the clergy as well. In making this point, one writer recently wrote in the official publication of the American Jewish Congress the following: "No American of the postwar era has been more admired on native grounds than the Rev. Billy Graham; and *his* claim that 'there is no American I admire more than Richard Nixon,' 'a man of moral integrity and Christian principles,' might give pause to even the most enthusiastic champions of the need to pay more attention to clergymen. . . . those in clerical garb are treated with an indulgence out of proportion to the moral illumination they possess."[6] Such an observation is not necessarily borne out of any cynicism toward religion in general or Christianity in particular, but is a generalization that may be applied at one time or another to virtually all of the major religious traditions.

This is not to suggest that religion in America is without some redeeming moral value, quite to the contrary. Rather, this phenomenon is mentioned here simply to make the point that there is a great disparity in American society between professed religious beliefs, even relating to morality, and the actual level of moral behavior of those claiming a religious identity. This recognition is needed not only as a reminder that communities of faith must struggle with the failure of their own members to reflect the moral values of their own religious tradition, but also to view more realistically the limits to be placed on the role of law. Through efforts that are made to advance government sponsorship and support of religion, religious communities are often inclined to use political means for the accomplishment of their own ends. Indeed, history is replete with examples of efforts made by religion to turn to the state or the political order to use legal means to effect standards of personal morality that the religious communities could not accomplish through religious means even among their own members. This may be seen historically in laws bearing on adultery, Sunday blue laws, Prohibition, and, to some extent, in many of the efforts of some groups to outlaw abortion. Unfortunately, the disparity between religion and morality has reached epidemic proportions in contemporary American society.

From a normative or theological perspective, there is clearly a firm basis in both Judaism and Christianity for the claim that religion is the foundation of morality even to the point of its being joined. Indeed, in both Judaism and Christianity, religion and morality are conjoined, first in an ethical monotheism in which God is altogether holy and righteous in his very being and a biblical faith which affirms that morality is essential to genuine faith.[7] Both traditions are rooted in two commandments that enjoin, "You must love the Lord your God with all your heart and with all your soul and with all your might"[8] *and* "you shall love your neighbor as yourself."[9] Before quoting the second commandment, Jesus declared, "The second commandment is like unto it" and concluded quoting these two commandments, by saying, "On these two commandments depend the whole Law and the Prophets."[10] In both Judaism and Christianity these commands are held not only in juxtaposition and given supreme value, but each is used to validate the other. In the Scriptures of both Judaism and Christianity, observance of religious ritual is condemned where there is lacking any corresponding observance of basic moral norms.[11] In a similar vein, Confucianism condemns religious ritual that is not accompanied by morality.[12] While it is common to think of religion as including some moral code, it does not follow that a moral code is essential to religion or that morality is dependent upon religion. Adding to the complexity is the fact that in some of the major religions of the world, moral norms and religious norms are often joined, leading to the point of there not being a differentiation between the two. In Judaism, this becomes readily apparent when examining the 613 commands of *halakhah*. Similarly, both religious and moral commands permeate the teachings or laws of *shari'ah* in Islam and *dharma* in Hindusim and Buddhism.

The argument that religion is essential to morality and that, therefore, without religion there is no foundation for morality, claims too much for religion and ignores the infinite variety of religious norms and practices. The argument is flawed, first of all, as already noted, because it fails to take into account that morality is not necessarily integral to all religious experience nor is it an essential element in the vast diversity of religion throughout history and in today's world. In some religious traditions, both in principle and in practice, orthodox belief and performance of ritual clearly dominate over any moral code of conduct or morality as such. While not rejecting morality, it is made nonessential.[13] Morality, as perceived by persons and societies throughout the world is as varied as religion. The religions of the world do not offer a harmonious code of ethics that could be made the foundation of morality in any given society. To contend that morality is dependent on religion is to pose serious problems for free, democratic, and religiously pluralistic societies. As William K. Frankena rightly observed, "If morality (and hence politics) is dependent on religion, then we must look to religion as a basis for any answer to any personal or social problem of any importance. . . . If morality is dependent on religion, then we cannot hope to solve our problems, or resolve our differences of opinion about them, unless and in so far as we can achieve agreement and certainty in religion (not a lively hope)."[14] Religious obligations in one religion as well as legally and morally sanctioned forms of behavior in a given society may be, and often are, in conflict with moral norms in other religions and in society at large.

The attempt to make religion the foundation of morality inevitably also raises questions of *whose* religion and *whose* morality? Entire volumes have been written on defining religion,[15] but the problem is one that all too often presupposes that the world's religions and their myriad subdivisions share some common apprehension of human existence and ethical norms of behavior. Thus, religion is often defined as "a sense of the sacred" or "a feeling of dependence" on some non-human entity and as involving "worship" or some form of "devotion." These terms fail the tests of both inclusivity when applied to the variant forms of religion and compatibility with what is quintessential in the religions themselves in light of their profound and fundamental differences at their core.

Even the notion of the divine or deity, the transcendent "other," so basic to the religious traditions of the Near East and the West, have no corresponding reality in most of the major traditions of the East. Thus, Rudolph Otto's identification of the sense of the holy (*mysterium tremendum et fascinosum*)[16] and Martin Buber's use of the "I and Thou" as lying at the heart of religion[17] are to be found wanting when applied even to the major religions of the world. References to a personal relationship to deity, which Jewish and Christian theologians are inclined to claim as lying at the heart of religion, have no place, for example, in the religions of Jainism, Theravada Buddhism, or Confucianism. Jainism holds the view that there is no Supreme Ruler of the world, for there is no god higher than man himself.[18] Similarly, Theravada Buddhism rejects the notion of any transcendent eternal Being or Creator or philosophical speculation as the way of salvation; rather each person must rely upon himself for salvation, on his own power and self-discipline.[19] In an even more radically humanistic focus, the founder of Confucianism explicitly denied even any personal interest in the world of the unseen or supernatural and affirmed that the measure of man is man.[20]

Differences between religion extend beyond their rational apprehension of human existence or claims of a mystical union with ultimate reality or divine revelation to ethical and moral behavior as well. While there are many striking similarities in certain ethical teachings in the major religions of the world, there are also numerous differences to be found relating to such issues as sexual behavior, the structure of the family, the killing of human beings, the treatment and eating of animals, acts of violence, and war. These differences appear not only as between the major world religions, but with considerable frequency in the various groupings or subdivisions within each of the major religions. The teachings of some religions apply to the tribe, some to the nation, while some, such as Buddhism, Judaism, Christianity, and Islam, hold that their moral teachings are to be held as universal. Simply to assume, or even to imply, that religion in some generic form is the foundation of morality in a country like the United States is to fail to take into account the great diversity of ethical teachings among the religions themselves, not to mention the historical record of religion which has often reflected a wide disparity between the teachings of the religions and their historical expression. Alas, it must be said, all religions have failed to live up to their own teachings.

Much good has been done in the name of religion, but also much evil has been done. It has often been said that perhaps more wars have been fought and persecutions carried out in the name of religion than for any other cause. As one historian has written, "Nowhere does the name of God and justice appear more frequently than on the banner and shield of the conqueror."[21] The world witnessed with horror the revolution in Iran when a particular form of Islam transformed the nation into what is called a church-state, i.e., a state ruled by the laws and precepts of a particular religious community. Immediately, non-Muslims were subjected to dire persecution, adulterers were executed, the rights of women were abridged, and the hands of those who were caught stealing were cut off. Under given circumstances, a wide range of acts of violence, including war, has long enjoyed the sanction of religion. During the past decade in India in the bloody encounters between Sikhs and Hindus, one Sikh leader was widely reported in the press to have declared that it is our "religious duty to send opponents to hell." In Israel, fanatical Muslims and Jews have for several decades engaged in acts of violence against each other, usually in the name of religion.

The history of Christianity is replete with similar examples. At the Ecumenical Council of the Lateran in 1215, Pope Innocent III decreed the obligation of every Catholic to "exterminate" heretics. The violent forms of anti-Semitism perpetrated and supported by Catholic, Protestant, and Eastern Orthodox churches remains as one of the black chapters in the history of Christianity. Here it is well to recall the words of the French philosopher, Blaise Pascal, himself a deeply religious man, who wrote, "Men never do evil so completely and so cheerfully as they do from religious conviction."[22] When viewed broadly as to its actual role in history, the ambiguous character of religion becomes quite evident. As the late William E. Hocking of Harvard University wrote, "Religion has fostered everything valuable to man and has obstructed everything; it has welded states and denigrated them; it has rescued races and it has oppressed them, destroyed them, condemned them to perpetual wandering and outlawry. It has raised the value of human life, and it has depressed the esteem of that life almost to the point of vanishing; it has honored womanhood, it has slandered marriage. Here is an energy of huge potency, but of ambiguous character."[23] Based upon its historical record, there is ample evidence to substantiate the claim that religion is not necessarily good, but neither is law nor morality in their given historical expression.

II

The problem of religion and morality becomes particularly acute, as in American society, with the growth of religious pluralism and the diversity of religious beliefs and practices, whenever the moral teachings of the latter come into conflict with the legal and moral code of American society. The first major church-state case to reach the United States Supreme Court involved the Mormon practice of polygamy, as divinely instituted, and seen to be, therefore, completely consistent with the teachings of the Church of Jesus Christ of Latter-day Saints.[24] The confrontation between church and state in this case centered on the question of the free exercise of religion, which was the result of a conflict between the tenets of a particular religious community with a moral code that had come to be embodied in law. More recently, the United States Supreme Court upheld the right of a state to outlaw the use of peyote in religious ceremonies by members of the Native American Church, again a law that resulted from a moral stance that held that the use of peyote was a practice not to be condoned even though it was held to be essential for religious ceremonial use by the Native American Church. The religious community known as The Family continues to suffer from social disapproval and discrimination and some measure of legal harassment because of its teachings that condone sex outside of marriage between persons who profess to have a genuine love relationship.

In addressing the question of religion and morality, attention needs to be given to their relationship in the much larger purview of history and the phenomenon of religion. In the ancient world, there was no distinction made between religion and morality or, for that matter, between religion and the state. In each case, they— religion and morality and religion and the state— were simply indistinguishable. There was, however, by the time of Plato and other Greek philosophers a growing tension between religion and morality. As J. Milton Yinger obverved, "When Socrates, Plato, Aristotle, and most of the other philosophers [of ancient Greece] sought to discover the nature of moral obligation, the source of the distinction between right and wrong, they did not relate their answer to a religious system."[25] In Plato's *Euthyphro*, Socrates asks, "Is what is holy holy because the gods approve it, or do they approve because it is holy?" The question was one Thomas Aquinas addressed centuries later. According to Aquinas, God commands what is right; the commands are not right because God commands them.[26]

Centuries later, with the Enlightenment, the differentiation between religion and moralilty became even more distinct. A wide range of theories was propounded that separated norms of moral behavior from religion per se by arguing that the real rationale of morality and moral conduct is to be found in reason. For those less inclined to favor religion, or at least to be skeptical of the claims of religion, by holding forth the prospect of rewards and punishments the relationship of religion to morality was inclined to be seen simply as a way of providing sanction of and support to the moral norms of society. Thereby, religion was perceived as a means of social control. Thus, religion came to be interpreted by many, and even defined, essentially in terms of "socially recognized values." In his own way, Karl Marx conceived of religion in this way and since religion was the creation of the bourgeoisie, it represented socially recognized bourgeoise values that further reenforced a form of social control over the masses. It is by no means unreasonable to see how those most hostile to religion would be so inclined to define religion and thereby come to explain religion as but the creation of society as a means of social control on the part of the privileged and the powerful. Such a view, of course, denies the supernatural or transcendent dimension of religion and the claim of a divine creator who has revealed himself in history. Even without a negative view of religion, the symbiosis of religion and morality inevitably revolves around the questions: Is morality the consequence of religion or is religion the result of moral awareness? As in centuries past, these questions continue to engage the attention of philosophers and theologians. Advances in the history and phenomenology of religion, as well as in anthropology and the social sciences, have added greatly to understanding the complexity of both religion and morality in the modern world.

As noted earlier, the claim that morality does not depend upon or stem from religion has a long history, both in the West and the East. There were in the ancient world, Greek, Roman, and Chinese thinkers who saw religion as primarily serving to provide sanction of and support to morality. With the Enlightenment came a new wave of intellectual freedom which argued against the nexus between religion and morality and instead contended for a morality not dependent upon religion but based upon human concerns and reason. For some, morality dependent upon religion, with its promise of rewards and punishments, represented a primitive or kindergarten stage of human development. For those, like Marx, who saw religion as a way of sanctioning and supporting the moral values of the powerful as over against the powerless, religion would naturally be viewed negatively. For still others, like Sigmund Freud, religion was attacked because, he maintained, it destroys a sense of moral responsibility and encourages irrationality.[27] For a variety of reasons, from thinkers of both positive and negative views of religion, morality with its norms of behavior came to have an autonomy of its own, independent of religion, with human reason and individual conscience made the final arbiters to which even religious teachings were to be subject.

It is well to be reminded that the concept of ethical and moral norms not only exist without religion, but antedate major religions of today's world. Long before Moses and the beginning of the nation of Israel, peoples of the Fertile Crescent had developed systems of moral conduct. The Code of Hammurabi (c. 2100-1800 B.C.) affords some striking parallels with moral laws in the early history of Israel. Before the dawn of Christianity, Greek and Roman civilizations produced philosophers of profound moral acuity—Sophocles, Socrates, Plato, and Aristotle—of renown to this day. Six centuries before the birth of Christianity, the Buddha in India and Lao-tzu and Confucius in China produced profound moral philosophy which became the basis of the religious traditions of Buddhism, Taoism, and Confucianism.[28]

The concept of a universal moral awareness has a long history in both Judaism and Christianity, for both traditions affirm that all of humanity is created in the image of God. The New Testament categorically affirms that "God has not left himself without witness"[29] and speaks of "the true Light, which lighteth every man that cometh into the world."[30]

Christianity, in both the Catholic and Protestant traditions, accepted and reaffirmed, with varying interpretations, the concept of natural law, as proclaimed earlier by Greek and Roman philosophers and jurists, namely that there is a moral awareness or set of moral principles that may be derived from human reason which are the possession of all people and by which they should be governed in their relations with one another. In tracing the origin and development of natural law, Ernest Barker, a highly regarded historian of political thought, observed:

The origin of the idea of natural law may be ascribed to an old and indefeasible movement of the human mind (we may trace it already in the *Antigone* of Sophocles) which impels it towards the notion of an eternal and immutable justice; a justice which human authority expresses, or ought to express—but does not make; a justice which human authority may fail to express by the diminution, or even the forfeiture, of its power to command. This justice is conceived as being the higher or ultimate law, proceeding from the nature of the universe — from the Being of God and the reason of man. . . .

The movement of the mind of man towards these conceptions and their consequences is already apparent in the *Ethics* and the *Rhetoric* of Aristotle. But it was among the Stoic thinkers of the Hellenistic age that the movement first attained a large and general expression and that expression . . . became a tradition of human civility which runs continuously from the Stoic teachers . . . to the American Revolution of 1776 and the French Revolution of 1789. Allied to theology for many centuries—adopted by the Catholic Church. . . . the theory of Natural Law had become . . . and continued . . . an independent and rationalist system, professed and expounded by the philosophers of the secular school of natural law.[31]

Thus, natural law became an integral part of Western political thought and the foundation of the Universal Declaration of Human Rights, as adopted by the United Nations, 10 December 1948. With this declaration, a body of nation-states throughout the world, for the first time in history, without a dissenting vote, committed themselves to the concept of universal human rights —including, the dignity and worth of all persons and the equal rights of all persons—by means of a constitutional document of the world community to be binding upon nations with the force of positive international law. Article I declares, "All human beings are born free and equal in dignity and rights. They are endowed with reason and conscience and should act towards one another in a spirit of brotherhood."

The notion of human rights as embodied in the Declaration only gradually emerged after centuries of philosophical thought on natural law and natural rights. The concept came to the fore primarily out of the Enlightenment, although earlier examples might be cited, such as the English Magna Charta and the Royal Oaths of the Nordic Kingdoms, in which the authority of the sovereign was limited by the natural rights of the people. Later during the seventeenth century, English Puritans developed further the meaning of human rights with the Rights of Parliament and the Bill of Rights which affirmed the right of religious liberty and the right of protection from illegal imprisonment. The late Roman Catholic historian-philosopher, Christopher Dawson, as also the renowned Protestant historian-theologian, Ernst Troeltsch, found the modern movement of human rights as stemming from seventeenth-century England. "The momentum of its religious impulse," Dawson wrote, "opened the way for a new type of civilization based on the freedom of the person and of conscience as rights conferred absolutely by God and nature."[32] Largely derived from rationalistic natural law and a legacy of Judeo-Christian and classical thought, the concept of human or natural rights came to be forthrightly enunicated as a political principle in the latter part of the eighteenth century by the American and French revolutions, in which the natural rights of the human person were expressed in the American Declaration of Independence and the French Declaration of the Rights of Man.

While a theological basis of human or natural rights may be found in both Judaism and Christianity, in retrospect the historical record of Christianity (as by far the dominant single religion in Western civilization) on behalf of natural or human rights is far from clear and not without much ambivalence. Admittedly, the history of Christianity has often been in contradiction to the norms of Christian faith and morality. Certainly, it would be a gross distortion of history if one were to base the record of Christianity on Christian theological foundations of human rights and then to infer that human rights as such were generally espoused by Christianity. For such was not the case. For centuries, even up to the present time, human rights have been repeatedly and oftentimes flagrantly violated by institutional Christianity as well as other religions. It is well to acknowledge that with regard to natural or human rights, the historical record of Christianity, as with other religions, has been sometimes good, and sometimes bad.

Whatever one's own view of religion or faith commitment may be, it is important to recognize that to contend that all morality is based on religion is beset with serious and irreconcilable divisions in society, both for the adherents of a wide array of religious traditions as well as those citizens who claim no religious affiliation. The separation of morality from religion, however, is not to suggest here that there is no relationship between religion and morality, but rather to avoid making the broad assumption that morality is founded on religion. As has already been noted in the brief references to Greek, Roman, and Chinese philosophers, as well as to one of the greatest of Christian theologians, Thomas Aquinas, the view that morality is not dependent on religion is by no means a view necessarily antagonistic to religion. Immanuel Kant, a devout Christian philosopher, vigorously argued for the autonomy of moral commitments, based on the dictates of reason and conscience, which are the possessions of every person, but still he held that religion and morality are mutually obligatory. When, however, a person asks what he or she ought to do, the response comes because he or she feels within the "categorical imperative" to do so, not because of any external moral norms or for the sake of any rewards or punishments.[33] Writing at the beginning of this century, Troeltsch vigorously argued that "morality has to stand on its own."[34]

In the relationship between religion and morality, there is clearly an important role for religion to play. Beyond reason and conscience, religion may give added meaning to morality while, at the same time, providing inspiration and motivation for moral conduct. In his recently published work, *Faith and Order: The Reconciliation of Law and Religion*, Harold J. Berman rightly cautions, at the pragmatic level, against a purely intellectual or philosophical view of morality without a faith commitment:

> the trouble with a purely intellectual or philosophical analysis of morality is that the very inquiry, by its exclusive rationality, tends to frustrate the realization of the virtues it proclaims. The intellect is satisfied, but the emotions, without which decisive actions cannot be taken, are deliberately put aside. . . . To say, for example, that it is against human nature to tolerate indiscriminate stealing and that every society condemns and punishes certain kinds of taking of another's property is not the same thing as to say that there is an all-embracing moral reality, a purpose in the universe, which stealing offends.[35]

Out of the autonomous status given to morality, i.e., the independence of moral norms from religion, has come the increasingly widely held view of the universality of basic moral principles. In the twentieth century, particularly since World War II, many of these moral principles have been made a part of international law, e.g., prohibitions against genocide and discrimination based upon ethnic and religious identity. The independence of moral norms over religious and pragmatic considerations have increasingly been made applicable to all societies and to all persons everywhere. As G. J. Warnock has written:

> If conduct is to be seen as regulated only *within* groups, we have still the possibility of unrestricted hostility and conflict *between* groups— which is liable, indeed, to be effectively ferocious and damaging in proportion as relations between individuals within each group are effectively ordered toward harmonious co-operative action. Thus, just as one may think that a Hobbesian recipe for 'peace' could securely achieve its end only if all Hobbesian individuals were engrossed within a single irresistible Leviathan, there is reason to think that the principles of morality must, if the object of morality is not to be frustrated, give consideration to *any* human, of whatever special group or none he may in fact be a member.[36]

Here it is well to recall that for Kant, in order for an act to be moral, it should meet the test of universality. With the principle of the universality of moral norms has come the concept that some patterns of conduct are morally wrong even if they are widely accepted in certain societies.

What has come to be recognized as "the moral point of view" is rooted in that conduct that impartially serves to benefit others and society at large. There is for the moralist, goodness for goodness sake, since goodness has its own reason for being beyond any element of self-interest or personal advantage. For Kant, with all of his emphasis on the principle that moral norms must be autonomous, based on the dictates of conscience and reason, he became convinced that moral commitments require a belief in "a morally intentioned governor of the universe. . . . but [he] also recognized the difficulty of providing any clear and incontestable rational justification for being moral."[37]

III

In addition to the many questions and ramifications that revolve around the relationship between religion and morality, there is the inevitable question of the bearing of this relationship on law and society. Since by its very nature, morality has to do with the regulation of human conduct primarily in interpersonal relationships, but by no means exclusively, there can be little disagreement with the premise that morality is an essential ingredient of the fabric of a stable and civil society, without which no free and pluralistic society can exist, let alone survive. For it is only through the regulation of human behavior, as one writer aptly expressed it, "that cooperative living is possible," for without some restraint human beings could not have "community life."[38] Lord Devlin went so far as to argue that "an established morality is as necessary as good government to the welfare of society."[39] In arguing against the thinking of John Stuart Mill that "the only purpose for which power can be rightfully exercised over any member of a civilised community, against his will, is to prevent harm to others,"[40] Devlin maintained that society has a right to punish legally what it regards as morally unacceptable behavior. Thus, for many years a number of states had laws forbidding the sale, prescription, or even the use of contraceptives and, until 1965, the very *use* of contraceptives in Connecticut was by law regarded as a criminal act. This Connecticut state law was overturned by the United States Supreme Court, in *Griswold v. Connecticut*, by a vote of seven to two.[41] In arguing their case, the lawyers for the plaintiffs maintained that the law violated basic human rights, including the right to privacy, and that the state must show an objective relationship between the regulation of morality and the public welfare, without which the "promotion of morality," the alleged basis of the Connecticut law, could be used as a justification for almost any law. The significance of the *Griswold* decision extends far beyond the question of the use of contraceptives, since the Court found, for the first time, that the right to privacy has grounding in the Constitution. It was this principle which eight years later the Court was to use, in large measure, to base its decision of denying the right of the state to prohibit abortion, particularly during the first trimester of a woman's pregnancy.[42]

If morality is essential to a stable and civil society, the question arises as to how to establish and maintain the morality of society. The first response has to be that any civil and democratic society must ultimately depend upon the voluntary commitment of a majority of its citizens to a recognized moral code of behavior. Without this principle a democratic or civil society could not be realized. Indeed, a distinguishing feature of morality is its requisite of moral sanction or pressure upon which it relies for support. More than a century ago, John Stuart Mill, in his essay, "Utility of Religion," rightly understood that the ultimate sanction for morality was not religion, but public opinion, which he argued "is a source of strength inherent in any system of moral belief . . . whether connected with religion or not." Public opinion, Mill observed, does much to mold and shape the human conscience. "When the motive of public opinion acts in the same direction with conscience," he wrote, "it is then of all motives which operate on the bulk of mankind the most overpowering."[43] More recently, H. L. A. Hart has argued that moral sanction is not only an essential element in the concept of morality, it is also, practically speaking, necessary to sustain it.[44] As a political theorist, Konvitz noted that the principle of public opinion as the final arbiter of morality is amply confirmed in American society today.

Examples of this phenomenon [are] everywhere. Until very recently, it was generally assumed that all major religions condemned abortion as sinful and evil, yet today it is widely approved by public opinion, not only in the United States, but also in the Western Catholic and Protestant countries. A similar observation may be made with respect to divorce. Sexual relations outside of marriage have been condemned by Christianity and Judaism, yet today "cohabitation" has become widely accepted as a substitute for marriage. Dormitories shared by students of both sexes are today common on all major campuses, and curfew regulations are a thing of the past. Mill's conclusion is validated all about us: religious precepts work only when aided by public opinion, and the operative ingredient is public opinion.[45]

Mill also discounted that the prospect of rewards and punishments held forth by religion had a powerful effect on moral behavior. "Rewards and punishments," he wrote, "postponed to that distance of time, and never seen by the eye, are not calculated, even when infinite and eternal, to have on ordinary minds, a very powerful effect in opposition to present temptations."[46] The effect of the prospect of rewards and punishments, Mill reasoned, was weakened further by their remoteness in time and their uncertainty. They clearly do not possess the power over morality that results from the sanction of public opinion. In his view of the relationship of morality to law, Mill held to limited government and the limited role of law by asserting what he called "one very simple principle," namely, as mentioned earlier, "that the only purpose for which power can be rightfully exercised over any member of a civilised community, against his will, is to prevent harm to others."[47]

The force exerted by the sanction of public opinion as the final arbiter of the morality of society and the rising tide of belief in the principle enunciated by Mill that "the only purpose" for which the restraints of law and government over moral conduct can be justified "is to prevent harm to others" have had a profound impact on liberal democracies of the West, including the United States. Here, aided by the concept of America as a secular or limited state, constitutional provisions that guarantee the institutional separation of church and state and the free exercise of religion, and judicial interpretations' reenforcing the "right to privacy," the subject of religion, morality, and law has come to be regarded by many as crucial to the nation's self-identity.

The subject has come to occupy a major place in the great judicial and political debates in contemporary American society.[48] On the one hand, there are those who vigorously argue that society has every right to uphold recognized moral values and lifestyles of the majority whether or not their violation results in any injury or "harm to others." The justification for such moral laws are at least twofold: one, that the majority has the right to legislate its moral values, as Devlin maintained, to punish legally what it condemns morally; and two, that moral laws are needed ultimately to preserve and protect the very existence of an orderly society and its institutions. On the other hand, there are those just as committed who maintain that the purpose of law is to protect and prevent harm or injury to others and, therefore, where such a threat is generally not present, law should aim at the freedom and privacy of its adult citizens and their right to live out their lives so long as their behavior does not threaten the rights of others, or themselves, or the social order.[49] Strong arguments are made by protagonists on both sides, but the two views represented here on morality and law are fundamentally in conflict and, therefore, irreconcilable, and so the debate continues.

Many hold that the problem of morality and law in American society has been directly eroded by the libertarian directions of

the United States Supreme Court in its interpretations of the
First Amendment, particularly its interpretation of the
Establishment Clause, in which the Court for almost fifty years
has affirmed that the First Amendment means "nothing less than
the separation of church and state." One result of its rulings, it is
alleged, has been too radical a separation not only of religion
and law, but of morality and law as well. As a result, it is
charged, the Court has lowered the norms of traditional morality
that have long been embodied in American law, such as statutes
requiring prayer and Bible reading in the public schools and
prohibiting abortion, certain forms of sexual activity, legalized
gambling, the operation of businesses on Sunday, and explicit
sexual expressions in art, literature, and the mass media. These
changes in law have, it is argued, resulted in the denial of
traditional moral values in American society.

In recent years, books by writers such as Richard John
Neuhaus, William J. Bennett, and Stephen L. Carter suggest for
many that America has lost its moral compass and forsaken its
spiritual heritage.[50] Organizations such as the Christian
Coalition are bent upon redeeming American politics and
restoring traditional Christian morality and values to the public
square and to American society. Strongly supportive of laws
restoring prayer and Bible reading to the public schools and laws
aimed at prohibiting acts of immorality, as they view them, these
individuals and groups generally show little hesitation in
translating their religious views into political commitments. For
them, there can be no real conflict between what is moral and
what is legal and, conversely, they believe that what is legal
should be moral. The morality that they seek to embody into
law tends to be a morality based not on what Mill called "public
opinion," the will of the majority or prevailing moral view of
society, but on their own particular understanding of the moral
rightness of the acts themselves.

While there is a sense in which law reflects some kind of
moral consensus of society, it does not by any means follow that
for the average individual the question of legality is synomous
with morality. In a free and democratic society, laws are
necessarily rooted in the concept of limited government or a

limited state and a large measure of personal or individual freedom. Freedom of press or freedom of speech, for example, does not carry with it the notion that in the exercise of these civil liberties the moral values of society are being necessarily upheld in the speech and publications themselves, but rather the value of individual freedom and civil rights of the citizenry are to be upheld and respected by the state. As David A. J. Richards has written, "Laws are not, as a matter of definition or fact, always or necessarily moral."[51] For example, the inherent limitations of law bearing on interpersonal relations in prohibiting discrimination against other persons in education, employment, housing, and public accommodations preclude its fulfilling the moral imperatives of compassion and genuine regard for other persons. The American Bill of Rights quite rightly occupies a lofty place in American jurisprudence, but these rights are necessarily couched in largely negative terms since they impose restrictions on civil or government authority over the lives of citizens.[52] To be sure, laws are based upon some form of consensual morality in the regulation of human behavior, but law is not, and cannot be, the final arbiter of morality.

It is, however, the increasing tendency of the United States Supreme Court to uphold the limited role of government in order to protect the citizen's right to privacy, as in its rulings upholding the right of abortion, and to guarantee the separation of church and state, as in its decisions prohibiting religious exercises in the public schools, that has created a tremendous furor over the denial by government of its endorsement of both religion and morality in American society. In recent years, national presidential campaigns, as well as state and local political campaigns, have been waged over questions relating to the role of government in promoting "traditional" moral values and an accommodationist rather than a separationist view in church-state relations.

While showing some concern for the erosion of moral values and the radical separation of law and religion and morality and law in contemporary American society in that it may endanger respect for law, Harold J. Berman recently rightly warned, at the same time, that

> we must avoid . . . the dangers of making too close an interconnection between them. . . . Each is . . . in some tension with the other; each challenges the other. Religion by standing outside the law, helps to prevent legal institutions from being worshipped. Conversely, law, by its secularity, leaves religion free to develop in its own way. The separation of law and religion thus provides a foundation for the separation of Church and State, protecting us against caesaropapism, on the one hand, and theocracy on the other.[53]

Meanwhile, the argument that court decisions have brought about a moral decline in America runs counter to the religious resurgence in American society during the past several decades. For example, organized religion experienced one of its greatest periods of growth in membership in the period following the Supreme Court's decisions on prayer and Bible reading in the public schools. The emergence in the late seventies of the New Religious Right with its political agenda aimed at restoring the nation's moral and spiritual values by putting prayer back in the public schools may be viewed not only as overly simplistic, but fails to take seriously the causes for major moral problems of the day, such as wanton acts of violence, child abuse, crime, drugs, racism, poverty, and sexual promiscuity. The means by which these problems will be alleviated will ultimately require far more than legislation and the enactment of laws, but all the moral and spiritual resources society can provide.

NOTES

1. See, for example, Plato's *Euthyrphro*; Thomas Aquinas's, "Treatise on the Law," in *Summa Theologiae*, 2.7.90-97; Immanuel Kant's *Critique of Practical Reason* (1788) and *Religion within the Limits of Reason Alone* (1793); John Stuart Mill's *Three Essays on Religion*; Soren Kierkegaard's *Fear and Trembling*; Edward A. Westermarck, *The Origin and Development of the Moral Ideas*, 2 vols., 2nd ed. (London: Macmillan Co., 1924); Edward A. Westermarck, *Christianity and Morals* (Freeport, N.Y.: Books for Libraries Press, 1969); Bernard Haring, *Faith and Morality in the Secular Age* (New York: Doubleday

and Co., Inc., 1973); J. Roland Pennock and John W. Chapman, *Religion, Morality, and the Law* (New York: New York University Press, 1988); Basil Mitchell, *Law, Morality, and Religion in a Secular Society* (London: Oxford University Press, 1970) and *Morality, Religious and Secular: The Dilemma of the Traditional Conscience* (Oxford: Clarendon Press, 1980); Arthur Leon Harding, ed., *Religion, Morality, and Law* (Dallas: Southern Methodist University Press, 1956); W. W. Bartley, *Morality and Religion* (London: Macmillan, 1971); Gene H. Outka and John P. Reeder, Jr., eds. *Religion and Morality: A Collection of Essays* (Garden City, N.Y.: Anchor Press/Doubleday, 1973); and Ronald M. Green, "Morality and Religion," in *The Encyclopedia of Religion*, ed. Mircea Eliade et al. (New York: Macmillan Publishing Co., 1987), 10:105.; St. John A. Robilliard, *Religion and the Law* (Manchester: Manchester University Press, 1984); and Peter Hinchliff, *Holiness and Politics* (Grand Rapids, Mich.: William B. Erdmans Publishing Co., 1982), note particularly, chaps. "Morality and Power" and "Public and Private Morality."

2. John Milton Yinger, for example, stated this view cryptically, when he wrote, "In theological terms, religion is concerned with 'is-ness,' morality with 'oughtness.' Morality seeks, for example, to control conditions that lead to death--to prohibit cruelty and murder, to reduce sources of illness and hunger. Religion seeks to help one adjust to the fact of death. Morality is concerned with the relationship of man to man; [while] religion is concerned with the relationship of man to some higher power or idea"; see Yinger, *The Scientific Study of Religion* (New York: Macmillan Co., 1970), 51. Yinger found "the distinction" between religion and morality to be "in terms of the authority and the sanctions that are attached to the codes [of each]"; ibid.

3. *Dallas Morning News*, 24 August 1984, 8A.

4. Milton R. Konvitz, "Is Religion the Foundation of Morality?" *Midstream* (June/July 1985): 17; the following month in Utah, President Reagan reaffirmed these views and added that the Founding Fathers who wrote the Constitution "knew that morality derives chiefly from religious faith."

5. There are studies that clearly indicate behaviorial differences among members of certain narrowly defined religious communities, but such distinctions are clearly lost in the patterns of the population at large, the great majority of whom profess some religious identity.

6. Stephen J. Whitfield, "Church and State: A View from the Right," *Congress Monthly* 61(April/May 1994): 8.

7. See, for example, John P. Reeder, *Religion and Morality in Judaic and Christian Traditions* (Englewood Cliffs, N.J.: Prentice-Hall, 1988). Perhaps the closest definition of religion in the Bible is to be found in *Micah* 6:8, in which religion is defined primarily in moral terms: "He has told you, O man, what is good; and what does the Lord require

of you but to do justice, and to love kindness, and to walk humbly with your God?"

8. *Deuteronomy* 6:5; *Matthew* 22:37.

9. *Leviticus* 19:18; *Matthew* 22:39.

10. *Matthew* 22:40.

11. *Amos* 5:21-24 reads as follows: "I hate, I despise your feasts, and take no delight in your solemn assemblies. Even though you offer up to Me burnt offerings and your grain offerings, I will not accept them; and I will not *even* look at the peace offerings of your fatted beasts. Take away from Me the noise of your songs; I will not even listen to the sound of your harps. But let justice roll down like waters, and righteousness as an ever-flowing stream"; *James* 1:27 states, "Pure religion and undefiled before God and the Father is this: to visit the fatherless and widows in their affliction, and to keep oneself unspotted from the world."

12. *The Analects of Confucius* 3.3 asks, "A man who is not good, what can he do with ritual?"

13. Two illustrations may be cited here, one having to do with ancient China and the other with the United States today. Writing of religion in ancient China, the Chinese scholar, C. K. Yang, wrote the following: "From an early date in Chinese culture, the major role of religion was not as the fountainhead of moral ideals but the magical one of inducing the gods and spirits to bring happiness to man, to ward off evil, to cure sickness, to obtain rain in a drought, to achieve victory in war and peace in crisis"; C. K. Yang, *Religion in Chinese Society* (Berkeley: University of California Press, 1961), 279. In a study of church members in California by sociologists Rodney Stark and Charles Glock, it was found that approximately 10 percent of those surveyed rejected moral conduct as irrelevant to their Christian salvation. Only half believed that "doing for others" and "loving thy neighbor" were necessary for salvation; see Rodney Stark and Charles Glock, *American Piety: The Nature of Religious Commiment* (Berkeley: University of California Press, 1968), 71-76.

14. William K. Frankena, "Is Morality Logically Dependent on Religion?" in *Religion and Morality*, 295.

15. See, for example, Alan G. Widgery, *What Is Religion?* (New York: Harper and Brothers, 1953); Joseph Dabney Bettis, comp., *Phenomenology of Religion: Eight Modern Descriptions of the Essence of Religion* (New York: Harper and Row, 1969); and Mircea Eliade and David Tracy, eds., *What Is Religion: An Inquiry for Christian Theologians* (Oxford: Oxford University Press, 1950).

16. See Rudolph Otto, *The Idea of the Holy: An Inquiry into the Nonrational* (Oxford: Oxford University Press, 1950).

17. See Martin Buber, *I and Thou* (New York: Charles Scribner, 1958).

18. See *The Gaina Sutras* in *The Sacred Books of the East*, ed. F. Max Muller, 50 vols. (Oxford: Clarendon Press, 1879-1910), 22: 152.

19. *Majjhima Nikaya* 63 in *Buddhism in Translation*, trans. Henry Clarke Warren (Cambridge: Harvard University Press, 1922), 122.

20. *The Analects of Confucius*, trans. and anno. Arthur Waley (London: G. Allen Unwin, Ltd., 1938), passim. In characterizing Confucianism, Hu Shih declared, "Teaching a moral life is the essential thing: and the way of the gods are merely one of the possible means of sanctioning the teaching. That is in substance the Chinese concept of religion"; quoted by Wing-tsit Chan, *Religious Trends in Modern China* (New York: Columbia University Press, 1953), 246.

21. Hubert Muller, *Religion and Freedom in the Modern World* (Chicago: University of Chicago Press, 1963), 52.

22. Blaise Pascal, *Pensees: The Thoughts of Blaise Pascal* (1844), trans. William F. Trotter (New York: Temple Classics, 1904), No. 895, p. 363.

23. William E. Hocking, *The Meaning of God in Human Experience: A Philosophical Study of Religion* (New Haven: Yale University Press, 1912), 11.

24. See *Reynolds v. United States*, 98 U.S. 145 (1878).

25. Yinger, *The Scientific Study of Religion*, 53.

26. In making the distinction between what is contrary to natural law is contrary to the order of God, Aquinas wrote, "The theologian considers sin chiefly as an offense against God, and the moral philosophers, as something contrary to reason"; *Summa Theologiae* 1-2, q. 71, a.6.

27. See Sigmund Freud, *The Future of an Illusion* (New York: Norton, 1975).

28. This may be readily illustrated in the sacred writings of these traditions: *The Dhammapada* of Buddhism, *The Tao Te Ching* of Taoism, and *The Analects of Confucius* of Confusianism. A recent volume by R. P. Peerenboom, *Law and Morality in Ancient China: The Silk Manuscripts of Huang-Lao* (Albany: State University of New York, 1993), based upon recently discovered manuscripts after being lost for over two thousand years, further validates the strong tradition of law and morality in ancient China.

29. *Acts* 14:17.

30. *John* 1:9. Among other passages, Paul wrote, "Is he the God of the Jews only? Is he not also of the Gentiles? Yes, of the Gentiles also" *Romans* 3:29).

31. Ernest Barker, *Traditions of Civility: Eight Essays* (Cambridge: Cambridge University Press, 1948), 312-13.

32. Christopher Dawson, *The Judgment of the Nations* (New York: Sheed and Ward, 1942), 50-51.

33. See Immanuel Kant's publications, *Critique of Practical Reason* (1788) and *Religion Within the Limits of Reason Alone* (1793).

34. Ernst Troeltsch, "The Essence of the Modern Spirit," in *Religion in History* (Minneapolis: Fortress Press, 1991), 261; originally published in German in 1907.

35. Harold J. Berman, *Faith and Order: The Reconciliation of Law and Religion* (Atlanta: Scholars Press, 1993), 14-15.
36. G. J. Warnock, *The Object of Moralilty* (London: Metheun, 1971), 150.
37. Green, "Morality and Religion," 96.
38. K. O. L. Burridge, "Levels of Being," in *Religion and Morality*, 49ff.
39. Patrick Devlin, *The Enforcement of Morals* (Oxford: Oxford University Press, 1965), 13.
40. John Stuart Mill, *On Liberty*, Chap. 1.
41. *Griswold v. Connecticut*, 381 U.S. 479 (1965).
42. *Roe v. Wade*, 410 U.S. 113 (1973).
43. John Stuart Mill, *Three Essays on Religion* (New York: Henry Holt and Co., 1874; reprinted New York: Greenwood Press, 1969), 84-85; in this same essay, Mill notes that "the names of all the strongest passions (except the merely animal ones) manifested by human nature, are each of them a name for some one part only of the motive derived from . . . public opinion. The love of glory; the love of praise; the love of admiration; the love of respect and deference; even the love of sympathy, are portions of its attractive power"; ibid., 85.
44. H. L. A. Hart, *The Concept of Law* (Oxford: Clarendon Press, 1961), 176-77.
45. Konvitz, "Is Religion the Foundation of Morality?", 19.
46. Mill, "Utility of Religion," 89.
47. Mill, *On Liberty*, ch. 1.
48. See, for example, Edmond Cahn, *The Moral Decision: Right and Wrong in the Light of American Law* (Bloomington: Indiana University Press, 1955); Devlin, *The Enforcement of Morals*; Michael J. Perry, *Morality, Politics, and Law: A Bicentennial Essay* (New York: Oxford University Press, 1988); Robert N. Baird and Stuart E. Rosenbaum, eds., *Morality and the Law* (Buffalo, N.Y.: Prometheus Books, 1988); and D. Don Welch, ed., *Law and Morality* (Philadelphia: Fortress Press, 1987); Kent Greenawalt, *Conflict of Law and Morality* (New York: Oxford University Press, 1987); and Kent Greenawalt, *Religious Convictions and Political Choice* (New York: Oxford University Press, 1987).
49. In recent years, increasing attention is being given to laws aimed at protecting the environment and threatened animal species and preventing cruelty to animals.
50. See, for example, Richard John Neuhaus, *The Naked Public Square* (Grand Rapids: Wm. B. Eerdmans, 1984); William J. Bennett, *The De-valuing of America: The Fight for Our Culture and Our Children* (New York: Summit Books, 1992); and Stephen L. Carter, *The Culture of Disbelief: How American Law and Politics Trivialize Religious Devotion* (New York: BasicBooks, 1993). See also, R. Randall Rainey, S.J., "Law and Religion: Is Reconciliation Still Possible?" *Loyola of Los Angeles Law Review* 27 (November 1993):

147-92, in which the author argues that there is presently a growing estrangement between religion and law that has resulted "in the virtual banishment of religious belief and practice from the public life of the political community," a view particularly "widespread among intellectuals, media elites, and law school faculties" and "periodically expressed in the opinions of the United States Supreme Court" (p. 150).

51. David A. J. Richards, *The Moral Criticism of Law* (Encino, Cal.: Dickinson Publishing Co., 1977), 178.

52. See H. L. A. Hart, *Law, Liberty, and Morality* (Stanford: Stanford University Press, 1963), ch. 1, "The Legal Enforcement of Moralilty." Illustrations of the limited role of government in controlling the morality of its citizens may be found in the Wolfenden Committee's Report in England in 1954, which provoked much spirited debate, with its declaration that "there must remain a realm of private morality and immorality which is, in brief and crude terms, not the law's business" (sec. 61); the following year, the American Law Institute Mode Penal Code, after considerable debate, adopted the following: "There is the fundamental question of the protection to which every individual is entitled against state affairs when he is not hurting others."

53. Berman, *Faith and Order*, 216.

2

Morality as a Perennial Source of Indeterminacy in the Life of the Law

CALVIN WOODARD

The approach of this essay to "the relationship between law and morality" stands *independently* of particular "moral" issues, or specific constitutional law cases. It is a generic topic that has troubled legal thinkers at *other times* (as well as the present), and in *other places* (as well as in the U.S.) that deserves to be addressed as such. [1]

Be that as it may, despite the fact that the relationship between law and morality (two of the fuzziest words in the English language) is only a rope of sand, it is nonetheless absolutely essential to understanding any legal system, including that of the United States. For morality is an organic part of that experience which, as Justice Oliver Wendell Holmes long ago noted,[2] is "the life of the law." Further, and as such, morality is also a major cause of the uncertainty or indeterminacy of law that has for so long bedeviled legal critics, leading to countless efforts—in the form of codes, statutes, and written constitutions— to make the law more certain.

This essay shall first offer a few samples of contemporary definitions of morality to indicate just how wildly different are the meanings ascribed to it in current usage. Then, shifting to the meaning of law and drawing on the major legal theories that have appeared since c.1800, it will be shown how law has been redefined in ways embodying different meanings of morality —

and hence incorporating into its very meaning strikingly diverse "relationships" with morality. Finally (moving gingerly into legal history), an attempt will be made to describe some ways in which the very uncertainty of the "law and morality" relationship has influenced our history.

AMBIGUITIES IN THE MEANING OF "MORALITY"

Though I can claim no mastery of contemporary moral philosophy, I am confident that there is no unanimous agreement, or even consensus among philosophers as to the meaning of "morals" or "morality." I offer, however, a few randomly selected examples to illustrate the wide diversity of meanings found in contemporary usages.

A. "What is the relationship between morality and rationality? The answer depends, of course, on how we characterize 'rationality' and 'morality.' We can begin with the definition of rationality found in contemporary microeconomics: rationality is utility maximization. . . . Defining rationality in this way enables one to give a simple and minimal definition of morality: *morality is constrained utility maximization.*"[3]
B. "As for what 'morality' means . . . let it suffice here to say that it concerns at least the domain of the right and the good, and questions of obligation, duty, fairness, virtue, character, the nature of the good life, and the good society, and, behind these, assumptions about the nature of man, the preconditions for social life, the limits of its possible transformation, and the grounds of practical judgement."[4]
C. "Moral debate nowadays is 'like playing croquet with flamingoes,' for there is no generally accepted view of the nature or the content of morality."[5]

The foregoing quotations indicate why law's relationship with morality is, and must remain, ambiguous; even among philosophers, morality defies definition in part because its meaning apparently varies so sharply from moralist to moralist. But in the world of practical affairs, the "law and morality" question is usually raised not by moral philosophers but by practical persons moved by some perceived moral outrage which they believe law should (or should not) address.[6] Thus, in the 1840s Henry David Thoreau refused to pay federal taxes to finance what he believed to be an "immoral war" against Mexico, though the federal government had approved it; following World War II, the Allies, outraged by the atrocities of the German Third Reich, prosecuted its leaders as war criminals, for their grotesquely inhumane and immoral policies (though the defendants claimed that they acted in accordance with duly enacted German law); Martin Luther King led a moral crusade against the immorality of racial segregation laws; George Bush, as a presidential candidate, challenged the morality of a penal system that "furloughed" a convicted felon; and Sen. Jesse Helms attacked the use of funds raised by federal laws to finance an art exhibit displaying what he judged to be "immoral" photography.

Trying to draw any meaningful conclusions regarding the meaning of "moralist" or the nature of the relationship between morality and law from these and other such wildly diverse issues seems utterly futile. Beyond this, the language of "morality/immorality" seems to be invoked by members of the public to express their approval or disapproval of some condition they believe to be grotesquely offensive; and the resort to that form of language becomes the basis for some demand, or denial of the need for law.

Perhaps the most crucial jurisprudential inquiry regarding the relationship between law and morality is not concerning the nature of law, or the meaning of morality, but the *function* that morality (as measured by the tone of voice and the kind of language used) plays in the actual evolution of our law and legal system. It would seem that functionally the law-morality relationship serves to give private individuals and groups a kind of appeal on controversial issues, over the head of officials, legal and otherwise, wielding political authority. Thus, through expressions of morality, "the people" (who under our Constitution are "sovereigns" as well as subjects of the law) assert their power, as a kind of unempaneled jury, passing judgment on law itself.

THE MEANING OF "MORALITY"
IMPLICIT IN VARIOUS CONCEPTS OF "LAW":
A JURISPRUDENTIAL PERSPECTIVE

Persons interested in exploring the relationship between law and morality might be expected to seek the answer in legal theory or legal philosophy. However, all such persons must surely be struck not so much by the different definitions of law (which are perhaps to be expected) as by the different versions of morality built into the various definitions of law.

During the two hundred or so years since this nation came into being, many new approaches to law have emerged, defining and refining the concept of law itself. Most of the innovations have been in reaction to the limitations inherent in the traditional forms of natural law dominant in the eighteenth century.[7] Orthodox natural law theory envisioned a cosmic whole embracing "divine law" and the "law of nations" as well as national law; it also posited a relationship between law and morality, both of which were organic parts of a single seamless whole. Thus any attack on natural law cast doubt on the relationship between law and morality. Hence the intellectual ferment caused by attacks on, or retreats from, orthodox natural law theory raised profound questions about the nature of the relationship between law and morality. The result has been various modern (post-natural law) concepts of law with diverse relationships with morality.

Despite the diversity of views concerning the relationship between law and morality, however, it is possible to discern in modern jurisprudence six (6) basic relationships, or paradigms, which describe the relationship between these two ambiguous words. Identifying them may help to clarify some of the current confusion. Tersely put, they are as follows: law may be said to be *inseparable from* morality (natural law); law may be said to differ qualitatively from morality and hence the two must be kept (at least analytically) *separate* (positivism); law may be said to be morally *neutral* (legal process); law may be said to be moral only insofar as it leads to good *results* (utilitarianism); law and morality may each be said to be different *stages in the evolving development* of a society's value system (historical jurisprudence); or law may be said to be institutionalized *immorality* (Marxism). A fuller explanation of each of these paradigms is in order.

PARADIGM A: *Law and morality are inseparable. Law divorced from morality is not law at all; it is naked power to which one defers only out of fear.*

According to this (natural law) theory, law and morality are, if not the same, in extremely close harmony with each other. The old phrase (from Sir William Blackstone) was clear enough: "Law commands that which is right and prohibits that which is wrong."

This philosophy of law is based on the premise that the universe and everything in it, including human life, derives its meaning from some supernatural authority. That higher authority ordained two kinds of law: first, a kind of "absolute natural law" (NL-1) mandating those things (such as aging, sleeping, and dying) to which all mortals are subject, and *must* obey, simply because they have no choice; and, second, a kind of "exhortory natural law" (NL-2), pertaining to those obligations mortals *ought* to recognize and obey.

This second form of natural law, NL-2, though consisting of rules of conduct human beings ought to obey is not absolutely enforceable (as are the NL-1 mandates) because all persons possess a measure of autonomy. Hence, whereas no one has the power to stem the passage of time, *all* persons have the power to act as they will— and many, they being human, persist in (willfully or otherwise) deviating from what they "ought" to do. Thus the eternal human problem is how to make free-agents exercise their autonomy as they "should"— that is, morally.

Traditionally, human societies have developed, and relied upon, a number of social institutions to curb the baleful tendency of human beings to act foolishly, stupidly, irresponsibly, or worse. In Western societies the major social institutions developed to train and keep individuals in line were the family, the church, various educational institutions, and government, each of which exerted different kinds of influence on the individuals subject to their authority. Working together, they sought to induce or, where necessary, to force (including terrorizing) their fellow human beings into complying with the rules of behavior necessary for social coexistence. The various rules imposed upon individuals came to be known, by analogy to NL-1, as "Natural Law" (NL-2).

Natural law, of course, as a legal theory, has reflected all the richness and contradictions of human thought. (One modern commentator noted that there have been more kinds of natural law than there are pies at the Leipzig Fair.) Besides the Judeo-Christian God, its authority has been derived from graven images, the "blind forces of nature," the Cosmos and what J.M. Finnis, a contemporary natural law advocate, calls "the essential conditions of human survival."[8]

In recent times, natural law (NL-2) commentators have rediscovered certain individual rights that governments are bound to respect. Thus, according to Ronald Dworkin, these rights (which stem from law, not policy) "trump" decisions made on utilitarian grounds for the community as a whole.[9] Though the actual source of these rights remains unclear, they do seem to flourish only in democracies where a rule of law prevails. Thus, whether the rule of law is itself based on natural law, or some form of morality, remains an unanswered question.

The traditional natural law (NL-2) theory has had an enormous impact on our civilization as well as the relationship between law and morality. For it seemed to invest *all* laws, including those made by human lawmakers, with the authority of both God and nature. As a result, the law of the state was easily conflated with the "higher moral law." This tendency was, and remains, especially evident in criminal law where immoral (as well as sinful and illegal) behavior are conjoined in a unique fashion. Evidence of criminal intent (demonstrating malice or spite) distinguishes crime from civil liability (tort) and serves as a major justification for capital punishment. Sir James Fitzjames Stephen, uncle to Virginia Woolf as well as a famous Victorian criminal law scholar and judge, spoke for many moralists when he said that it was "morally right to hate criminals."[10] Likewise, liability in tort (injury to others) was itself limited to "fault," a moral concept implying a breach of a duty owed; and contractual obligations were long based on "promises," yet another moral concept.

The natural law (NL-2) supposition that law and morality are the same points to two antithetical conclusions. If, on the one hand, law and morality really are the same, then surely human beings have *both* a moral and legal duty to obey the law. If, however, on the other hand, a particular law clashes with morality, then it clearly is not real law and hence it carries no moral authority whatever. As such it can impose no obligation, moral or otherwise, upon anyone to obey it. To the contrary, one may be morally bound to disobey such law. Thus, paradoxically, natural law theory, by linking law with morality, contributed both to the development of (a) a rule of law (based in part on a moral obligation to obey law) and (b) civil disobedience (based on the notion that immoral law, no matter how legal, is not law at all). Both of these developments have played central roles in our legal history.

PARADIGM B: *Law and morality are qualitatively different from each other: the former exists in the form of an (empirical) "IS"; the latter is a (normative) "OUGHT," based not upon fact but upon (non-empirical) preferences or aspirations.*

In modern jurisprudence, this paradigm takes two diverse forms, both of which lead to legal positivism and the proposition that law and morality are separate.

1. In the original Anglo-American form of legal positivism (attributed to the English legal thinkers, Jeremy Bentham, and his lieutenant, John Austin),[11] law was conceived to be more than a rule or body of rules. To them it was one of several sanctions (including morality and religion) that societies had developed over time to induce their members to act in an acceptable manner. Through various pleasures/inducements (calculated to encourage) or pains/penalties (to discourage), societies molded their free-willed members into patterns of behavior that broadly conformed with social needs. But it had not been

done rationally in accordance with a humanly contrived agenda. The English Benthamites called for a "root-and-branch" reorganization of society; first, by positing a specific, humanly-prescribed goal (promoting the greatest happiness of the greatest number); and, second, by using the reformed legal sanction, "positive law," as a means for inducing individual members of society to choose voluntarily (on the basis of their own "pleasure/pain" calculations) to comply with the law, thereby promoting the posited goals of society. (According to this scheme the legal and moral sanctions differed from each other; they could be used most effectively by analyzing them separately as to source, form, and manner of enforcement.)

2. In a later, European version of positive law (usually associated with the Austrian, Hans Kelsen),[12] "law" is regarded as a logically closed system of "norms" all derived, through a process of ratiocination, from a single basic norm (the *Grundnorm*) which is not law itself but the source of law. This form of positivism has two distinct aspects: First, the *Grundnorm* (which is similar in some ways to Immanuel Kant's a priori "Categorical Imperative" and also to the U.S. Constitution) expresses the nation's justification for its law and its aspirations. As such it is a form of morality as well as law; and, as the basis of law, it is not subject to empirical or logical proof. It is a normative "ought." Second, "laws" are legal norms logically deduced from the "Grundnorm" and, as such, they make up a series of "pure" laws based on reason, not morality.

All positivists insist that law can be understood only if it is separated from its moral, or normative aspects. For, as David Hume long ago asserted, one cannot logically infer a normative *ought* from an empirical *is*.[13] Whereas Kelsen was more likely to say one cannot infer the *Grundnorm* of law from laws, the English positivists, especially Bentham, were far more reform-minded. The latter would point out the fact that merely because law exists empirically in form X, it does not follow that X *should* exist either as a law or in the form X.

Of course, the English positivist approach to law demands some (moral) standard by which to evaluate, and to determine, the normative value of the empirical laws. Since the late eighteenth century, the dominant moral standard relied upon for determining the morality of law has been an empirical one, tied to the actual results produced; that is, no law, legal institution, or practice should be tolerated unless it can be empirically shown to promote some agreed upon moral standard. As already noted, that standard has long been utilitarianism, that is, "promoting the greatest happiness of the greatest number" of the members of society. (The utilitarian maxim will be considered more directly as Paradigm D.)

Returning to law as a "sanction," the English legal thinkers of the eighteenth and nineteenth centuries introduced a strikingly novel approach to law that necessitated the seeming "unnatural" conclusion that law and morality must be separated. They focused their attention not on the *source* of law but on the *results* it produces and, later still, its *function* (a concept developed by twentieth-century anthropologists and borrowed by such twentieth-century American legal thinkers as Karl Llewellyn and Felix Cohen).

Bentham and his followers concluded that law is but one of the four major sanctions societies rely upon in getting their individual members, each of whom is vested with his/her own self-interest, autonomy, and free will, to live together with a minimum of friction and to do the "work" necessary to sustain the society itself. There are four major social sanctions. The first is the *religious sanction,* which was the threat of eternal damnation instilled by high ritual to encourage (and on occasion terrorize) the public into obeying the teachings of the church. The second sanction, the *natural,* or *physical sanction,* is self-enforcing in that people's appetites and yearnings for the approval and rewards of cooperative living, as well as the necessities of life, are so strong that they can make even the most refractory mortals willingly pull themselves out of warm beds on cold mornings in order to report to workplaces they detest. Why? To earn paychecks, which they can spend in satisfaction of their own private wants and needs. Thus, appetites are both incentives and sanctions. The third sanction, the *moral sanction,* is wielded and imposed upon people by their ever-observant contemporaries (elders, betters, inferiors, and equals), all of whom make up an ever-changing but perennial review board, which is constantly watching and evaluating people's behavior, approvingly or otherwise, urging them to modify and moderate their conduct so as to comport with the "board's" expectations and preferences. When they refuse to comply with the "board's" demands, they risk the consequences: they may do nothing; but the "board" may react violently, expressing its disapproval in unpredictable ways calculated to make the people regret their daring to deviate from the demands or expectations placed upon them. In other words, the indeterminate "oughts" imposed upon people, and the consequences of people's failure to comply with such demands can be fatal. (Consider, for example, a civil rights activist in South Africa who, taking a moral stand, ignores the "oughts/ought nots" of his neighbors.) Though people may regard the demands placed upon them by neighbors and the general public as "immoral," or worse, most people comply — out of fear of the unknown and unpredictable consequences. This fear is what Bentham meant by the "moral sanction." Whatever it is, it is different from law; and we can never understand it, or law, unless we examine each of them separately. For fear of the public reaction (whether or not "moral") is surely one of the great motivating factors influencing human conduct. The fourth sanction, the *legal sanction*, is the threat of legal punishment which includes the innate fear of being caught and then adjudged guilty of violating the law.

Together, these sanctions impinge upon all human beings, enveloping them in a shroud of fears, inhibitions, perceptions, impressions, and aspirations that shape their conduct as they try to comport with the religious, natural, moral, and legal sanctions.

While all four social sanctions push and pull individuals, though not necessarily in the same manner or even in the same direction, only one— the "legal sanction" is capable of doing it rationally in an accountable manner. For laws, proper, or properly so called, can be defined to mean only those demands made upon people by a determinate human (as opposed to a superhuman) sovereign; and such a human sovereign can be held accountable to the larger society in ways that neither a divine lawgiver nor the faceless persons who wield the "moral sanction" can. For a rationally responsible human lawmaker can frame laws (that will be enforced by the legal sanction) strategically, as a mighty lever, imposing pleasures/benefits /pains/costs upon those subject to the laws so as to induce private parties to act in ways that benefit the greatest number of the members of society.

This paradigm obviously conflates two totally distinct ideas, each of which impinge upon the law and morality question differently. The first idea is result-oriented: law "should" be used to attain some humanly prescribed "purpose," the morality of law depending upon the morality of the purpose to which it is put and its effectiveness in realizing that purpose. In that result-oriented context, the first idea in the paradigm is properly associated with utilitarianism. The second notion is that law must be separated from morality for analytical purposes. It is widely associated with positivism, a form of jurisprudence that may, but need not be linked to utilitarianism.

Generally speaking, positivism concerns law as a *means*; utilitarianism focuses on the *ends* to which law should be put. Both positivism and utilitarianism have been major causes of contention in modern debates about the relationship between law and morality, partly because they imply two different forms of morality. As each of them raises quite different questions regarding that relationship, the two are treated here separately. Specifically, Paradigm B is confined to the positivistic idea that law and morality are two distinct social sanctions that must be kept separate for analytical reasons. The utilitarian idea, that law should be used to attain a humanly-prescribed (moral) goal or purposes, will be discussed under Paradigm D.

Undoubtedly, a large part of the present-day confusion about the relationship between law and morality is attributable to the fact that the two different usages of morality implicit in utilitarianism and positive law have been, historically, part of a single system of legal thought. In the present century, however, the two ideas— positivism and utilitarianism— have drifted apart, and have taken on lives of their own. As such they often appear in modern law and morality discourse under the aegis of different groups of legal thinkers, making quite different claims.

For the purpose of clarifying the two, I shall try to show how they came to be conflated in the first place.

In Anglo-American jurisprudence, the original source of both positivism and utilitarianism was Jeremy Bentham (1748-1832). A root-and-branch reformer, he wanted to rebuild a corrupt society (as he perceived the England of his day to be) on a rational and morally sound foundation. For that purpose he regarded "positive law" (i.e., law defined as a social sanction and separated from the other social sanctions, including morality) to be the rational means by which a morally good society could be attained (i.e., a society in which the greatest number of persons enjoy the greatest happiness).

Bentham's notions of positive law, and the separation of law from morality, were given new life in the twentieth century by both Hans Kelsen and Prof. H.L.A. Hart. In his *Concept of Law*, published in 1955, Hart posited a model legal system consisting of "rules" and, distinguishing law from morality, he explored the limits of the usefulness of legal rules.[14] More than any other modern legal philosopher, Hart demonstrated the need to separate law from morality in order to determine when and where the legal sanction can be used effectively.

The relationship between law and morality in the modern world has been deeply influenced by Benthamite utilitarianism, by Austinian analytical jurisprudence, and, more recently, by Professor Hart's updated version of both. Still, many reasonable persons do not understand how or why law and morality came to be separated in modern jurisprudence. They believe law (in a quasi-natural law sense) to be something other than a social sanction wielded by a human lawmaker. Still other persons refuse to think of morality as a "social sanction" wielded by a faceless public and expressed in the form of negative or positive reactions. They therefore look askance, and often in anger born of deep hurt, at the assertion that law can, or should be separated from morality.

PARADIGM C: *Law is morally neutral.*

This paradigm might be called the "due process-neutral principles" paradigm. Unlike natural law, it equates law with a humanly contrived institutional process by which policies are framed by legislatures (in the form of substantive law), implemented by administrative officials or agencies, applied by the judiciary, and enforced by the constabulary. All are parts of a single process that, like an enormously complicated yet delicate mechanism, must be constantly fine-tuned so that all of its parts work in harmony.

Of capital importance to this paradigm are the procedures and practices that define the legality of the process "in motion." Unlike the rules of substantive law that are subject to sudden change by a legislature (reflecting moral crisis), the procedures and practices governing the legal process, and especially in judicial matters, are relatively non-political in character and rarely change. But it is precisely the steady allegiance to such technical points of procedure and practice that make law more than just another good idea or an abstract idealistic theory. For the technical points of procedure and practice add to the process a kind of institutional disinterestedness based on professional expertise that assures everyone a public forum in which they are entitled to a hearing with "due process of law." That assurance — as a legal fact, not as an elegant but empty right— is very possibly the most valuable contribution law has to offer. As such, the neutrality of law is the source of its morality, and is the "ideal" relationship between law and morality.

According to the "due process-neutral principles" paradigm, then, the true morality of law is not to be found in substantive rules, and not in the results reached in specific cases, but in its continued operation in compliance with established procedures (including its own "inner" morality) that, through time, protects law itself from the extremes of political and moral passion.

But the neutrality of law does more; it also leads society, according to its own invisible agenda, in directions unforseen by lawmakers. Through incremental changes based on reason, tempered by the discipline of legal procedures, yet made in response to practical need, some of the most valuable human changes have come about. Thus, as Sir Henry Maine noted, one of the most seminal developments in all of human history was brought about in Roman law not by royal fiat, and not by statute, but by learned jurisconsulats working on a case-by-case basis over long spans of time.[15] Gradually, they changed the very foundation of Roman law "from status to contract." That is, Roman citizens, whose place in society and prospects in life had long been determined exclusively by their family status, gradually won from the courts the legal standing to act in their own capacity, and not as members of their family. As such they were free for the first time to make their own arrangements, through mutual agreement, or contract, with others irrespective of the status of their family or their status within their family. Thus was born the Western version of individualism based on equality before the law.

The English common law developed in a similar fashion. One looks in vain for the name of the English Justinian who promulgated the law of "torts" or "contracts" or "bailments." For there were no lawgivers and, in fact, down to the eighteenth century, there was no body of substantive law rules as such. Those rules remained inchoate, buried in countless judicial opinions delivered orally and reported haphazardly over many generations. They were not, and possibly could not have been, extricated from the procedural aspects of the writ system and cast in the form of substantive rules prior to the post-Blackstone era. But the point is that the common law system, preoccupied with resolving private disputes with a minimum of concern for any purpose other than resolving disputes in a manner that afforded specific parties a fair trial, generated the legal tradition and precedents out of which the body of substantive law that we now call the common law subsequently emerged.

Thus, it was the combination of professional discipline and the semi-autonomous momentum (from case to case) of the legal process— rather than a body of rules handed down by some omnipotent lawgiver— that brought about the substantive body of common law. It was built up over long spans of time, not in accordance with any preconceived blueprint or the will of any omniscient lawgiver, but silently and slowly— like the Mississippi delta.

The "due process-neutral principles" paradigm posits that the morality of law lies in workings of the legal process itself; in the present, it assures private persons a kind of access to legal justice that is impervious to the vicissitudes of political passion; and, through time, it conduces to unanticipatable long-term changes that, being based on the discipline of the legal process itself, are beneficial in effect. In short, law (in the form of the legal process) generates its own invaluable forms of morality. All other forms of morality obtrude, and disrupt the natural fulfillment of law's own morality.

PARADIGM D: *The morality of law is determined by the morality of the uses to which it is put and the results it brings about in the real world.*

This oft-derided "result-oriented" paradigm cuts a wide swath in modern legal thought and it cannot be associated exclusively with any single school of jurisprudence. However, as already suggested, its most seminal modern expounder was Jeremy Bentham, who is also properly labeled a "utilitarian-positivist."

One of the really great moments in the history of law occurred when Bentham, who had heard Blackstone and others endlessly extol the virtues of English law, looked out his window and saw not— as he had been led to expect— a smiling land full of happy and prosperous people. He saw, rather, a nation rife with poverty, crime, misery, and woe. Whereupon he asked himself what was so wonderful about any legal system that produced, condoned, or contributed to the perpetuation of such grim circumstances? Should not the purpose of law be to enrich the quality of life of those who live under it? And is not its *true* relationship with morality to be determined by the results it produces?

As noted earlier, Bentham's belief that law should be useful in dealing with the problems of society led him to develop his own version of utilitarianism. Long a favorite target of ridicule by moral philosophers, lawyers, among others, should not forget that Bentham wrote at a time when less than 5 percent of the English public had a voice in government. Thus, whatever the moralists may say about the crudity of Bentham's moral philosophy, his bold assertion, made under those unhappy circumstances, that law should be used to "promote the greatest happiness of the greatest number," inspired badly needed reform in law itself and, no less important, numerous social reforms through law.[16]

Bentham's inspiring humanitarian message spurred more than one generation of lawyers and legal thinkers, especially in the United States, to worry about the law and morality problem in terms of the real world results attributable to law. Thus in the earlier parts of the present century, the advocates of "sociological jurisprudence" seized upon this aspect of Bentham's message and, like him, insisted that law has a practical, real world moral purpose, though they defined that purpose more in terms of social justice than "the greatest happiness of the greatest number." Also like him, they believed that the morality of law was to be measured by its success in realizing that (moral) purpose.

Later still, the "legal realists" of the 1930s and 1940s, following the lead of both Bentham and sociological jurisprudence, constantly worried about what they called "the social performance of law." It is probable that those same concerns lie close to the heart of the "Critical Legal Studies" movement of the present day as well.

Thus, the Benthamite concern for the "results" of law added a valuable dimension to modern jurisprudence and also pointed moral inquiry in a new direction. It also complicated the relationship between morality and law. For it leaves us, like Bentham, wondering if there exists a better measure of the value of a legal system, or indeed of the rule of law itself, than the quality of life of those subject to it? And if this approach stresses the morality of results, it also imposes a heavy moral burden on the hand that wields the tool of law.

PARADIGM E: *Law grows out of morality, the latter being an essential earlier stage in the evolution of the former.*

This paradigm, reflecting the ideas of the now largely ignored historical school of jurisprudence, assumes that though law and morality are different, they are linked, through time, in a symbiotic relationship; as puberty grows out of infancy, and adulthood out of puberty, so law grows out of morality which has itself evolved earlier from custom. In this sense, both morality and law stem from the same experience that gives a people its distinctive national character. (So Holmes and the "life of the law.")[17]

A nation's character is molded by the dialectic interplay between and among normless habits, customs, morality, and law. Some, but not all of those habits and customs are followed simply out of unthinking inertia; some, but not all, are invested with moral authority and deferred to because people think — and are taught that they ought to do so; some, but not all are enforced as law by the legal sanction. Which, of all the habit-based customs, are to be invested with normative content (and to be regarded as moral), and which moral obligations are to be enforced as law, are questions that have to be answered anew as time passes, new ideas appear, aspirations change, and issues, old and new, occur and recur in different lights.

Thus, whether a given practice (such as owning firearms, or smoking cigarettes in public places, or using steroids) is a matter of normless custom (and therefore left to each person's own unfettered discretion), or a matter of morality (and therefore subject to the extra-legal, but often crushing force of moral approbation/disapprobation imposed by an ever-observant public), or a matter of law (and therefore legal or illegal and enforced by governmental authority) is not solely the result of rationally agreed upon decisions. It is, at least in part, the result of each society's own unique cultural history and the state of affairs existing at a particular time. As law may be used to create slavery at one time, so it may be used to establish racial equality at another time— both usages (according to this paradigm) saying as much about the changing nature of morality and its relationship with law as it does about the goodness or badness of racial discrimination.

Thus, according to this paradigm, the relationship between law and morality is not so much a matter of legal responses to immorality, as it is rather a matter of public sentiments (measured by degrees of outrage or indifference) and timing; if, and when, a consensus emerges on a given issue (when, that is, the majority of the people seem to believe some thing or some state of affairs is no longer tolerable), legal action is possible, and usually forthcoming. Lacking such a consensus, however, recourse to law will be at best a dead letter or worse. Such were the lessons of the *Dred Scott* decision and Prohibition.

PARADIGM F: *Law is institutionalized immorality.*

This Marxist paradigm defines the relationship between law and morality with remarkable clarity: Law is an instrument of oppression created by the governing classes to protect and to further their own interests. As those interests are in derogation of those of the people generally, it follows that law, like the interests it preserves, is immoral. Law and morality are, in short, contradictory notions.

Though the United States Constitution ordains that the people are sovereign, one need not be a Marxist to worry about who, and which interests, actually control American law, and to what ends. Thus our aim, consistent with this paradigm, ought not to be to keep our law untainted by private interests, certainly not by entrusting our well-being to the wisdom and philanthropic goodness of some elite group, class, or party. To the contrary, it should be to keep American law open to the influence of *all* private interests, making the points of contact more a matter of public record and establishing clear lines of accountability between private and public officials. After all, the people have "interests" and (as Roscoe Pound and the champions of "sociological jurisprudence" never tired of saying) our law exists to protect, not to destroy, those interests.[18] Morality, however, demands that our law should seek not only to protect private interests, but to do so in ways that further the higher interests of society as well.

Here, then, are six different paradigms of law positing quite different relationships with morality. It takes no great insight to see that each of the paradigms conceives of law as having an altogether different function; and it is therefore a truism to say that under each paradigm, law has a different relationship with morality.

This observation, unhelpful as it is, does remind us that the relationship between law and morality depends, in large part, on our reason for wanting to know. It is undoubtedly impossible to explain, psychologically or otherwise, why some persons are drawn to, and become more attached to one or another of the paradigms. Why, for example, does one person gravitate towards the certainty of the "neutral principles" approach and another to the open-ended uncertainty of "legal realism?" Or why does one generation enthusiastically adopt the "law and economics" agenda, with economic "efficiency" as its goal, and another generation, with no less zeal, is inspired by the idea of "sociological jurisprudence" and take the eradication of racial prejudice and poverty as the special mission of law?

Though these questions are perhaps unanswerable, it is worth remembering that *all* the paradigms are, in fact, part of our legal tradition. As such, we can legitimately have recourse to them when and where appropriate. And all of them, taken together, enrich our understanding of law.

LAW AND MORALITY: A HISTORICAL PERSPECTIVE

So much for the relationship between law and morality seen from the point of view of modern legal theory. The same problem will now be viewed from an historical point of view.

Two points stand out: first, the law and morality problem is as old as law itself; and, second, in the modern era the relationship between law and morality has been profoundly influenced by extra-legal, non-moral developments not involving law or morality as such. A brief word about each of these points is in order.

A. *Law and Morality: Traditional Answers to an Ancient Problem*

The omnipresence of morality not only raises the familiar "right/wrong" and "ought/ought not" questions about every aspect of law; it also raises antecedent questions of a less clearly defined moral character. These questions are: first, what form of morality will be recognized?, second, who will decide?, and third, what role do private citizens play in determining what morality should be recognized? The practical answers a society gives to these questions, not the answers provided by moral philosophy, determine the de facto nature of the relationship between law and morality. Moreover, they are questions that admit of historical answers.

1. *What form of morality will be recognized*? Philosophers, legal and otherwise, have long been troubled by the relationship between law and morality. In fact the two have always been so closely entwined that they have been virtually inseparable. Even when and where law has taken the form of an authoritative written code ascribed to, or derived from, a lawgiver of supreme moral (as well as legal) authority, the meaning of the promulgated law has inevitably remained, in certain circumstances, unclear. Consequently every social order based on *any* form of law has had to make provision for "interpreting" and "clarifying" ambiguities in the law itself.

a. The nature of such provisions necessarily have great bearing on the relationship between law and morality. For, at the minimum, the interpreters (or exegetes) of law inevitably infuse into law their own sense of what the law "ought" to be, and how it "should" be interpreted in the particular circumstances before them. Like the famous Roman scholars who rediscovered the Code of Justinian in medieval Bologna, these interpreters added "glosses" to the blackest black-letter— and those glosses included their own (moral) "oughts."

b. The status, qualifications, and standing of those persons responsible for interpreting and clarifying the law, and the means they adopt for that purpose, differ from legal system to legal system, from society to society, and from time to time. But they are all responding to a need endemic to law itself: any authoritatively promulgated legal rule must take a fixed form, and (therefore) it is, by definition, limited by that form. But life is not so limited. To that extent, law is static in character, and life is dynamic. Hence all law-based societies are compelled to seek means to keep the authoritatively promulgated law alive in a world of changing times and circumstances. One way or another, they all do so by introducing some form of morality into the law.

(1) Historically, most societies have accomplished this end by entrusting the custody of law to a carefully selected corp of exegetes, lay or otherwise, whose personal preferences are tempered by long training and rigorous discipline.

(2) Familiar examples include the rabbis of Jewish law and the juriconsulats of Roman law.

(3) In English legal history, a distinct professional guild of barristers, serjeants, and judges, all members of one of the Inns of Court, gave the common law its form and content. As such, that law (inevitably) reflected the moral, as well as legal values of the members of the guilds of barristers. When, however, the courts' practices and policies became too legalistic and formulistic, private parties (who use law, as well as being subject to it) turned to the King, as the fountain of justice, for relief from the law, they were appealing to the royal conscience (another form of morality) for more justice and less law. In time these appeals led to that peculiar mixture of law and morality called equity.

(4) In the United States, where the Constitution takes the form of a written document, the question of its (current) meaning, and who has the authority to say so, continues to be a matter of public concern. Of course, ever since John Marshall held that our Constitution was a legal document, its interpretation has been regarded as a matter of law (rather than politics or morality or religion). As such, its "interpretation" has naturally been left to the members of the United States Supreme Court.

(a) At times, the Supreme Court has "construed" the Constitution literally; at other times in accordance with the "original intent" of the Framers; and at still other times as an "organic" document that grows through time, its being kept alive by constant reinterpretation in accordance with changing circumstances. The moral values of the justices, including their ideas about what the Constitution "ought" to be and do, account in large part for these changes in the meaning given to the Constitution.

(b) In the American legal system, the relationship between constitutional law and morality has long been

established on a case by case basis by the Supreme Court's
sitting as a court of law, not as a court of morality. Even so, the
Court has never been able to exclude morality from legal matters
coming before it. Perhaps the moral values of the justices have
been most often expressed, indirectly, through the paradigm of
law they adopted. As such, the morality issue may well have
been concealed from the justices themselves. For they have
consistently insisted that they were guided in their work only by
law, not morality.

2. *Who will decide?* The foregoing instances illustrate ways
by which various societies have permitted some form of a
dynamic "ought" (morality) to be infused into the black-letter "is"
of their law. History suggests, in effect, that those persons who
have the authority to decide what law "is" and what law
"means," inevitably establish a relationship, often formalized,
between law and morality and therefore what the law "ought" to
be. Thus, the official relationship between law and morality is
usually a carefully guarded one, the morality being that of
persons assiduously trained and disciplined to adopt and
maintain the integrity of a particular image of the law itself.

3. *The role of private citizens.* Even so, private individuals
may also be strongly motivated by a personal sense of morality;
and, as noted at the outset, in a law-oriented democracy, such
persons tend to expect law to uphold, if not enforce, their sense
of right and wrong. When it fails to do so, they perceive conflicts
between law and morality, and they protest in the name of
morality.

B. *Law and Morality: Modern Dimensions*

Few would deny that American law has dramatically
changed during the last hundred or so years. So much so that its
looming presence in everyday life has become, like shopping
malls, a virtual hallmark of modernity. Much of that law differs,
qualitatively as well as quantitatively, from that of the pre-
twentieth century. Yet popular ideas and attitudes toward law,
and especially its assumed relationship with morality, often
remain those of an earlier era. As such, they may themselves be
a source of frustration as well as confusion.

Modern law, and public attitudes towards that law, have
been overwhelmingly conditioned by the looming presence of
the federal government which, in the last half of the twentieth

century, casts a long shadow across the whole of American life. Thus, the relationship between law and morality in the United States, certainly in this century, has been profoundly influenced by the phenomenal growth of government. Many of the innovations in legal theory discussed above, and some of the bitterest law and morality controversies in the modern era, have in fact involved law only indirectly. The real bone of contention has been government or, more specifically, the federal government and its policies. Since the government can act officially only through law, major changes in the dominant philosophy of government or the pursuit of new policies by government must have enormous legal (as well as political) ramifications.

This essay began with the assertion that the relationship between law and morality is both complex and confusing. Some of the sources of confusion have been attributed to the variety of concepts of law itself. Thus (to restate the paradigms discussed above): law may be said to reflect morality; law may be said to be what "is," which differs intrinsically from the "oughts" of morality; law may be said to be morally "neutral"; law may be said to be moral only insofar as it leads to moral results; law may be said to be a stage in the development of a society's value system, as certain non-normative habits become social values to be protected by, or pursued through, the powers of government; and law may be said to be institutionalized (and legitimized) immorality.

Other confusions arise from the fact that law is, in one sense, the voice of the government; and as the role of government changes, so its forms and functions must also change. Such changes bring about different relationships and conflicts with morality.

Then, of course, there is the question of the meaning of morality itself. Is it our conscience telling us intuitively what is right and wrong? Or is it some objective standard, outside ourselves, signifying what is right and wrong? Or is it our principled conclusions derived from a dispassionate, rational analysis of the dilemma we face in life and act upon in good faith? Or is it a system of values shared by, and in some senses, peculiar to, the members of a given society that find expression in the collective conscience of a society?

Confusion abounds. As noted long ago, we are lost in a forest of sign posts. But that observation confirms one of the dicta of the old "legal realists": where there is room for choice, there is not only indeterminacy— there is also the possibility of change for the better.

If that be true, the morality of American law, and indeed of American society, depends upon the choices made by the nation's people, their motives, and the ways they act upon them. So put, the relationship between law and morality is itself a very personal moral problem for everyone. But it is more. For, ultimately, the relationship between law and morality in our day will be defined empirically, not philosophically, by peoples' choices, including their choice of one of the available "paradigms of law." The legal history of our times will tell the tale.

NOTES

1. Mark Twain somewhere observed that the difference between the "right word" and "*almost* the right word" is the difference between "lightening" and "lightening-bug," from which I conclude that one can never learn much about "lightening" by focusing on "lightening bugs." In the present context, this means that approaching the "relationship between law and morality" in terms of particular problems (such as teen-age pregnancies), or particular Supreme Court cases (such as *Roe v. Wade*), is "almost" the same as discussing the general topic itself.
2. O.W. Holmes, *The Common Law* (Boston, Mass.: 1881), 1.
3. J.S. Kraus and J.L. Coleman, "Morality and the Theory of Rational Choice," *Ethics* 97 (1987): 715 (emphasis added).
4. Stephen Lukes, *Marxism and Morality* (New York: Oxford, 1987), 2.
5. Stephen Clark, review of Basil Mitchell, "Morality: Religious and Secular," *Times Literary Supplement*, 28 November 1980.
6. The "law-morality" problem has two entirely distinct dimensions, each of which raises two qualitatively different types of questions: First, is a given "moral" issue one that law *can*, in its nature, deal with effectively? Second, assuming law *can* deal with a given problem effectively, *should* it be used? The first ("can") question raises a practical, or empirical issue having to do with the nature of law itself, its inherent limitations, and the scope of its effectiveness in a particular context. (Example: given the number, and patterns of dispersal, etc., of children in the U.S., no law is capable of effectively controlling their tooth brushing habits. Any legislative attempt to do so would fail.) The second question raises a (*non*-empirical) normative issue: Assuming law *can* effectively address a given problem, *should* it be used to do so? (Example: evidentiary rules banning the use of unlawfully seized evidence. Often officials can,

and do, seize such evidence. The issue is a normative one: should it be admissable in court trials? The U.S. Constitution, which guarantees every defendant "due process of law," also prohibits "unlawful searches and seizures.") Of course persons differ for numerous reasons on legal questions. Still, whether law "ought" to be used is intrinsically different from whether it "can" deal with the issue in question. As a result, many persons who acknowledge and deplore the existence of certain conditions which they (morally) deplore, may also believe that law simply *cannot*, in its nature, effectively deal with it and therefore assert that it *should not* be used. But this is true not because they morally condone the condition, or are morally indifferent to its consequences, but because they believe law is simply incapable of dealing with it.

7.   In and following the period during which the U.S. Constitution was framed and ratified, there were three perceived shortcomings of traditional natural law that were addressed during the nineteenth century: (a) *Natural law is "over" human society and fatalistically ordains the destiny of all human beings.* Like Goethe's *Faust*, many of the revolutionaries of the period, including many of the founders of the new nation in the New World, rejected the notion that human possibilities or prospects were limited *by anything*, divine or otherwise. Bold and rash men alike regarded traditional boundaries on human accomplishment to be challenges rather than innate human limitations; and they sought a form of (human) law of their own (human) making which they, *qua* human beings, themselves could make, control and change to meet their needs. (b) *By positing that law was a part of morality, some version of natural law doctrine not only sanctioned the laws of unjust regimes, it also made obedience to their laws morally obligatory.* (c) *As natural law stemmed from superhuman (divine or natural) sources it must be universal. Yet law obviously was no more universal than language.*

8.   J.M. Finnis, *Natural Law and Natural Rights* (New York: Oxford University Press, 1981).

9.   See, generally, Ronald Dworkin, *Taking Rights Seriously* (Cambridge, Mass.: Harvard University Press, 1977). More specifically, see "Is There a Right to Pornography?" *Oxford Journal of Legal Studies* 1 (1981).

10.   Sir James Fitzgerald Stephen, *A History of the Criminal Law of England* 3 vols. (London: Macmillan, 1883), 2: 81.

11.   A general reference (i) to Bentham is to Jeremy Bentham, *An Introduction to the Principles of Morals and Legislation*, ed. J.H. Burns and H.L.A. Hart (London: The Athelone Press, University of London: 1970); and (ii) to John Austin is *The Province of Jurisprudence Determined*, ed. H.L.A. Hart (London: 1954). See, also, Jeremy Bentham, *Of Law in General*, ed. H.L.A. Hart (London: The Athelone Press, University of London, 1970). For a discussion

of the latter, see H.L.A. Hart, *Essays on Bentham: Studies in Jurisprudence and Political Theory* (Oxford: Clarendon Press, 1982), esp. ch. 2.

12. For Kelsen, see Hans Kelsen, *The Pure Theory of Law* (Berkeley, Calif.: University of California Press, 1934).

13. See David Hume, *A Treatise on Human Nature* (1777), quoted in Lord Lloyd of Hampstead, QC and M.D.A. Freeman, *Lloyd's Introduction to Jurisprudence*, 5th ed. (London: Stevens and Sons, 1985), 33; note also, Hume's famous comment: "If we take in our hand any volume; of divinity or school metaphysics, for instance, let us ask, *Does it contain any abstract reasoning concerning quantity or number?* NO. *Does it contain any experiental reasoning concerning matter of fact and existence?* NO. Commit it then to frames: for it can contain nothing but sophistry and illusion." David Hume, *An Enquiry Concerning Human Understanding*, 3rd ed., ed. P.H. Niddich (1975), t. 3.

14. H.L.A. Hart, *The Concept of Law* (Oxford: Clarendon Press, 1961).

15. Sir Henry Maine, *Ancient Law* (London: J. Murray, 1861), 170; see generally, Peter G. Stein, *Legal Evolution: The Story of an Idea* (New York: Cambridge University Press, 1980), esp. ch. 4.

16. See generally, Elie Halvy, *The Growth of Philosophic Radicalism*, trans. Mary Morris (London: Faber and Faber, 1928); see also John Dinwiddy, *Bentham* (New York: Oxford University Press, 1989).

17. See n. 1.

18. See Lloyd and Freeman, *Lloyd's Introduction to Jurisprudence*, 564-70, 606-14.

3

The Idea of Human Rights: Is the Idea of Human Rights Ineliminably Religious?

MICHAEL J. PERRY

The conception of human rights, based upon the assumed existence of a human being as such, broke down at the very moment when those who professed to believe in it were for the first time confronted with people who had indeed lost all other qualities and specific relationships — except that they were still human. The world found nothing sacred in the abstract nakedness of being human.[1]

We almost all accept . . . that human life in all its forms is *sacred*. . . . For some of us, this is a matter of religious faith; for others, of secular but deep philosophical belief.[2]

The name of the state where I was born and raised — Kentucky— derives from an Indian word meaning "the dark and bloody ground."[3] Were there an Indian word for "the dark and bloody time," it would aptly name this century in which we have been born and raised, a century as unrelentingly dark and bloody as any in human history. In the midst of all the terrible inhumanity of the twentieth century, however, there is a hopeful story: the emergence in international law of the idea of human rights.[4]

The increased and increasing protection of human rights by international law in the period since the end of the Second

World War is an important and hopeful story, amply recounted elsewhere.[5] But it is not a story that should dispel our skepticism about the extent to which many basic human rights, notwithstanding their protection by international law, are really any better off now than they were before 1945. (Even as the twentieth century ends, the furious slaughter of innocents continues— most famously, perhaps, in the former Yugoslavia.[6] Neither that story nor that skepticism is the subject of this essay, however. The internationalization of human rights— and the attendant rhetoric of human rights so pervasive in world today, especially in the Western world— present an important occasion, in my view, for addressing several fundamental questions about the idea of human rights.

The idea of human rights— the idea that has emerged in international law in the period since the Second World War— i s complex. In this chapter the main constituents of the idea will be explored. In this essay, however, I am interested only in one constituent— albeit, a foundational one: the conviction that every human being is sacred. Is that conviction inescapably religious— and the idea of human rights, therefore, ineliminably religious?

I

"The International Bill of Human Rights," as it is sometimes called, consists of three documents. The first of the these, the Universal Declaration of Human Rights (1948), speaks, in the Preamble, of "the inherent dignity . . . of all members of the human family" and of "the dignity and worth of the human person." In Article I, the Declaration proclaims: "All human beings . . . should act towards one another in a spirit of brotherhood." The second and third documents are the International Covenant on Civil and Political Rights (1976) and the International Covenant on on Economic, Social, and Cultural Rights (1976). The Preamble common to both covenants echoes the Universal Declaration in speaking of "the inherent dignity . . . of all members of the human family." The Preamble then states:

"These rights derive from the inherent dignity of the human person. . . ." A fourth document, the American Declaration of the Rights and Duties of Man (1948), begins: "The American peoples have acknowledged the dignity of the individual. . . . The American states have on repeated occasions recognized that the essential rights of man are not derived from the fact that he is a national of a certain state, but are based upon attributes of his human personality. . . ." The Preamble to the American Declaration proclaims: "All men . . . should conduct themselves as brothers to one another." A fifth document, the American Convention on Human Rights (1978), echoes the American Declaration in stating, in the Preamble, that "the essential rights of man are not derived from one's being a national of a certain state, but are based upon attributes of the human personality." Similarly, the African Charter on Human and Peoples' Rights (1986) states, in the Preamble, that "fundamental human rights stem from the attributes of human beings."

The idea of human rights that informs these various international human rights documents (and many others) is, in part, the idea that *there is something about each and every human being, simply as a human being, such that certain things ought not to be done to him or her and certain other things ought to be done for him or her.*[7] The "every human being, simply as a human being," is represented in the Universal Declaration of Human Rights (Article 2) by this language: "Everyone is entitled to all the rights and freedoms set forth in this Declaration, without distinction of any kind, such as race, colour, sex, language, religion, political or other opinion, national or social origin, property, birth or other status."[8] The International Covenant on Economic, Social and Cultural Rights and the International Covenant on Civil and Political Rights each contain identical language.

The question to which this formulation of the idea of human rights gives rise is this: What, precisely, is that "something about each and every human being, simply as a human being"— what is it about us "simply as human beings"— such that certain things ought not to be done to us and certain other things ought to be done for us? To ask the question in the words of the

American Declaration, the American Convention, and the African Charter, what are the relevant "attributes" of each and every human being— the attributes on which "the essential rights of man" are based? The principal such attribute, according to the documents of the International Bill of Human Rights, is "the inherent dignity of all members of the human family" (from which derive human rights).

What are we to make of such talk: talk about "the inherent dignity" of all human beings, about all human beings as members of one "family," and about the importance, therefore, of all human beings acting towards one another "in a spirit of brotherhood"? It is easy enough to understand such talk as *religious* talk.[9] But is it possible, finally, to understand such talk in a nonreligious ("secular") sense? Is there, at least, a nonreligious equivalent for such talk, and, if so, what is it? Or must we conclude that the idea of human rights is indeed ineliminably religious, that a fundamental constituent of the idea, the conviction that every human being is sacred (has "inherent dignity," is "an end in himself," or the like), is inescapably religious?[10]

II

What does it means to say that a conviction (belief, idea, worldview, etc.) is or is not "religious"?[11]

In *Sources of the Self: The Making of the Modern Identity*, Charles Taylor has observed that "the problem of the meaning of life is . . . on our agenda, however much we may jibe at the phrase."[12] The problem of the meaning of life does not arise for everyone, it is not on everyone's agenda (even if, as Taylor says, it is on the agenda of "our" age). But it does arise for many. The problem can even arise *again* for someone, after it had been resolved, or repressed— someone who had been convinced of the meaningfulness of life, and especially of her own life, but whose conviction has been gradually eroded or perhaps suddenly shattered. A principal occasion of its arising (or arising again)— at least, of its arising in an existential, as distinct from merely intellectual, way— is a searing encounter with such common but elemental events as sickness, old age, and death. Another principal occasion is an encounter, whether personal or vicarious, with evil and the terrible, primal suffering evil causes. Such experiences, and experiences of other kinds, can leave one with a feeling that she is, or might be, a stranger, an alien, an exile, homeless, anxious, vulnerable, threatened, in a world, a universe, that is, finally and radically, unfamiliar, hostile, perhaps even pointless, absurd. Albert Camus wrote: "What, then, is that incalculable feeling that deprives the mind of the sleep necessary to life? A world that can be explained even with bad reasons is a familiar world. But, . . . in a universe suddenly divested of illusions and lights, man feels an alien, a stranger. His exile is without remedy since he is deprived of the memory of a lost home or the hope of a promised land. This divorce between man and his life, the actor and his setting, is properly the feeling of absurdity."[13]

Because of its radically alienating character, any such experience can be an occasion of existential confrontation with the problem of meaning: *Am I indeed an alien, an exile, homeless, in a world, a universe, that is strange, hostile, pointless, absurd? Or, instead, is the world, finally and radically, familiar, even gracious; does the world have a point, is it a project; is the world, in that sense, meaningful: meaning-full, full of meaning rather than bereft of it (and therefore meaning-less, absurd)? In particular, is the world hospitable to me in my deep yearning to be at home, rooted, connected?*[14] For the person deep in the grip of, the person claimed by, the problem of meaning, "the cry for meaning is a cry for ultimate relationship, for ultimate belonging," wrote Abraham Heschel. "It is a cry in which all pretensions are abandoned. Are we alone in the wilderness of time, alone in the dreadfully marvelous universe, of which we are a part and where we feel forever like strangers? Is there a Presence to live by? A Presence worth living for, worth dying for? Is there a way of living in the Presence? Is there a way of living compatible with the Presence?"[15]

One fundamental response to the problem of meaning is "religious": the trust that the world is finally ("at the end of the day") meaningful, meaningful in a way hospitable to our deepest yearnings. The word "religion" derives from the Latin verb "religare," which means to bind together again that which was once bound but has since been torn or broken; to heal.[16] A "religious" vision, then, etymologically understood, is a vision of final and radical reconciliation, a set of beliefs about how one is or can be bound or connected to the world— to the "other" and to "nature"— and, above all, to Ultimate Reality in a profoundly intimate way. If an ideology is not grounded or embedded in a vision of the finally or ultimately meaningful— the ultimately reconciled/reconciling— nature of the world, it is a confusion, on the understanding of religion presented here, to think of that ideology as "religious"— even if the ideology, like Marxism, is all-encompassing.[17]

Throughout human history it has been the so-called religious "mystics" who have trusted most deeply and affirmed most passionately the ultimate meaningfulness of reality.[18] Although her experience that the world is ultimately meaningful is deeply personal, the religious mystic denies that the experience is reducible to an idiosyncratic, perhaps even pathological, psychological state. Notwithstanding its noetic quality, however, and for all its potency, the mystical experience is often, if not invariably, transitory.[19] Moreover, not everyone is graced by such experience (or graced as often, or to the same degree). In the aftermath of mystical experience, therefore, or in its absence, fundamental questions about the meaningfulness of human existence— questions that so thoroughly pervade, and so relentlessly subvert, our lives— remain in need of answers that are intellectually satisfying and emotionally resonant. In Milan Kundera's *The Unbearable Lightness of Being,* the narrator, speaking of "the questions that had been going through Tereza's head since she was a child," says that "the only truly serious questions are ones that even a child can formulate. Only the most naive of questions are truly serious. They are the questions with no answers. A question with no answer is a barrier than cannot be breached. In other words, *it is questions with no answers that set the limits of human possibilities, describe the boundaries of human existence.*"[20] Communities, especially historically extended communities— "traditions"— are the principal matrices and repositories of religious answers to such questions:[21] Who are we? Where did we come from; what is our origin, our beginning? Where are we going; what is our destiny, our end?[22] What is the meaning of suffering? Of evil? Of death? And there is the cardinal question, the question that comprises many of the others: Is the world ultimately meaningful or, instead, ultimately bereft of meaning, meaning-less, absurd? If any questions are fundamental, *these* questions — "religious or limit questions"[23] — are fundamental. Such questions — "naive" questions, "questions with no answers," "barriers that cannot be breached"— are "the most serious and difficult . . . that any human being or society must face. . . . To formulate such questions honestly and well, to respond to them with passion and rigor, is the work of all theology. . . . Religions ask and respond to such fundamental questions. . . . Theologians, by definition, risk an intellectual life on the wager that religious traditions can be studied as authentic responses to just such questions."[24]

To say that a conviction is "religious," therefore, is to say that the conviction is embedded in— that it is an aspect, a constituent, of— a religious vision or cosmology: a vision according to which the world is ultimately meaningful (in a way hospitable to our deepest yearnings). (Of course, not every religious tradition tells the same story about the way in which the world is ultimately meaningful; often the stories are different, even if sometimes the stories are quite similar.) To ask if the conviction that every human being is sacred— the conviction that every human being has "inherent dignity," is "an end in himself," or the like— is inescapably religious is to ask if the conviction can be embedded in, if it can cohere with, if it can be supported by, either a nonreligious cosmology, according to which the world is, at the end of the day, not meaningful but meaningless, or a cosmological agnosticism that neither affirms nor denies the ultimate meaningfulness of the world.

Real moralities— the moralities that various human communities have actually lived— have always been cosmologically embedded: In every human community across time and space, "moral norms are closely linked to beliefs about the facts of human life and the world in which human life is set. To know what people find good in human action, we must know something about the powers and vulnerabilities they find characteristically human, and about how they explain the constraints that nature, power, finitude, and mortality impose on persons. . . . When they formulate moral norms and impose them on themselves and others, [persons] are trying to formulate relationships between realities and human purposes that allow them 'to live as [they] would in a world that is the way it is.'"[25] The conviction that every human being is sacred is cosmologically embedded; it is (as the reader shall see) embedded in a religious cosmology.[26] Indeed, in one or another version the conviction is embedded in more than one religious cosmology.[27] The question before us is whether the conviction can be embedded either in a nonreligious cosmology or in cosmological agnosticism.

III

As stated earlier, it is easy to understand talk about "the inherent dignity" of all human beings and related talk— for example, about all human beings as members of one "family" — as religious talk. But can we understand such talk in a secular sense? Perhaps it would now be useful to present a religious version of talk about the inherent dignity of all human beings; that is, a religious version— the Christian version, or at least [a Christian version]— of the conviction that every human being is sacred. We will then be in a better position to discern whether there is— indeed, whether there can be— a coherent secular version of the conviction.

For Christians the basic shape of the good life is indicated by the instruction given by Jesus at a Passover seder on the eve of his execution: "I give you a new commandment: love one another; you must love one another just as I have loved you."[28] The "one another" is radically inclusive: "You have heard how it was said, You will love your neighbor and hate your enemy. But I say this to you, love your enemies and pray for those who persecute you; so that you may be children of your Father in heaven, for he causes his sun to rise on the bad as well as the good, and sends down rain to fall on the upright and the wicked alike. For if you love those who love you, what reward will you get? Do not even the tax collectors do as much? And if you save your greetings for your brothers, are you doing anything exceptional? Do not even the gentiles do as much? You must therefore set no bounds to your love, just as your heavenly Father sets none to his."[29]

But, *why* should we "love one another as I have loved you"? The answer, in the vision of Judaism and Christianity, a vision nourished by what David Tracy has called "the analogical imagination,"[30] is that the Other (the outsider, the stranger, the alien), too, no less than onself and the members of one's family or tribe or nation, is a "child" of God — God the creator and sustainer of the universe, imag(in)ed, analogically, as loving "parent"[31] — and therefore a "sister"/"brother." As Hilary Putnam has written, the moral image central to what Putnam calls the Jerusalem-based religions "stresse[s] equality and also fraternity, as in the metaphor of the whole human race as One Family, of all women and men as sisters and brothers."[32] (At the beginning of its "Pastoral Letter on Catholic Social Teaching and the U. S. Economy," titled *Economic Justice for All*, the National Conference of Catholic Bishops wrote: "This letter is a personal invitation to Catholics to use the resources of our faith, the strength of our economy, and the opportunities of our democracy to shape a society that better protects the dignity and basic rights of our *sisters and brothers both in this land and around the world*."[33] In a recent essay on "The Spirituality of The Talmud," Ben Zion Bokser and Baruch M. Bokser state: "From this conception of man's place in the universe comes the sense of the supreme sanctity of all human life. 'He who destroys one person has dealt a blow at the entire universe, and he who sustains or saves one person has sustained the whole world'."[34] They continue:

The sanctity of life is not a function of national origin, religious affiliation, or social status. In the sight of God, the humble citizen is the

equal of the person who occupies the highest office. As one talmudist
put it: 'Heaven and earth I call to witness, whether it be an Israelite or
pagan, man or woman, slave or maidservant, according to the work of
every human being doth the Holy Spirit rest upon him. . . ." As the
rabbis put it: "We are obligated to feed non-Jews residing among us
even as we feed Jews; we are obligated to visit their sick even as we visit
the Jewish sick; we are obligated to attend to the burial of their dead
even as we attend to the burial of the Jewish dead."[35]

Friedrich Nietzsche was relentlessly critical of what he called
"the concept of the 'equal value of men before God'." That
concept, he wrote,

is extraordinarily harmful; one forbade actions and attitudes that were
in themselves among the prerogatives of the strongly constituted—as if
they were in themselves unworthy of men. One brought the entire
tendency of the strong into disrepute when one erected the protective
measures of the weakest (those who were weakest also when
confronting themselves) as a form of value."

Confusion went so far that one branded the very virtuosi of life
(whose autonomy offered the sharpest antithesis to the vicious and
unbridled) with the most opprobrious names. Even now one believes
one must disapprove of a Cesare Borgia; that is simply laughable. The
church has excommunicated German emperors on account of their
vices: as if a monk or priest had any right to join in a discussion about
what a Frederick II may demand of himself. A Don Juan is sent to hell:
that is very naive. Has it been noticed that in heaven all interesting men
are missing?— Just a hint to the girls as to where they can best find
their salvation.— If one reflects with some consistency, and moreover
with a deepened insight into what a "great man" is, no doubt remains
that the church sends all "great men" to hell— it fights against all
"greatness of man."

The degeneration of the rulers and the ruling classes has been the
cause of the greatest mischief in history! Without the Roman Caesars
and Roman society, the insanity of Christianity would never have come
to power.

When lesser men begin to doubt whether higher men exist, then the
danger is great! And one ends by discovering that there is *virtue* also

among the lowly and subjugated, the poor in spirit, and that *before God* men are equal— which has so far been the *non plus ultra* of nonsense on earth! For ultimately, the higher men measured themselves according to the standard of virtue of slaves— found they were "proud," etc., found all their higher qualities reprehensible.

When Nero and Caracalla sat up there, the paradox arose: "the lowest man is worth more than the man up there!" And the way was prepared for an image of God that was as remote as possible from the image of the most powerful— the god on the cross![36]

One might respond to the religious vision sketched here, if not like Nietzsche, then this way: "Even if I assume, for the sake of argument, that the Other is a 'child' of God and therefore my 'sister/brother,' still, why should I love the Other? In particular, why should I give a damn about the well-being of her or him who is, in some deep sense, my sister or my brother?" For us — or, at least, for most of us— it is a fundamental conviction, born not merely of our own experience, but of the experience of the historically extended communities ("traditions") that for many of us have been formative, that an important constituent of one's own well-being— of one's authentic flourishing as a human being— is concern for the well-being of one's sisters and brothers. We believe, based on that experience, that a life of loving connection to one's sisters and brothers is, to that extent, a flourishing life and that a life of unloving, uncaring, alienation from one's sisters and brothers is, to that extent, a withering life. This fundamental conviction about human good— about what it means to be (truly, fully) human, about what is of real and ultimate value in life, about what makes a life most deeply meaningful[37] — is, for us, bedrock; this is where our spade is turned.[38] There may be little of resonance for us to say, if indeed there is anything, *to* one who rejects the conviction— which, it bears emphasis, is not necessarily, for a person whose conviction it is, a religious conviction. But there is this to say *about* one who rejects it: He is, by our lights, no less in the grip of a pathology of estrangement than if he were to reject that an important constituent of one's own well-being is concern for the well-being of one's child, or spouse, or parent.[39] The serious question among us— some of whom count ourselves religious, but others of whom do not— is not whether a life of loving connection to our sisters and brothers is (to that extent) a flourishing life, but this: "Who is my sister? Who is my brother?"[40] Or, in a different but spiritually equivalent terminology: "Who is my neighbor?"[41] — which is the very question to which, according to Luke's Gospel, Jesus responded with the Parable of the Good Samaritan.[42]

One response to the question, a religious response, is that the Other, too, is, in the deepest possible sense, i.e., as a child of God, your sister/brother. To fail to "see" the Other as sister/brother is (according to this religious response) to succumb to a kind of blindness: blindness to the true nature or being both of the Other and of oneself, which nature/being consists partly in a profound kinship between self and Other. And to fail to love the Other as sister/brother— worse, to hate the Other— is to succumb to the pathology of estrangement; it is, to that extent, to wither as a human being rather than to flourish.[43] That the estrangement is radical— indeed, that it is estrangement even from "the Lord your God"[44] — and involves the most fundamental and enduring failure to achieve human well-being, is emphasized in the searing "Last Judgment" passage of Matthew:

When the Son of man comes in his glory, escorted by all the angels, then he will take his seat on his throne of glory. All nations will be assembled before him and he will separate people from one another as the shepherd separates sheep from goats. He will place the sheep on his right hand and the goats on his left. Then the King will say to those on his right hand, "Come, you whom my Father has blessed, take as your heritage the kingdom prepared for you since the foundation of the world. For I was hungry and you gave me food, I was thirsty and you gave me drink, I was a stranger and you made me welcome, lacking clothes and you clothed me, sick and you visited me, in prison and you came to see me." Then the upright will say to him in reply, "Lord, when did we see you hungry and feed you, or thirsty and give you drink? When did we see you a stranger and make you welcome, lacking clothes and clothe you? When did we find you sick or in prison and go to see you?" And the King will answer, "In truth I tell you, in so far as you did this to one of the least of these brothers of mine, you did it to me." Then he will say to those on his left hand, "Go away from me, with your curse upon you, to the eternal fire prepared for the devil and his angels. For I was hungry and you never gave me food, I was thirsty and you never gave me anything to drink, I was a stranger and you never made me welcome, lacking clothes and you never clothed me, sick and in prison and you never visited me." Then it will be their turn to ask, "Lord, when did we see you hungry or thirsty, a stranger or lacking clothes, sick or in prison, and did not come to your help?" Then he will answer, "In truth I tell you, in so far as you neglected to do this to one of the least of these, you neglected to do it to me." And they will go away to eternal punishment, and the upright to eternal life.[45]

The response of the Gospel to "Who is my sister/bro-ther/neighbor?"— and kindred responses— are religious in the fundamental sense that such a response is embedded in a religious vision of the world and of our place in it. Of course, there are differences among religious visions within the relevant range— sometimes large differences, sometimes small. The analogical imagination does not yield precisely the same vision in every time or in every place. How a person or a community arrives at a religious vision is a difficult question— as is the question how one brings another to such a vision. Moreover, different religious traditions, and even different theologies within the same broad religious tradition, proffer different answers to such questions.

It bears emphasis that a theistic religious vision does not necessarily include a conception of "God" as a kind of divine legislator, issuing directives for human conduct. (Indeed, a religious person may well believe that such a "God"— such an idol— is dead.)[46] The imperative to "love one another as I have loved you" can be understood (and in my view should be understood) not as a piece of divine legislation, but as a (truly, fully) human response to the question of how to live. However, to say that the response is a human one does not entail that it is not also a religious response. What makes the imperative a *religious* human response and not merely a secular one is that the response is the existential yield of a religious conviction about how the world (including we-in-the-world) hangs together: in particular, the conviction that the Other is, finally, one's own sister/brother— and should receive, therefore, the gift of one's loving concern.[47]

Indeed, a theistic religious vision is not necessarily attended by confident, much less dogmatic, God-talk. (I have developed the point elsewhere.)[48] If that statement seems strange, consider what one scholar has recently stressed about Thomas Aquinas, perhaps the greatest Christian theologian: "Much of [Aquinas'] doctrine about talking about God is in truth a carefully qualified *via negativa*. . . . Aquinas would simply agree with modern antitheists that we cannot say what God is; and that human language is inadequate to the claimed reality of God; and that there is something improper even in saying that God is a being. But not only does Aquinas think that none of these admissions disqualifies him from theism; he actually thinks that the theist should make these admissions."[49] Of course, and as Aquinas understood, to insist that we cannot say what God is— that we can only follow a *via negativa* and say what God is not— is not to deny that we can try to mediate our experience of Ultimate Reality analogically— for example, by speaking of God as *like* a loving "parent," and of the Other as *like* a "sister"/"brother." In addition to his "carefully qualified *via negativa* . . . Aquinas also has, of course, a *via positiva* about God-talk, namely, the 'doctrine of analogy.' . . ."[50] However, to insist, with Aquinas, that in talking about God we must either follow a *via negativa* or speak analogically is *not* to say that God-talk is merely metaphorical or figurative or poetic. Aquinas was, after all, a committed theological realist.[51]

To forestall predictable misunderstanding, two important points should be made. First, in presenting a religious version of the conviction that every human being is sacred, I have relied on the religious materials I know best. In relying primarily on Christian materials, however, I do not mean to suggest that there are not ample materials in other religious traditions out of which one can construct, or reconstruct, a relevantly similar version of the conviction. Of course, just as there are differences among the precise religious visions adhered to by different traditions within Christianity, there are differences among the precise visions adhered to by different world religions. (Again, the analogical imagination does not yield precisely the same vision in every time or place.) But such differences as there are ought not to obscure the fact that the experience of all human beings as sacred is widely shared among different sects and religions, albeit expressed— mediated— differently in different traditions. And that common ("ecumenical") ground helps to explain the emergence of the idea of human rights as a point of convergence among peoples from different religious traditions.[52]

Second, in presenting a religious version of the conviction that every human being is sacred, and in relying primarily on Christian materials in doing so, I do not mean to deny that the lived practice, as distinct from the professed ideals, of every religious tradition, including Christianity, offers at best equivocal support for what we now call human rights. Indeed, I do not mean to deny even that the professed ideals of religious traditions— at least on some quite plausible construals of those ideals— fail to support, and may even oppose, some of what we now think of as human rights. Christianity is a conspicuous example.[53] There has been an obvious tendency on the part even of the world's "great" religious traditions to tribalism, racism, and sexism. No person who takes seriously the resources of one or another religious tradition should deny "the brokenness and ambiguity of every tradition" or repress "one's own inevitably ambivalent relationship to [the tradition]."[54] A self-critical attitude towards one's own tradition is "the route to liberation from the negative realities of [the] tradition."[55]

For believers to be unable to learn from secular feminists on the patriarchal nature of most religions or to be unwilling to be challenged by Feuerbach, Darwin, Marx, Freud, or Nietzsche is to refuse to take seriously the religion's own suspicions on the existence of those fundamental distortions named sin, ignorance, or illusion. The interpretations of believers will, of course, be grounded in some fundamental trust in, and loyalty to, the Ultimate Reality both disclosed and concealed in one's own religious tradition. But fundamental trust, as any experience of friendship can teach, is not immune to either criticism or suspicion. A religious person will ordinarily fashion some hermeneutics of trust, even one of friendship and love, for the religious classics of her or his tradition. But, as any genuine understanding of friendship shows, friendship often demands both critique and suspicion. A belief in a pure and innocent love is one of the less happy inventions of the romantics. A friendship that never includes critique and even, when appropriate, suspicion is a friendship barely removed from the polite and wary communication of strangers. As Buber showed, in every I-Thou encounter, however transient, we encounter some new dimension of reality. But if that encounter is to prove more than transitory, the difficult ways of friendship need a trust powerful enough to risk itself in critique and suspicion. To claim that this may be true of all our other loves but not true of our love for, and trust in, our religious tradition makes very little sense either hermeneutically or religiously.[56]

IV

The religious-cosmological context of the conviction that every human is sacred (the context sketched in the preceding section) is not appealing to everyone. It was very unappealing to Nietzsche. And even for one to whom it is greatly appealing, it may not be credible. It is not credible, for example, to Jürgen Habermas, who has written: "[By confronting] the conscientious question about deliverance for the annihilated victims[,] we become aware of the limits of that transcendence from within which is directed to this world. But this does not enable us to ascertain the *countermovement* of a compensating transcendence from beyond. That the universal covenant of fellowship would be able to be effective retroactively, toward the past, only in the weak medium of our memory . . . falls short of our moral need. But the painful experience of a deficit is still not a sufficient argument for the assumption of an 'absolute freedom which saves in death'."[57]

Even if one finds incredible the religious-cosmological context of the conviction that every human being is sacred, the question persists whether the religious version of the conviction is not the only coherent version. Can there be a coherent secular version— a version not finally rooted in a religious vision of the world and of our place in it? Can the conviction be embedded either in a nonreligious cosmology or in cosmological agnosticism? Consider Glenn Tinder's statement:

Nietzsche's stature is owing to the courage and profundity that enabled him to make all this unmistakably clear. He delineated with overpowering eloquence the consequences of giving up Christianity, *and every like view of the universe and humanity.* His approval of those consequences and his hatred of Christianity give force to his argument. Many would like to think that there are no consequences— that we can continue treasuring the life and welfare, the civil rights and political authority, of every person without believing in a God who renders such attitudes and conduct compelling. Nietzsche shows that we cannot. We cannot give up the Christian God— *and the transcendence given other names in other faiths*— and go on as before. We must give up Christian morality too. If the God-man is nothing more than an illusion, the same thing is true of the idea that every individual possesses incalculable worth. The standard of *agape* collapses. It becomes explicable only on Nietzsche's terms: as a device by which the weak and failing exact from the strong and distinguished a deference they do not deserve. Thus the spiritual center of Western politics fades and vanishes.[58]

Tinder's emphasis on the Christian tradition will surely and understandably be, for some non-Christians, a provocative distraction from his fundamental point. Tinder's and Nietzsche's point loses nothing, however, if the emphasis is placed not on the Christian tradition but on the Jewish, for example. Recall the comment on the Talmud quoted earlier in this essay.[59]

Is Tinder right? While one might agree with Charles Larmore that morality is now widely understood (or, at least, understood by those of us, religious or not) to be independent of God conceived of as the supreme moral legislator.[60] But is it plausible to think that morality can be independent of *any* cosmological convictions— any convictions about how the

world (including we-in-the-world) hangs together? After
Nietzsche, is it plausible to think that a morality embedded in
religious convictions about how the world hangs together can be
more or less equivalent to a morality embedded in the
conviction that the world is nothing but a great cosmic process
utterly bereft of ultimate meaning and therefore, from a human
point of view, absurd?[61] As Bruce Ackerman expressed it,
"There is no meaning in the bowels of the universe."[62] Nietzsche
declared: "'Naivete: as if morality could survive when the *God*
who sanctions it is missing! The 'beyond' absolutely necessary if
faith in morality is to be maintained."[63] Writing recently of
"anthropocentrism, [which] by abolishing all horizons of
significance, threatens us with a loss of meaning and hence a
trivialization of our predicament," Charles Taylor has said: "At
one moment, we understand our situation as one of high
tragedy, alone in a silent universe, without intrinsic meaning,
condemned to create value. But at a later moment, the same
doctrine, by its own inherent bent, yields a flattened world, in
which there are not very meaningful choices because there aren't
any crucial issues."[64]

Consider a cosmology according to which the world is,
finally and radically, meaningless— or, even if meaningful in
some sense, not meaningful in a way hospitable to our deepest
yearnings for what Heschel called "ultimate relationship,
ultimate belonging."[65] Consider, for example, Clarence Darrow's
bleak vision (as recounted by Paul Edwards):

Darrow, one of the most compassionate men who ever lived, . . .
concluded that life was an "awful joke." Darrow offered as one of his
reasons the apparent aimlessness of all that happens. "This weary old
world goes on, begetting, with birth and with living and with death," he
remarked in his moving plea for the boy-murderers Loeb and Leopold,
"and all of it is blind from the beginning to the end." Elsewhere he
wrote: "Life is like a ship on the sea, tossed by every wave and by every
wind; a ship headed for no port and no harbor, with no rudder, no
compass, no pilot; simply floating for a time, then lost in the waves." In
addition to the aimlessness of life and the universe, there is the fact of
death. "I love my friends," wrote Darrow, "but they all must come to a

tragic end." Death is more terrible the more one is attached to things in the world. Life, he concludes, is "not worthwhile," and he adds . . . that "it is an unpleasant interruption of nothing, and the best thing you can say of it is that it does not last long."[66]

One prominent contemporary proponent of a Darrowian cosmology, the physicist and Nobel laureate Steven Weinberg, "finds his own world-view 'chilling and impersonal'. He cannot understand people who treat the absence of God and of God's heaven as unimportant."[67]

Where is the place in a cosmological view like Weinberg's for the conviction that every human being is sacred (has inherent dignity, is an end in himself, etc.) to gain a foothold? Indeed, embedded in the view that the world is merely a process devoid of ultimate meaning, what would the conviction that every human being is sacred even mean? If the only coherent version of the conviction is religious, if indeed the only *intelligible* version is religious, then cosmological agnosticism, which neither affirms nor denies the ultimate meaningfulness of the world, entails agnosticism about the sacredness *vel non* of human beings.

In writing recently about abortion and euthanasia, Ronald Dworkin has asserted that "we almost all accept, as the inarticulate assumption behind much of our experience and conviction, that human life in all its forms is *sacred*. . . ."[68] Dworkin then observes that "for some of us, [the sacredness of human life] is a matter of religious faith; for others, of secular but deep philosophical belief."[69] Now, many folks who believe that every human being is sacred do not count themselves religious; some of them even embrace nonreligious views like Weinberg's. The question nonetheless persists whether there is a coherent secular version of the conviction about the sacredness of every human being. Imagine a nonreligious person saying: "That every human being is sacred is not, for me, a religious tenet; it is a secular but deep philosophical belief." We may ask: "Please tell us something about the constellation of views — views about how the world, including we-in-the-world, hangs together— in which, for you, that philosophical belief is

embedded." Imagine this answer: "For me the conviction that
every human being is sacred is not only axiomatic; it is
unconnected to any of my views about how the world hangs
together." (Perhaps the answer includes this statement: "I have
no confident views about how the world hangs together. I'm
agnostic about all such 'religious' or 'cosmological' matters.") It
seems, then, that the premise that every human being is sacred
is, for our nonreligious interlocutor, less a conviction about (a
part of) the world than a kind of free-floating aesthetic
preference. In Dworkin's view, however, the premise is, even
for most nonreligious persons who hold it, much more than an
aesthetic preference.

In his book on abortion and euthanasia, Dworkin writes that
"one of [his] main claims [is] that there is a secular as well as a
religious interpretation of the idea that human life is sacred."[70]
Dworkin purports to explain, in his book, how the conviction
that every human being (or, as Dworkin says, "life") is sacred
"may be, and commonly is, interpreted in a secular as well as in a
conventionally religious way."[71] To say that a human life is
sacred is partly to say, according to Dworkin, "that it has *intrinsic*
and *objective* value quite apart from any value it might have to
the person whose life it is."[72]   Emphasizing in particular the
notion of "intrinsic" value, Dworkin writes: "Much of our life is
based on the idea that objects or events can be valuable in
themselves. . . . The idea that some events or objects are valuable
in and of themselves . . . is . . . a familiar part of our experience.
The idea of intrinsic value is commonplace, and it has a central
place in our shared scheme of values and opinions. . . .
Something is intrinsically valuable . . . if its value is *independent*
of what people happen to enjoy or want or need or what is good
for them."[73]

Dworkin's comments about "intrinsic" value obscure rather
than clarify that value is always and everywhere value *for*
someone(s) or something(s). The notion of something being
valuable independently of a beneficial relation to anyone or
anything— whether a human being, a nonhuman but living
entity, or God— is perfectly opaque. Putting aside things that
are values either for nonhuman entities or for God, we may say

that "the category of values is anthropocentric, in that it corresponds to interests which can only take root in creatures with something approaching our own affective make-up. . . . Values are only ascribable from points of view constituted by human patterns of affective response. A wholly dispassionate eye would be as blind to them as a black-and-white camera to chromatic colors."[74] The relevant distinction here is between "intrinsic" value and "instrumental" value. To say that something has intrinsic value is to say, not that something has value even if it has no value for anyone (not even God) or anything— what would *that* mean?— but that something has value for someone (or something) *as an end in itself rather than merely as a means to an end: the end of attaining something else that is valued.* And to say that something has "objective" value and not (or not merely) "subjective" value is to say that something has value for someone (for example, that it is good for her, that it is conducive to or perhaps even constitutive of her flourishing) even if she is unaware that it has value for her— indeed, even if she believes that it has disvalue for her.[75] Now, that something has both objective and intrinsic value for someone does not mean that it is sacred. An end to my itch has both objective and intrinsic value for me (or so we may assume), but it is not thereby sacred. For some persons who count themselves religious, to say that every human being is sacred is to say (speaking analogically) that every human being is the beloved child of God (God who is love). For persons who do not count themselves religious, what does it mean to say that every human being is sacred?

According to Dworkin, "The nerve of the sacred lies in the value we attach to a process or enterprise or project rather than to its results considered independently from how they were produced."[76] The sacredness of human beings is rooted, for nonreligious persons, in two basic facts about human beings (argues Dworkin). First, every human being is "the highest product of natural creation. . . . The idea that human beings are special among natural creations is offered to explain why it is horrible that even a single human individual life should be extinguished."[77] Second, "each developed human being is the product not just of natural creation, but also of the kind of deliberative human creative force that we honor in honoring art."[78] "The idea that each individual human life is inviolable is therefore rooted . . . in two combined and intersecting bases of the sacred: natural *and* human creation."[79]

> The life of a single human organism commands respect and protection, then, no matter in what form or shape, because of the complex creative investment it represents and because of our wonder at the . . . processes that produce new lives from old ones, at the processes of nation and community and language through which a human being will come to absorb and continue hundreds of generations of cultures and forms of life and value, and, finally, when mental life has begun and flourishes, at the process of internal personal creation and judgment by which a person will make and remake himself, a mysterious, inescapable process in which we each participate, and which is therefore the most powerful and inevitable source of empathy and communion we have with every other creature who faces the same frightening challenge. The horror we feel in the willful destruction of a human life reflects our shared inarticulate sense of the intrinsic importance of each of these dimensions of investment.[80]

This, then, is Dworkin's rendering of a secular version of the conviction that every human being is sacred. Even if in truth the world is nothing but a process bereft of ultimate meaning, every human being is nonetheless sacred, according to Dworkin, because "each human being . . . is a creative masterpiece"[81] — a masterpiece of "natural *and* human creation."[82]

Does Dworkin succeed in portraying a coherent secular version of the conviction that every human being is sacred? Important questions need to be answered— or so it seems to me. How does the fact that something is a masterpiece of natural and human creation make that something not merely a creative masterpiece but sacred? What is the precise sense of "sacred" in play in Dworkin's portrayal? Let us agree that every human being is a creative masterpiece and, as such, inspires (or should inspire) awe in us. That something justifiably inspires awe in us, however— James Joyce's *Ulysses*, for example — entails neither that we believe it to be sacred nor that it is sacred.

To say that every human being is sacred (and therefore inviolable) is ordinarily to say something about (what is believed to be) the true nature of every human being. Of course, something may inspire awe in us, and we may therefore value it — it may have value for us, both objective value and intrinsic value— because it is sacred (or, at least, because we believe it to be sacred). But to suggest, as in his book Dworkin at least sometimes does, that something is sacred *because* it inspires awe in us, because we value it, is to reverse the ordinary order of things. (Recall, for example, Dworkin's statement that "the nerve of the sacred lies in the value we attach to a process or enterprise or project rather than to its results considered independently from how they were produced."[83]   Or his statement that "the life of a single human organism commands respect and protection . . . because of our wonder at the . . . processes that produce new lives from old ones . . .")[84] Dworkin seems to be using "sacred" in what we may call a weak, or "subjective," sense— something (e.g. a human life) is sacred *because*, or *in the sense that*, it inspires awe in us and we attach great value to it— rather than in the strong, or "objective," sense — something is sacred and *therefore* it inspires awe in us and we attach great value to it. Moreover, in using "sacred" in the weak or subjective sense, Dworkin is trading on the greater strength of the objective sense in which the word is ordinarily used.

That rhetorical strategy, however, is problematic. The premise that every human being is sacred-in-the-subjective-sense cannot begin to bear the weight of the premise that every human being is sacred-in-the-objective-sense. Imagine someone saying to a Bosnian Serb: "The Bosnian Muslim, too, no less than you, is sacred. It is wrong for you to rape her." If "sacred" is meant in the subjective sense, the Bosnian Serb may reply: "Sacred to you and yours, perhaps, but not to me and mine. In the scheme of things, we happen not to attach much value to her life." By contrast, "sacred" in the objective sense is not fundamentally a matter of "sacred to you" or "sacred to me"; it is, rather, a matter of how things really are. (Of course, one may disbelieve the ontology, but that's a different problem.) If every human being is sacred in the objective sense, then, in violating the Bosnian Muslim, the Bosnian Serb does not merely violate what some of us attach great value to; he violates the very order of creation.

Now, Dworkin may insist that he has been misunderstood. He may insist that he means "sacred" in the objective sense, and that on his account of "sacred" the Bosnian Serb is indeed violating the very order of creation. He may say that the Bosnian Muslim has intrinsic value even for the Bosnian Serb — and objective value too: that the welfare of the Bosnian Muslim is an intrinsic good for the Bosnian Serb even if the Bosnian Serb will remain forever unaware of that fact. But if Dworkin wants to respond in some such way, then he must forswear any explanation of the sacredness of someone or something in terms of, or by reference to, "the value we attach to" that someone or something. He must explain it solely in other terms. It is not clear, however, what that other explanation might be; in particular, it is not obvious that either a secular cosmology or cosmological agnosticism can yield the requisite conviction about how things really are. How do we get from "the universe is (or might be) nothing but a cosmic process bereft of ultimate meaning" to "every human being is nonetheless sacred (in the strong or objective sense"?) Of course, even in an absurd universe, a universe bereft of transcendent meaning, there can be creative masterpieces. But, again, that something is a creative masterpiece and understandably inspires awe in us entails neither that it is sacred nor even that we believe it to be sacred (in the strong sense).

Has Dworkin identified a coherent secular version of the conviction that every human being is sacred? It seems not, if "sacred" is meant in the objective sense. If, however, "sacred" is meant in the subjective sense, perhaps Dworkin has identified a coherent secular version. But if he has, Dworkin's secularized claim that every human being is sacred is a substantially weaker claim— it claims much less— than the paradigmatic claim about the sacredness of all human beings. In any event, Dworkin has said nothing to diminish suspicion that the conviction that every human being is sacred— *sacred in the strong/objective sense, sacred because of how the world really is, and not because of what we attach value to in the world—* is inescapably religious. The challenge is to identify a coherent secular version of *that* conviction. The challenge is to identify a coherent secular version of *that* conviction. In his review of Dworkin's book for the *London Times Literary Supplement*, Robert Grant concluded that "in *Life's Dominion*, Professor Dworkin makes considerable play with, indeed frankly exploits, the idea of the sacred, but shows no understanding of it."[85]

V

If— *if* the conviction that every human being is sacred is ineliminably religious, it follows that the idea of human rights is ineliminably religious, because the conviction is an essential, even foundational, constituent of the idea. The possibility that the idea of human rights is ineliminably religious poses a problem for the secular or agnostic enthusiast of human rights. One response to the problem is to try to defend the establishment in international law (and elsewhere) of the particular human rights, or of some of them, that have in fact been established in international law during the last fifty years, not by relying on the conviction that every human being is sacred, but by means of a justificatory strategy that avoids reliance on that conviction— that avoids reliance, therefore, on "the idea of human rights." Two such strategies may be identified here.[86]

The Definitional Strategy

There is today no way of "proving" that napalming babies is bad except by asserting it (in a louder and louder voice), *or by defining it as so, early in one's game, and then later slipping it through, in a whisper, as a conclusion.*[87]

The idea of human rights, again, is that because each and every human being is, simply as a human being, sacred, certain

things ought not to be done to any human being and certain
other things ought to be done for every human being. The
definitional strategy is a different way of trying to ground the
proposition that certain things ought not to be done to any
human being and certain other things ought to be done for every
human being— a way that does not rely on the premise that
human beings are sacred. According to the definitional strategy,
certain things ought not to be done and certain other things
ought to be done simply because "the moral point of view" —
understood as the "impartial" or "universal" point of view —
requires it. In commenting on "that sort of impartiality that
constitutes the moral point of view," James Griffin has written
that "we all agree that to look at things morally is to look at
them, in some sense or other, impartially, granting every person
some sort of equal status. Of course, we should have to make
this notion of equal status more determinate— say through one
interpretation or other of the Ideal Observer or Ideal Contractor.
In any case, principles of equality can be principles of
impartiality in this sense: they can express the spirit with which
one will, if one is moral, consider the facts of the matter."[88]

The definitional strategy is deeply problematic, because it
fails even to address what David Tracy has called the "limit-
question" of morality: "Why be moral at all?"[89] The definitional
strategy fails to respond to this fundamental challenge:

You claim that we ought not to do certain things to any human being,
and that we ought to do certain other things for every human being.
We ask why. You say that the moral (impartial, universal) point of
view requires it. For the sake of argument we will stipulate to your
definition of "moral." Our challenge remains, but now we'll express it
this way: Why ought we to adopt "the moral point of view"; why ought
we to be "moral" in the stipulated sense? Why ought we to give a damn
about being "moral" or doing the "moral" thing? We are right back
where we started: What reasons— what real-world, flesh-and-blood
reasons— are there for doing for every human being those certain
things that the moral point of view requires be done for every human
being and for not doing to any human being those certain other things
that the moral point of view forbids be done to any human being?

The fundamental challenge to each and every human-rights-claim— to each and every claim about what ought not to be done to any human being or what ought to be done for every human being— is a demand for reasons. James Nickel has distinguished between two different interpretations of the demand: one according to which it is "a demand for prudential reasons" and another according to which it is "a request for moral reasons."[90] (The distinction between "prudential" and "moral" is deeply problematic, at least for anyone with an Aristotelian understanding of morality.)[91] The second interpretation, Nickel suggests, "assumes that one's audience has transcended egoism and is prepared to accept arguments that appeal directly to what is reasonable from the moral point of view, whether or not it can be shown that adopting this perspective is likely to promote the long-term interests of the individual."[92] But the problem is larger, much larger, than "egoism": One may favor, not oneself, or even one's family, but one's tribe, or nation, or race, or religion. The assumption that those to whom human-rights-claims are addressed have "transcended" such favoritism is wildly implausible. The fundamental challenge to human-rights-claims is a real-world challenge: Many to whom such claims are addressed have conspicuously not adopted anything like "the moral (impartial, universal) point of view." The moral point of view is not a justificatory basis for human-rights-claims— at least, not a fundamental basis. The moral point of view is itself in dire need of justification, especially in a world— *our* world, the *real* world — that is often fiercely partial/local rather than impartial/universal. The real world is full of what Primo Levi called "us-ism": "Those on the Rosenstrasse who risked their lives for Jews did not express opposition to anti-semitic policies per se. They displayed primarily what the late Primo Levi, a survivor of Auschwitz, called 'selfishness extended to the person closest to you . . . us-ism.' In most of the familiar stories of Aryans who risked their lives for Jews to whom they were married, they withdrew to safety, one by one, the moment their loved ones were released. Their protests bring home to us the iron limits, the tragically narrow borders, of us-ism."[93]

The question remains: What reasons are there for adopting "the moral point of view"? Charles Taylor, commenting critically on moral theories that are variations on the definitional strategy — in particular, theories that exclude discourse about human well-being— has put the point this way: "[Such theories] leave us with nothing to say to someone who asks why he should be moral. . . . But this could be misleading, if we seemed to be asking how we could convince someone who saw none of the point of our moral beliefs. There is nothing we can do to 'prove' we are right to such a person. But imagine him to be asking another question: he could be asking us to make plain the point of our moral code, in articulating what's uniquely valuable in cleaving to these injunctions [e.g., act 'impartially']. Then the implication of these theories is that we have nothing to say which can impart insight. We can wax rhetorical and propagandize, but we can't say what's good or valuable about [the injunctions], or why they command assent."[94]

The definitional strategy is unavailing. Of course, a strategy is not definitional if it explains "the moral point of view" on the basis of a cosmological vision that yields something like the premise that every human being is sacred. But then we are back to the question whether such a premise is not inescapably religious.[95]

The Self-Regarding Strategy

The self-regarding strategy is yet another way— a way that does not rely on anything like the premise that human beings are sacred— of trying to justify the proposition that certain things ought not to be done to any human being and certain other things ought to be done for every human being. According to the self-regarding strategy, it is good for oneself or for one's family/tribe/nation/race/religion/etc. that certain things not be done to any human being and certain other things be done for every human being. This strategy needs to be distinguished from (lest it collapse into) the different (and ineliminably religious?) strategy according to which every human being is sacred; it is good for everyone to recognize that fact and act accordingly. According to the self-regarding strategy, it is good for oneself or for one's nation/etc. that certain things not be done and certain other things be done even if it is not the case that every human being is sacred.

The fundamental problem with the self-regarding strategy is twofold. First, it is not clear how much more than "a mere nonagression treaty"[96] — a treaty among persons who have reason to fear one another— the self-regarding strategy can support. A recent, prominent self-regarding strategy is David Gauthier's contractarian argument. Let's put aside the question whether the argument works and look simply at the aim of the argument, which, according to Gauthier, is to show "that rational persons will recognize a role for constraints, both unilateral and mutual, in their choices and decisions, that rational persons would agree ex ante on certain mutual constraints were they able to do so, and that rational persons will frequently comply with those mutual constraints in their interactions."[97] In particular, Gauthier's self-regarding argument does not aim to justify anything close to the range of rights established in international law— in the International Bill of Human Rights, for example. As one commentator has observed, "[Gauthier's] main interest is to give an account of rational and impartial constraints on conduct. If this does not capture the traditional conception of morality, so much the worse for the traditional conception. Rationality— not morality— is the important notion for him."[98]

Second, whatever rights beyond "a mere nonaggression treaty" the self-regarding strategy can support, it is not clear that the strategy can support them as *human* rights— as rights each and every human being should enjoy. It may be able to support them only as rights among persons who have reason to fear one another's aggression or to need one another's cooperation. Nietzsche wrote: "Justice (fairness) originates among those who are approximately *equally powerful*, as Thucydides . . . comprehended correctly. Justice is repayment and exchange on the assumption of an approximately equal power position.

Justice naturally derives from prudent concern with self-preservation; that means, from the egoism of the consideration: 'Why should I harm myself uselessly and perhaps not attain my goal anyway'?"[99] Even if you are not within the circle of those I happen to respect and for whom I happen to have concern, if you are my neighbor I may have reason to fear your aggression or to need your cooperation. But if you are a Somalian, or a Bosnian Muslim, we (as North Americans) may not have any realistic reason to fear *your* aggression or to need *your* cooperation.

On the other hand, even if you are only a lowly inhabitant of an alien, distant, and weak community, we or some of those within the circle of our respect and concern may eventually suffer in ways not always easy to predict or even foresee if we fail to act toward you as if you were within the circle of our respect and concern— if, in that sense, we fail to take you into the circle of our respect and concern. Although, again, their principal justificatory reliance is on the idea of human rights — their principal argument is other-regarding— even the Universal Declaration of Human Rights and the other documents of the International Bill of Human Rights contain at least a hint of a self-regarding argument, namely: If you want to enjoy the fruits of peace in the world, you must extend your respect and concern to all human beings. The Universal Declaration, the International Covenant on Economic, Social and Cultural Rights, and the International Covenant on Civil and Political Rights all state, in their preambles, that "recognition . . . of the equal and inalienable rights of all members of the human family is the foundation of freedom, justice *and peace* in the world" (emphasis added). Similarly, the European Convention for the Protection of Human Rights and Fundamental Freedoms (1953) states that the "Fundamental Freedoms" it affirms "are the foundation of justice *and peace* in the world" (emphasis added).

As a matter of domestic political debate— as a matter of domestic *realpolitik*— plausible self-regarding ("pragmatic") reasons for our nation taking even the lowliest of the low into the circle of those it happens to respect and for whom it happens to have concern are undoubtedly an important complement to the other-regarding argument (i.e., the idea of human rights) for our nation doing so.[100] Jerome Shestack's useful catalog of such reasons is quoted in the margin.[101] It seems quite doubtful, however, that self-regarding reasons can by themselves bear all the weight. Put another way, it seems doubtful that any domestic political argument that is not at least partly other-regarding— that does not appeal at least in part to the conviction that every human being is sacred— can do the required work.[102] The self-regarding reasons are highly speculative.[103] How confident are we that we Americans will eventually suffer if we fail to take the Bosnian Muslims, for example, or the Tibetan Buddhists, into the circle of our respect and concern? Confident enough to incur the costs of taking them in (if we do not also believe that they and all human beings are sacred)? In any event, the conviction that every human being is sacred is partly constitutive of the American identity.[104] The Declaration of Independence famously proclaims: "We hold these truths to be self-evident, that all men are created equal, that they are endowed by their Creator with certain inalienable Rights, that among these are Life, Liberty and the pursuit of Happiness." No political argument for our nation taking the human rights of distant peoples seriously will begin to have the power of an argument that appeals at least in part to the conviction that all human beings are sacred "created equal and endowed by their Creator with certain inalienable Rights." The power of that conviction for most Americans derives in part from the fact that in the United States, which remains a pervasively religious society, the conviction that human beings are sacred is for most persons a religious conviction, even if for some persons the conviction is not religious— indeed, even if the conviction is not inescapably religious.

Unlike the definitional strategy, then, the self-regarding strategy for insisting that certain things not be done to any human being and that certain other things be done for every human being should not be dismissed. But the self-regarding strategy is probably availing only or mainly as a buttress, a complement, to the strategy that relies on the idea of human rights— on the conviction that every human being, even the

lowliest inhabitant of the most alien, distant, and weak
community, is sacred. Significantly, neither individually nor
even cumulatively can self-regarding reasons by themselves
begin to account for the passionate other-regarding character of
most discourse in support of human rights.

VI

To suggest that the idea of human rights is ineliminably
religious— that there is, finally, no coherent secular version of
the idea of human rights, that the conviction that human beings
are sacred is inescapably religious— is *not* to deny that one can
take human rights very seriously indeed without being religious,
that agnostics, too, even atheists, can be take human rights
seriously, that they, too, can love the Other.[105] *Of course*
atheists— like Albert Camus[106] — can take human rights
seriously, *of course* they and other nonreligious persons can love
the Other. (Indeed, if the Other really is, in some deep sense,
one's sister/brother, then it would be surprising if every
nonreligious person were existentially disconnected from that
truth.[107] But, of course, as the example of Camus attests, to be
connected to that truth existentially, as Camus certainly was, is
not necessarily to affirm it philosophically.) However, as the
Polish philosopher Leszek Kolakowski has written: "When
Pierre Bayle argued that morality does not depend on religion,
he was speaking mainly of psychological independence; he
pointed out that atheists are capable of achieving the highest
moral standards . . . and of putting to shame most of the faithful
Christians. That is obviously true as far as it goes, *but this
matter-of-fact argument leaves the question of validity intact; neither
does it solve the question of the effective sources of the moral strength
and moral convictions of those 'virtuous pagans'.*"[108] That Camus
achieved the highest moral standards, that he loved the Other,
even that in doing so he understood himself to be engaged in a
profound act of resistance and rebellion— resisting and
rebelling against what he believed to be the ultimate absurdity,
or meaninglessness, of the universe[109]— "leaves the question of

validity intact." In particular, and as Nietzsche saw clearly, it leaves intact the question: Why should we give a damn about the well-being of all human beings, including the weak and the powerless— those whom the Gospel calls "the least of these brothers of mine"?[110]

Now, "the question of validity" (as Kolakowski calls it) is not always at issue, it is not always on the table. As stated earlier, one can, like Camus, love the Other without being religious.[111] If two citizens, one of them religious, the other not, happen to agree that the well-being of the Other is of fundamental importance, the question of validity does not arise *as between them*.[112] But that the question does not arise as between them does not mean that it does not arise as between or among others. After all, not everyone in the United States does, like Camus, love the Other; not everyone does agree that the well-being of all human beings— including the weak and the powerless— is of fundamental importance; not everyone agrees that he or she owes every human being respect or concern. The question of validity is often on the table— though often not explicitly— in the public square, as, for example, when redistributive issues are being debated.[113] "Why should *we* be taxed to support *them*? Frankly, I don't give a damn about them. And even if I did, I've worked hard for my money and it's all I can do to take care of my own." The mere fact that one can love the Other without being religious does not begin to respond to the question of validity when the question does arise, when it is at issue.[114]

There is not only the question of validity. There is also, as Kolakowski has said, "the question of the effective sources of the moral strength and moral convictions of those 'virtuous pagans.'"[115] Habermas is frank in acknowledging the problem — and bleak in what he has to say about it: "Who or what gives us the courage for such a total engagement that in situations of degradation and deprivation is already being expressed when the destitute and deprived summon the energy each morning to carry on anew? The question about the meaning of life is not meaningless. Nevertheless, the circumstance that penultimate arguments inspire no great confidence is not enough for the grounding of a hope that can be kept alive only in a religious language. The thoughts and expectations directed toward the common good have, after metaphysics has collapsed, only an unstable status."[116] Consider, with respect the problem of the adequacy of any nonreligious response to that question, the relevance of what Jackson has said about anti-realism: "Letting go of realism will in all probability leave a society without the wherewithal to found or sustain a commitment to liberty, equality, or fraternity— much less sorority. Such a society may live for a time on past cultural capital embodied in liberal institutions and traditions, but a purely conventional virtue will not last long. The issue is one of motivation and consistency."[117] The bleakness of Habermas's statement— about the "unstable status" that "thoughts and expectations directed toward the common good have after metaphysics has collapsed"— lends weight to Jackson's.

Many persons will have an understandable incentive to reject the possibility that the idea of human rights is ineliminably religious: persons who do not count themselves religious, including some who count themselves anti-religious, but who embrace the idea of human rights— who embrace, in particular, the conviction that every human being is sacred (has inherent dignity, is an end in himself, etc.). "The conviction that every human being is sacred cannot be inescapably religious, for if it were, how could *we*— we who are not religious, and who may even look at religion as always and everywhere little more than a childish superstition— defend the idea of human rights?" How indeed?

For many religious persons and even for some nonreligious persons, the idea of human rights simply does not make sense, it does not exert a claim, apart from, cut off from, the Gospel vision of the world and of our place in it— or from some equivalent religious vision.[118] (Simone Weil wrote: "The Gospel makes no distinction between the love of our neighbor and justice. . . . The supernatural virtue of justice consists in behaving exactly as though there were equality when one is stronger in an unequal relationship.")[119] Some even fear that the only conception of justice likely to flourish apart from the Gospel (or some equivalent) vision, once we have exhausted our "past cultural capital,"[120] is the dispiriting conception implicit in Nietzsche's genealogy of justice:

My dear Sir Long-Ears-and-Virtuous, we have no desire whatever to be better, we are very contented with ourselves, all we desire is not to harm one another— and therefore we forbid certain actions when they are directed in a certain way, namely against us, while we cannot sufficiently honor these same actions provided they are directed against enemies of the community— against you, for instance. We educate our children in them; we cultivate them— If we shared that "God-pleasing" radicalism that your holy madness recommends, if we were fools enough to condemn together with those actions the source of them, the "heart," the "disposition," that would mean condemning our own existence and with it its supreme prerequisite— a disposition, a heart, a passion we honor with the highest honors. By our decrees, we prevent this disposition from breaking out and expressing itself in an inexpedient way— we are prudent when we make such law for ourselves, we are also moral— Have you no suspicion, however faint, what sacrifice it is costing us, how much taming, self-overcoming, severity toward ourselves it requires? We are vehement in our desires, there are times when we would like to devour each other— But the "sense of community" masters us: please note that this is almost a definition of morality.[121]

Clearly it is not enough to retreat (*pace* Richard Rorty?)[122] into a kind of ethnocentrism, proclaiming proudly and loudly that although among us late-twentieth-century North Americans and Western Europeans (and perhaps a few others), a great fondness for human rights— or for "the moral point of view" — is nothing more an acquired taste, it is *our* acquired taste (and that, if necessary, we are willing to fight and even die for it). First, not even among all of us late-twentieth-century North Americans, etc., has the taste— the aesthetic preference— f o r human rights been acquired. Second, if the fondness for human rights that some of us have is, at bottom, nothing more than an acquired taste, there is little of consequence to say to those who have not acquired the taste— and who may even have acquired a taste for violating (what we call) human rights— other than, perhaps, "Try it, you'll like it (maybe)." Third, why should we not try to disabuse ourselves of our fondness for human rights (if it is only an acquired taste), once it becomes clear that indulging that fondness can be, politically, economically, militarily, etc., a rather costly proposition?

Let it be emphasized that nothing in this essay— nothing at all— is meant to defend, as credible or even as appealing, any religious-cosmological beliefs or any religious-moral beliefs, much less to commend any such beliefs to anyone.[123] One certainly need not count oneself a religious person in order to wonder— indeed, one can be one of those "good many professors and other intellectuals [who] display a hostility or skeptical indifference to religion that amounts to a thinly disguised contempt for belief in any reality beyond that discoverable by scientific inquiry and ordinary human experience"[124] and *nonetheless* wonder— whether the idea of human rights is not ineliminably religious. One need not count oneself religious in order to wonder whether much secular moral-philosophizing has not been, for a very long time now, a kind of whistling in the dark.[125]

Nietzsche asked: "Now suppose that belief in God has vanished: the question presents itself anew: 'who speaks'?"[126] Echoing Nietzsche's question a brutal century later, Art Leff wrote:

Napalming babies is bad.

Starving the poor is wicked.

Buying and selling each other is depraved.

Those who stood up to and died resisting Hitler, Stalin, Amin, and Pol Pot— and General Custer too— have earned salvation.

Those who acquiesced deserve to be damned.

There is in the world such a thing as evil.

[All together now:] Sez who?

God help us.[127]

NOTES

1. Hannah Arendt, *The Origins of Totalitarianism* (New York: Harcourt, Brace, 1973), (emphasis added).
2. Ronald Dworkin, "Life is Sacred. That's the Easy Part," *New York Times Magazine*, 16 May 1993, 36.
3. For an explanation, see Darcy O'Brien, *A Dark and Bloody Ground* (New York: HarperCollins, 1993), 1.
4. The idea of human rights, in one form or another, is very old. See Leszek Kolakowski, *Modernity on Endless Trial* (Chicago: University of Chicago Press, 1990), 214.

   It is often stressed that the idea of human rights is of recent origin, and that this is enough to dismiss its claims to timeless validity. In its contemporary form, the doctrine is certainly new, though it is arguable that it is a modern version of the natural law theory, whose origins we can trace back at least to the Stoic philosophers and, of course, to the Judaic and Christian sources of European culture. There is no substantial difference between proclaiming "the right to life" and stating that natural law forbids killing. Much as the concept may have been elaborated in the philosophy of the Enlightenment in its conflict with Christianity, the notion of the immutable rights of individuals goes back to the Christian belief in the autonomous status and irreplaceable value of the human personality.
5. See, e.g., Louis B. Sohn, "The New International Law: Protection of the Rights of Individuals Rather Than States," *American University Law Review* 32 (1982): 1; Robert Drinan, S.J., *Cry of the Oppressed: The History and Hope of the Human Rights Revolution* (San Francisco: Harper and Row, 1987). There are many good studies of different aspects of the international law of human rights. See, e.g., Philip Alston, *The United Nations and Human Rights: A Critical Appraisal* (Oxford: Clarendon Press, 1992); Theodore Meron, ed., *Human Rights in International Law: Legal and Policy Issues*, (Oxford: Clarendon Press, 1984), vols. I and II. For relatively brief overviews of the international law of human rights, see Thomas Buergenthal, *International Human Rights* (Washington: Department of State, National Commission for UNESCO); Scott Davidson, *Human Rights* (Philadelphia, Pa.: Open University Press,1993). Two good periodical sources of articles are the *Harvard Human Rights Yearbook* and the *Human Rights Quarterly*.
6. On the day I write these words, 2 June 1993, there is a story in the *New York Times* about "mortar shells explod[ing] today [June 1] amid a neighborhood soccer tournament, killing at least a dozen people and wounding at least eighty in the worst single incident in a year in the bombardment of [Sarajevo] by the Bosnian Serb forces.

Shrapnel-peppered cars, drying pools of blood, a few shreds of blood-soaked clothing and a worn-out soccer ball were all that remained afterward in the parking lot where about one hundred players and spectators had gathered for the game. The attack came on a day of chaotic violence across Bosnia and Herzogovina that was shocking even by local standards and conformed the fears of many people here that the war in this former Yugoslav republic, which has already claimed tens of thousands of lives, is only getting worse." Chuck Sudetic, "Mortar Fire Kills 12 at Soccer Game in Bosnian Capital," *New York Times,* 2 June 1993, A1.

7.   Some "certain things," the "ought" and the "ought not" may be presumptive rather than unconditional or absolute.

8.   Article 2 continues: "Furthermore, no distinction shall be made on the basis of the political, jurisdictional or international status of the country or territory to which a person belongs, whether it be independent, trust, non-self-governing or under any other limitation of sovereignty."

9.   But see Robert Ombres, OP, "The Ethics of Human Rights," *Law and Justice* 114/115 (1992): 140, states, "References to God, Nature and even Human Nature were deleted from the drafts of the 1948 Universal Declaration of Human Rights shortly before its adoption."

10. Nietzsche was unrelentingly contemptuous of the conviction that every human being is sacred— as, for example, in this bleak and sobering passage from *The Will to Power*:

In moving the doctrine of selflessness and love into the foreground, Christianity was in no way establishing the interests of the species as of higher value than the interests of the individual. Its real *historical* effect, the fateful element in its effect, remains, on the contrary, in precisely the enhancement of egoism, of the egoism of the individual, to an extreme — to the extreme of individual immortality). Through Christianity, the individual was made so important, so absolute, that he could no longer be sacrificed: but the species endures only through human sacrifice — All "souls" became equal before God: but this is precisely the most dangerous of all possible evaluations! If one regards individuals as equal, one calls the species into question, one encourages a way of life that leads to the ruin of the species: Christianity is the counterprinciple to the principle of *selection*. If the degenerate and sick ("the Christian") is to be accorded the same value as the healthy ("the pagan"), or even more value, as in Pascal's judgment concerning sickness and health, then unnaturalness becomes law— This universal love of men is in practice the *preference* for the suffering, underprivileged, degenerate: it has in fact lowered and weakened the strength, the responsibility, the lofty duty to sacrifice men. All that remains, according to the Christian scheme of values, is to sacrifice oneself: but this residue of human sacrifice that Christianity concedes and even advises has, from the standpoint of general breeding, no meaning at all. The prosperity of the species is unaffected by the self-sacrifice of this or that individual (— whether it be in the monkish and ascetic manner or, with the aid of crosses, pyres, and scaffolds, as "martyrs" of error). The species requires that the ill-constituted, weak, degenerate, perish: but it was precisely to them that Christianity turned as a conserving force; it further enhanced that instinct in the weak, already so powerful, to take care of and preserve themselves and to sustain one another. What is "virtue" and "charity" in Christianity if not just this mutual preservation, this solidarity of weak, this hampering of selection? What is Christian altruism if not the mass-egoism of the weak, which divines that if all care for one another each individual will be preserved as long as possible?— If one does not feel such a disposition as an extreme immorality, as a crime against life, one belongs with the company of the sick and possesses its instincts oneself— Genuine charity demands sacrifice for the good of the species— it is hard, it is full of self-overcoming, because it needs human sacrifice. And this pseudo humaneness called Christianity wants it established that no one should be sacrificed.

Friedrich Nietzsche, *The Will to Power*, trans. Walter Kaufmann and R.J. Hollingdale; ed. Walter Kaufmann (New York: Random House, 1967), 141-42.

11. My discussion here is adapted from a longer discussion elsewhere. See Michael Perry, *Love and Power: The Role of Religion and Morality in American Politics* (New York:Oxford University Press, 1991), ch. 5.

12. Charles Taylor, *Sources of the Self: The Making of the Modern Identity* (Cambridge, Mass.: Harvard University Press, 1989), 18. Taylor also observes that "those whose spiritual agenda is mainly defined in this way are in a fundamentally different existential predicament from that which dominated most previous cultures and still defines the lives of other people today." Ibid. On the "notorious vagueness" of the question "What is the Meaning of Life?," see W.D. Joske, "Philosophy and the Meaning of Life," in *The Meaning of Life*, ed. E.D. Klemke (New York: Oxford University Press, 1981), 248, 248 et seq. See also R.W. Hepburn, "Questions about the Meaning of Life," in ibid., 209.

13. Albert Camus, *The Myth of Sisyphus and Other Essays* (New York: Vintage Books, 1955), 5. See Leszek Kolakowski, *The Presence of Myth* (Chicago: University of Chicago Press, 1989), esp. ch. 8: "The Phenomenon of the World's Indifference." Cf. Blaise Pascal, *Pensees* 95 (New York: Viking, 1966): "The eternal silence of these infinite spaces fills me with dread."

14. See David Tracy, *Plurality and Ambiguity: Hermeneutics, Religion, Hope* (San Francisco: Harper and Row, 1987), 87: "Like strictly metaphysical questions, religious questions must be questions on the nature of Ultimate Reality. Unlike metaphysical questions, religious questions deliberately ask the question of the meaning and truth of Ultimate Reality not only as it is in itself but as it is existentially related to us. The religious classics are testimonies to the responses of the religions to those questions" (emphasis added).

15. Abraham Heschel, *Who Is Man?* (Stanford, Cal.: Stanford University Press, 1965), 75. Cf. Fyodor Dostoevsky, *The Brothers Karamazov* (New York: Norton, 1976), 235: "For the secret of man's being is not only to live but to have something to live for. Without a stable conception of the object of life, man would not consent to go on living, and would rather destroy himself than remain on earth, though he had bread in abundance." (This is one of the Grand Inquisitor's statements in ch. 5 of Book Five.)

16. Cf. "Religion," Oxford English Dictionary, 13th ed., (1989), 568.

17. See David Braybrooke, "Ideology," in *Encyclopedia of Philosophy* 8 vols., ed. Paul Edwards (New York: MacMillan, 1967), 4:124.

18. Harvey Egan has written that "there is a sense in which all great religions are mystical at heart and that mysticism is the full-flowering of any religious tradition." Harvey Egan, *What Are They Saying About Mysticism?* (New York: Paulist Press, 1982), 17. According to Wayne Proudfoot, the very ubiquity of mystical experience among the world religions suggests that mysticism may be regarded as "a *paradigm* of religious experience." Wayne Proudfoot, *Religious Experience* (Berkeley, Calif.: University of California Press, 1985), xviii. Some commentators distinguish between two fundamental types of mystical experience, two kinds of experience of union with God or the Absolute: (1) the experience of union but not identity with God (as attested to by mystics in theistic traditions such as Christianity, Judaism, and Islam), and (2) the experience of complete absorption into the divine. Cf. ibid., 121: "The terms in which the subject understands what is happening to him are constitutive of the experience; consequently those in different traditions have different experiences. Jewish and Buddhist mystics [for example] bring entirely different doctrinal commitments, expectations, and rules for identifying their mental and bodily states to their experiences, and thus *devekuth* and *nirvana* cannot be the same."

19. According to William James, "transience" is a third mark of mystical experience. Commenting on James, Proudfoot writes: "The two secondary marks by which James characterizes the mystical state, transience and passivity, are also related to the noetic quality of the experience. Passivity conveys the sense of being grasped and of being subject to some power beyond oneself.

Both passivity and transience reflect the perception that the experience is not under the subject's voluntary control. It cannot be manipulated or guaranteed by the subject's decision or by causes that he might set in motion. He can prepare himself for it, but the experience is finally not subject to his control. The rules for the identification of an experience as mystical include the condition that he judge it to be something other than an artifact of his own thought and actions;" Proudfoot, *Religious Experience*, 147-48.

20. Milan Kundera, *The Unbearable Lightness of Being* (New York: Harper and Row, 1984), 139 (emphasis added).

21. "Not the individual man nor a single generation by its own power, can erect the bridge that leads to God. Faith is the achievement of many generations, an effort accumulated over centuries. Many of its ideas are as the light of the star that left its source a long time ago. Many enigmatic songs, unfathomable today, are the resonance of voices of bygone times. There is a collective memory of God in the human spirit, and it is this memory which is the main source of our faith." From Abraham Heschel's two-part essay "Faith," first published in vol. 10 of *The Reconstructionist*, 3, 17 November 1944. For a later statement on faith, incorporating some of the original essay, see Abraham Heschel, *Man Is Not Alone* (New York: Harper and Row, 1951), 159-76. On community/tradition as a principal matrix of moral beliefs, see Michael Perry, *Morality, Politics, and Law* (New York: Oxford University Press, 1988), 24-33.

22. See Robert Coles, *The Spiritual Life of Children* (Boston: Houghton Mifflin Co., 1990), 37 : "The questions Tolstoy asked, and Gauguin in, say, his great Tahiti triptych, completed just before he died ('Where Do We Come From? What Are We? Where Are We Going?'), are the eternal questions children ask more intensely, unremittingly, and subtly than we sometimes imagine;" see Heschel, *Who Is Man?*, 28: "In an old rabbinic text three other questions are suggested: '*Whence* did you come?' '*Whither* are you going?' 'Before *whom* are you destined to give account?'"

23. Tracy, *Plurality and Ambiguity*, 86.

24. David Tracy, *The Analogical Imagination: David Tracy* (New York: Crossroads, 1981), 4.

25. Robin W. Lovin and Frank E. Reynolds, "Focus Introduction," *Journal of Religious Ethics* 14 (1986): 48, 56-57; see ibid, "In the Beginning," in *Cosmogony and Ethical Order: New Studies in Comparative Ethics*, ed. Robin Lovin and Frank Reynolds (Chicago: University of Chicago Press, 1985), 1.

26. See Nietzsche, *The Will to Power*, 184: "What is the counterfeiting aspect of morality?— It pretends to know something, namely what 'good and evil' is. That means wanting to know why

mankind is here, its goal, its destiny. That means wanting to know that mankind has a goal, a destiny— " What was Nietzsche's teleology? See ibid., "The Eternal Recurrence," 544-50.

27.   See n. 52 and accompanying text.

28.   John 13:34. See John 15:12, 17. (This and the other translations in this essay are those of *The New Jerusalem Bible* (1985);) see generally Edmund Santurri and William Werpehowski, eds., *The Love Commandments: Essays in Christian Ethics and Moral Philosophy* (Washington, D.C.: Georgtown University Press, 1992). See also Garth Hallett, *Christian Neighbor-Love: An Assesstment of Six Rival Versions* (Washington, D.C.: Georgetown University Press, 1989). (For a recent collection of secular philosophical essays on "altruism," see *Social Philosophy and Policy* 10 (1993): 1-245). On the relation between the commandment to "love God" and the commandment to "love one another," see n. 47; see Nietzsche, *The Will to Power*, 183: "'Love': the ideal state of the herd animal that no longer wants to have enemies."

29.   Matthew 5:43-48; see Luke 6:27-35. (Such a conception of the good is not confined to semitic spiritualities. For Buddhists, for example, the good life centrally involves compassion (*karuna*) for all sentient creatures and therefore for all human beings.) Cf.Nietzsche, *The Will to Power*, 120: "One drives nature out of morality when one says 'Love your enemies': for then the natural 'Thou shalt love thy neighbor and hate thy enemy' in the law (in instinct) has become meaningless; then this love of one's neighbor must also find a new basis (as a kind of love of God). Everywhere, God is inserted and utility withdrawn; everywhere the real origin of morality is denied: the veneration of nature, which lies precisely in the recognition of a natural morality, is destroyed at its roots— "

30.   See Tracy, *The Analogical Imagination*, 4.

31.   In the Bible, God— Ultimate Reality— is often imaged as "parent," sometimes as "father," sometimes as "mother." Cf. Elizabeth Johnson, *She Who Is: The Mystery of God in a Feminist Theological Perspective* (New York: Crossroads, 1992).

32.   Hilary Putnam, *The Many Faces of Realism* (LaSalle, Ill.: Open Court, 1987), 60-61.

33.   National Conference of Catholic Bishops, *Economic Justice for All* (1986); emphasis added.

34.   Ben Zion Bokser and Baruch M. Bokser, "Introduction: The Spirituality of the Talmud," in *The Talmud: Selected Writings* (New York: Paulist Press, 1989), 7.

35.   Ibid., 30-31.

36.   Nietzsche, *The Will to Power*, 466-68.

37.   See Martha Nussbaum, *Aristotle on Human Nature and the Foundations of Ethics* (St. Lawrence, Canada: St. Lawrence

University, 1990), 22: "To find out what our nature is seems to be one and the same thing as to find out what we deeply believe to be most important and indispensable [in a human life]."

38. See Ludwig Wittgenstein, "Philosophical Investigations," sec. 217, in Putnam, *The Many Faces of Realism*, 85: ("I have reached bedrock, and this is where my spade is turned.").

39. Robert Nozick, *Philosophical Explanations* (Cambridge, Mass.: Harvard University Press, 1981): 403. Recall Glaucon's challenge to Socrates in Plato's *Republic*: show that being moral is better for the agent, apart from its external consequences. To isolate these consequences, Glaucon imagines a ring that makes someone invisible. With this ring he is able to act immorally with no external penalty: he can rob, murder, and rape without being caught or punished. Is there any reason why he should not do this? Glaucon sharpens the issue by imagining that the immoral man has the reputation of being moral, he is honored and praised as moral, while another man is thought to be immoral and so is condemned and shunned. Glaucon asks Socrates to show, despite this, that the second moral person is better off than the first immoral one, that we would be better off being that second than the first.

'The answer that [Plato] puts into the mouth of Socrates is that the just man is happy because his soul is harmoniously ordered, because, as we would say, he has an integrated personality, whereas the unjust man's personality is disintegrated, and the man who represents the extreme of injustice is psychotic, his soul is a chaos of internal strife." John Mackie, *Ethics: Inventing Right and Wrong* (New York: Penguin Press, 1977), 190-91. Should we take Socrates' response seriously? See Bernard Williams, *Ethics and the Limits of Philosophy* (Cambridge, Mass.: Harvard University Press, 1985), 46: "There is also the figure, rarer perhaps than Callicles supposed, but real, who is horrible enough and not miserable at all but, by any ethological standard of the bright eye and the gleaming coat, dangerously flourishing. For those who want to ground the ethical life in psychological health, it is something of a problem that there can be such people at all. But it is a significant question, how far their existence, indeed the thought of their existence, is a cultural phenomenon. They seem sleeker and finer at a distance. Some Renaissance grandee fills such a role with more style than the tawdry fascist bosses, gangsters, or tycoons who seem, even as objects of fantasy, to be their chief contemporary instances. Perhaps we deceive ourselves about the past."

40. See James Burtchaell, "The Source of Conscience," *Notre Dame Magazine* 13 (Winter 1984-85): 20, 20-21: "The Catholic tradition embraces a long effort to uncover the truth about human behavior

and experience. Our judgments of good and evil focus on whether a certain course of action will make a human being grow and mature and flourish, or whether it will make a person withered, estranged and indifferent. In making our evaluations, we have little to draw on except our own and our forebears' experience, and whatever wisdom we can wring from our debate with others. . . . What we are trying to unpuzzle are things like childbearing and immigration and economic policy and infant mortality and drug use and family fidelity and so much else about which we must frame moral judgments. With our fellow communicants we share commitments and assumptions: that we are happier giving than getting, that there is no greater love than to put down your life for your neighbor, and that your neighbor always turns out to be the most unlikely person." On our neighbor always turning out to be the most unlikely person, see n. 42 and accompanying text, Parable of the Good Samaritan. (For a revised version of Burtchaell's essay, and for several other illuminating essays by Father Burtchaell, see James Butchaell, *The Giving and Taking of Life* (Notre Dame, Ind.: University of Notre Dame Press, 1989).)

41. See Matthew 22:34-40: "But when the Pharisees heard that he had silenced the Sadducees they got together and, to put him to the test, one of them put a further question, 'Master, which is the greatest commandment of the Law?' Jesus said to him, 'You must love the Lord your God with all your heart, with all your soul, and with all your mind. This is the greatest and the first commandment. The second resembles it: You must love your neighbor as yourself. On these two commandments hang the whole Law, and the Prophets too." See also Mark 12:28-34; Luke 10:25-28. (On the relation between the two commandments, see n. 47.) Cf. Mackie, *Ethics*, 243: "D. D. Raphael, in 'The Standard of Morals,' in *Proceedings of the Aristotelian Society* 75 (1974-75) follows Edward Ullendorff in pointing out that whereas 'Thou shalt love thy neighbor as thyself' represents the Greek of the Septuagint (Leviticus 19:18) and of the New Testament, the Hebrew from which the former is derived means rather 'You shall treat your neighbor lovingly, for he is like yourself.'" (Thus, Bruce Ackerman need not worry that he is being asked to love the "stranger" as himself. *That*, protests Ackerman, "[o]nly a God could do . . .: there are too many strangers with too many strangenesses." Bruce Ackerman, *The Future of Liberal Revolution* 21 (New Haven, Ct.: Yale University Press, 1992).)

42. See Luke 10:29-37: "But the man was anxious to justify himself and said to Jesus, 'And who is my neighbour?' In answer Jesus said, 'A man was once on his way down from Jerusalem to Jericho and fell into the hands of bandits; they stripped him, beat him and then made off, leaving him half dead. Now a priest happened to be

travelling down the same road, but when he saw the man, he passed by on the other side. In the same way a Levite who came to the place saw him, and passed by on the other side. But a Samaritan traveller who came on him was moved with compassion when he saw him. He went up to him and bandaged his wounds, pouring oil and wine on them. He then lifted him onto his own mount and took him to an inn and looked after him. Next day, he took out two denarii and handed them to the innkeeper and said, 'Look after him, and on my way back I will make good any extra expense you have.' Which of these three, do you think, proved himself a neighbour to the man who fell into the bandits' hands?' [The man] replied, 'The one who showed pity towards him.' Jesus said to him, 'Go, and do the same yourself.'" In the annotation of *The New Jerusalem Bible*, a footnote appended to "Samaritan" says that "[t]he contrast is between the element in Israel most strictly bound to the law of love, and the heretic and stranger, . . . from whom normally only hate could be expected."

43. I may love the Other even if I do not understand that the Other is my sister/brother. And I may understand that the Other is my sister/brother and yet fail to love the Other.

44. See n. 41.

45. Matthew 25:31-46. In Matthew's Gospel, these are Jesus' final words to his disciples before the beginning of the passion narrative. Matthew 26:1-2 states: "Jesus had now finished all he wanted to say, and he told his disciples, 'It will be Passover, as you know, in two days' time, and the Son of Man will be handed over to be crucified.'" In the view of great German Catholic theologian Karl Rahner— a view consistent with the eschatology of the Last Judgment passage— not only is there no tension between the commandment to love God and the commandment to love one another, there is "a radical identity of the two loves." Karl Rahner, *Theological Investigations* 6 (Baltimore, Md.: Helicon Press, 1969), 231, 236. In his "Reflections on the Unity of the Love of Neighbor and the Love of God," Rahner wrote: "It is radically true, i.e. by an ontological and not merely 'moral' or psychological necessity, that whoever does not love the brother whom he sees, also cannot love God whom he does not see, and that one can love God whom one does not see only by loving one's visible brother lovingly;" ibid., 247. Rahner's reference is to a passage in John's First Letter in which it is written: "Anyone who says 'I love God' and hates his brother, is a liar, since whoever does not love the brother whom he can see cannot love God whom he has not seen." I John 4:20. See n. 42 and accompanying text (Parable of the Good Samaritan). In Rahner's view, the two great commandments are really one; see Rahner, 232: Rahner argued that if and to the extent one loves one's neighbor one has achieved the ontological/exis-

tential state of being/consciousness that constitutes "love of God" even if one does not "believe in God;" ibid., 238-39. If Rahner is right, then it is a mistake, a confusion, to say that one should love the Other *because* we love, or should love, God and God wants us to— or *because* we fear, or should fear, God and God wants us to. We may say, instead, that to love the Other (who is "sister/brother") just is to love God (who is "parent")— and that we should achieve the ontological/existential state of being/consciousness that constitutes "love of the Other" (= "love of God") because that state is the highest human good; to have achieved that radically unalienated condition is to have become "truly, fully" human. "We are well aware that we have passed over from death to life because we love our brothers. Whoever does not love, remains in death"; 1 John 3:14.

Has Rahner pushed a good idea— that no one can be judged to love God who fails to love his/her neighbor— too far? One can accept that idea while rejecting Rahner's identification of love of God with love of neighbor. Tim Jackson has suggested, in correspondence, that "surely there is such a thing as the *direct* love of God, as for instance in the ecstatic prayer of some mystics or in Holy Communion. Human beings are social animals, no doubt, but they are also born for a vertical relation to the Supernatural;" Jean Porter, "Salvific Love and Charity: A Comparison of the Thought of Karl Rahner and Thomas Aquinas," in Santurri and Werpehowski, *The Love Commandments*, 240.

46. On the death of such a "God," see Charles Larmore, "Beyond Religion and Enlightenment," *San Diego Law Review* 30 (1993): 799, 799-802. Indeed, as my footnote references to Buddhism — whose "theological" discourse is, in the main, non-theistic — suggest, the vision is not necessarily even theistic in any conventional sense. Whether mainline Buddhism is theistic in an unconventional sense is a difficult question. See David Tracy, "Kenosis, Sunyata, and Trinity: A Dialogue With Masao Abe," in John B. Cobb, Jr. and Christopher Ives, eds., *The Emptying God: A Buddhist-Jewish-Christian Conversation* (Maryknoll, N.Y.: Orbis Books, 1990), 135.

47. In Buddhism, the relevant conviction is that the Other— who, appearances (illusions) to the contrary notwithstanding, is not really other at all, not, at any rate, in any deep sense— is an object of infinite compassion. (The Buddhist greeting "Namast*" means, roughly, "I greet the place within you where we are one.")

48. See Perry, *Love and Power*, 72-73. Nor is such a vision necessarily attended by belief in an afterlife; see Timothy Jackson, "The Disconsolation of Theology: Irony, Cruelty, and Putting Charity First," *Journal Religious Ethics* 20 (1992): 1, 19, (arguing that "a future heaven and/or hell ought not to play much of a role in [Christian] ethics, whatever role they may play in cosmology").

49. TD.J. Chappell, "Why Read Aquinas?," *Times Literary Supplement,* 1 May 1992, 25 (reviewing Brian Davies, *The Thought of Thomas Aquinas* (Oxford: Clarendon Press, 1992)).

50. Ibid., 25. David Tracy's comments about the richness, the variety, but, finally, the problematic character— the limits— of all talk about Ultimate Reality, and especially of God-talk (talk about God, "theo-logizing"), are compelling: In and through even the best speech for Ultimate Reality, greater obscurity eventually emerges to manifest a religious sense of that Reality as ultimate mystery. Silence may be the most appropriate kind of speech for evoking this necessary sense of the radical mystery— as mystics insist when they say, "Those who know do not speak; those who speak do not know." The most refined theological discourse of the classic theologians ranges widely but returns at last to a deepened sense of the same ultimate mystery: the amazing freedom with all traditional doctrinal formulations in Meister Eckhart; the confident portrayals of God in Genesis and Exodus become the passionate outbursts of the prophets and the painful reflections of Job, Ecclesiastes, and Lamentations; the disturbing light cast by the biblical metaphors of the "wrath of God" on all temptations to sentimentalize what love means when the believer says, "God is love"; the proclamation of the hidden and revealed God in Luther and Calvin; the *deus otiosus* vision of God in the Gnostic traditions; the repressed discourse of the witches; the startling female imagery for Ultimate Reality in both the great matriarchal traditions and the great Wisdom traditions of both Greeks and Jews; the power of the sacred dialectically divorcing itself from the profane manifested in all religions; the extraordinary subtleties of rabbinic writing on God become the uncanny paradoxes of kabbalistic thought on God's existence in the very materiality of letters and texts; the subtle debates in Hindu philosophical reflections on monism and polytheism; the many faces of the Divine in the stories of Shiva and Krishna; the puzzling sense that, despite all appearances to the contrary, there is "nothing here that is not Zeus" in Aeschylus and Sophocles; the terror caused by Dionysius in Euripides' *Bacchae;* the refusal to cling even to concepts of "God" in order to become free to experience Ultimate Reality as Emptiness in much Buddhist thought; the moving declaration of that wondrous clarifier Thomas Aquinas, "All that I have written is straw; I shall write no more"; Karl Rahner's insistence on the radical incomprehensibility of both God and ourselves understood through and in our most comprehensible philosophical and theological speech; . . . the "God beyond God" language of Paul Tillich and all theologians who acknowledge how deadening traditional God-language can easily become; the refusal to speak God's name in classical Judaism; the insistence on speaking that name in classical Islam; the hesitant musings on the

present-absent God in Buber become the courageous attempts to forge new languages for a new covenant with God in the post-*tremendum* theologies of Cohen, Fackenheim, and Greenberg. There is no classic discourse on Ultimate Reality that can be understood as mastering its own speech. If any human discourse gives true testimony to Ultimate Reality, it must necessarily prove uncontrollable and unmasterable. Tracy, *Plurality and Ambiguity*, 108–09; see Martin Buber, quoted in Hans Kung, *Does God Exist? An Answer for Today* (Garden City, N.Y.: Doubleday, 1980), 508: ["God"] is the most loaded of all words used by men. None has been so soiled, so mauled. But that is the very reason I cannot give it up. Generations of men have blamed this word for the burdens of their troubled lives and crushed it to the ground; it lies in the dust, bearing all their burdens. Generations of men with their religious divisions have torn the word apart; they have killed for it and died for it; it bears all their fingerprints and is stained with all their blood. Where would I find a word to equal it, to describe supreme reality? If I were to take the purest, most sparkling term from the innermost treasury of the philosophers, I could capture in it no more than a noncommittal idea, not the presence of what I mean, of what generations of men in the vastness of their living and dying have venerated and degraded.... We must respect those who taboo it, since they revolt against the wrong and mischief that were so readily claimed to be authorized in the name of God; but we cannot relinquish it. It is easy to understand why there are some who propose a period of silence about the "last things," so that the misused words may be redeemed. But this is not the way to redeem them. We cannot clean up the term "God" and we cannot make it whole; but, stained and mauled as it is, we can raise it from the ground and set it above an hour of great sorrow. For feminist-theological reflection on God-talk, see n.31, Johnson, *She Who Is*; Rosemary Ruether, *Sexism and God-Talk: Toward a Feminist Theology* (Boston: Beacon Press, 1983); Judith Plaskow and Carol Christ, eds., *Weaving the Visions: New Patterns in Feminist Spirituality* (San Francisco: Harper and Row, 1989), esp. part 2, "Naming the Sacred").

51.   As was Martin Buber and as is David Tracy; see n. 50. See David Hollenbach, S.J., "Afterword: A Community of Freedom," in R. Bruce Douglass and David Hollenbach, S.J., eds., *Catholicism and Liberalism: Contributions to American Public Philosophy*, (forthcoming):
"For Christian believers, it is a challenge to recognize that their faith in God and the way of life it entails is a historical reality—i t is rooted in historically particular scriptures and symbols and it is lived and sustained in historically particular communities. This historicity means that the task of interpreting the meaning of their

faith will never be done as long as history lasts. The God in whom they place their faith can never be identified with any personal relationship, social arrangement, or cultural achievement. God transcends all of these. Though Christians believe that in Jesus Christ they have been given a definitive revelation of who this God is, they cannot claim to possess or encompass God in any of their theologies or understandings of the ultimate good of human life. Thus, in the words of Avery Dulles, 'The Christian is defined as a person on the way to discovery, on the way to a revelation not yet given, or at least not yet given in final form'." (Quoting Avery Dulles, "Revelation and Discovery," in *Theology and Discovery: Essays in Honor of Karl Rahner, ed. William J. Kelly* (Milwaukee, Wis.: Marquette University Press, 1980), 27.) Hollenbach adds: "Because the Christian community is always on the way to the fullness of its own deepest faith, hope, and love, it must be continually open to fresh discoveries. Encounter with the other, the different, and the strange must therefore characterize the life of the church. Active participation in a community of freedom is a prerequisite to such discovery." Hollenbach, ibid., 23.

52. See David Cohn-Sherbok, ed., *World Religions and Human Liberation* (Maryknoll, N.Y.: Orbis Books, 1992); Hans Kung and Jürgen Moltmann, eds., *The Ethics of World Religions and Human Rights* (Philadelphia: Trinity Press International, 1990); Leroy Rouner, ed., *Human Rights and the World's Religions* (Notre Dame, Ind.: Notre Dame University Press, 1988); Arlene Swidler, ed., *Human Rights in Religious Traditions* (New York: Pilgrim Press, 1982); Robert Traer, *Faith in Human Rights: Support in Religious Tradtions for a Global Struggle* (Washington, D.C.: Georgetown University Press, 1991).

53. See Sandra Schneiders, "Does The Bible Have a Postmodern Message?," in *Postmodern Theology: Christian Faith in a Pluralist World*, ed. Frederic Burnham (San Francisco: Harper and Row, 1989), 56, 64-65: [There are] two problems: the ideological *use* of Scripture, which is, if you will, an exterior problem; and the ideological *content* of Scripture, which is intrinsic to the text. The question of the *use* of Scripture for purposes of oppression is being focused in the third-world struggle of the poor from domination by the rich and for participation in the societies and cultures which have been, for so long, controlled by the economically powerful for their own advantage. The struggle involves wresting the scared text from those who have used it to legitimate their oppressive regimes and strategies and delivering it into the hands of the oppressed as a resource for liberation. . . . The problem of the ideological use of Scripture is soluble and is slowly being solved.

The second problem, that of the ideological *content* of Scripture, is much more complicated. It is being focused in the struggle of women for liberation from patriarchal oppression in family, society, and church, and in the struggle of feminists, both men and women, to destroy the patriarchal ideology which grounds not only sexism but racism, classism, clericalism, and all the other forms of dualistic hierarchy in which the powerful dominate the weak in the name of God. Here the problem is not the Scripture has been *used* to legitimate oppression (although this is a continuing problem) but that the Bible itself is both a product and a producer of oppression, that some of its *content* is oppressive. Schneider's elaboration of the problem and her overview of the various responses of women (especially feminist theologians) and others to it (ibid., 63-71) are excellent. (Schneiders is a feminist Christian theologian.)

54. Tracy, *The Analogical Imagination*, 105.
55. Ibid., 100.
56. Tracy, *Plurality and Ambiguity*, 84-85, 86, 97-98, 112.
57. Jürgen Habermas, "Transcendence from Within, Transcendence in this World," in *Habermas, Modernity, and Public Theology*, ed. Don S. Browning and Francis Fiorenza (New York: Crossroads, 1992), 226, 238.
58. Glenn Tinder, "Can We Be Good Without God: The Political Meaning of Christianity," *Atlantic*, (December 1989), 69, 80 (passages rearranged and emphasis added).
59. Nor does the point lose anything if the emphasis is put, for example, on the (Mahayana) Buddhist tradition, with its insistence on compassion for all sentient creatures as the fitting response to the true— as distinct from the illusory— nature of the world.
60. See Larmore, "Beyond Religion and Enlightenment," 799, 799-802.
61. Cf. Nietzsche, *The Will to Power*, 169: "Man a little, eccentric species of animal, which— fortunately— has its day; all on earth a mere moment, an incident, an exception without consequences, something of no importance to the general character of the earth; the earth itself, like every star, a hiatus between two nothingness, an event without plan, reason, will, self-consciousness, the worst kind of necessity, *stupid* necessity— Something in us rebels against this view; the serpent vanity says to us: "all that *must* be false, *for* it arouses indignation— Could all that not be merely appearance? And man, in spite of all, as Kant says— "
62. Bruce A. Ackerman, *Social Justice in the Liberal State* (New Haven, Ct.: Yale University Press, 1980), 368.
63. Nietzsche, *The Will to Power*, 147.
64. Charles Taylor, *The Ethics of Authenticity* (Cambridge, Mass.: Harvard University Press, 1991), 68.
65. See Joske, "Philosophy and the Meaning of Life," 250: "If, as Kurt Vonnegut speculates in *The Sirens of Titan*, the ultimate end of

human activity is the delivery of a small piece of steel to a wrecked space ship wanting to continue a journey of no importance whatsoever, the end would be too trivial to justify the means." See also Nozick, *Philosophical Explanations*, 586: "If the cosmic role of human beings was to provide a negative lesson to some others ('don't act like them') or to provide needed food to passing intergalactic travelers who *were* important, this would not suit our aspirations— not even if afterwards the intergalactic travelers smacked their lips and said that we tasted good."

66. Paul Edwards, "Life, Meaning and Value of," *Encyclopedia of Philosophy* 4 (1967): 467, 470. Whether Clarence Darrow was in fact "one of the most compassionate men who ever lived" is open to serious question. For a revisionist view of Darrow, see Garry Wills, *Under God: Religion and American Politics* (New York: Simon and Schuster, 1990), ch. 8-9.

67. John Leslie, "Is It All Quite Simple? The Physicist's Search for a Theory of Everything," *Times Literary Supplement*, 29 January 1993, 3 (reviewing, inter alia, Steven Weinberg, *Dreams of a Final Theory* (New York: Pantheon Books, 1992)). Cf. Paul Davies, "The Holy Grail of Physics," *New York Times Book Review* , 7 March 1993, 11 (reviewing, inter alia, Weinberg's book): "Reductionism [in physics] may be a fruitful research method, but it is a bleak philosophy. . . . If the world is but a collection of inert atoms interacting through blind and purposeless forces, what happens to . . . the meaning of life?" For a controversial critique of such scientific reductionism, see Brian Appleyard, *Understanding the Present: Science and the Soul of Modern Man* (New York: Doubleday, 1992). On philosophical inquiry into cosmology, see Derek Parfit, "The Puzzle of Reality," Times Literary Supplement, 3 July 1992, 3.
Several papers in a fierce and ongoing debate about the consistency or inconsistency of claims made in evolutionary biology with Christian claims are relevant here. All the papers are by persons who identify themselves as Christians. In the September 1991 issue of *Christian Scholar's Review*, see Alvin Platinga, "When Faith and Reason Clash: Evolution and the Bible;" H. Van Till, "When Faith and Reason Cooperate;" Ernan McMullin, "Platinga's Defense of Special Creation;" Alvin Platinga, "Evolution, Neutrality, and Antecedent Probability: A Reply to McMullin and Van Till." In the June/July 1993 issue of *First Things*, see Howard Van Till and Philip Johnson, "God and Evolution: An Exchange."

68. Dworkin, "Life is Sacred," 36.

69. Ibid.

70. Ronald Dworkin, *Life's Dominion: An Argument About Abortion, Euthanasia, and Individual Freedom* (New York: Alfred A. Knopf, 1993), 195.

71. Ibid., 25. Curiously, elsewhere in his book Dworkin writes that
     that he "can think of no plausible account of the content that a
     belief must have in order to be deemed religious that would rule
     out convictions about why and how human life [is sacred], except
     the abandoned notion that religious belief must presuppose a
     god;" ibid., 163. He also says that "why and how human life is
     sacred" is an "essentially religious issue;" ibid., 165. It is not
     obvious why, if (as Dworkin insists) there is a secular
     interpretation or version of the idea that human life is sacred, the
     issue of why and how human life is sacred is *essentially* religious.
     If the idea that human life is sacred is *not* essentially religious, why
     is the issue of why and how human life is sacred essentially
     religious? Dworkin's principal incentive to claim that the idea that
     human life is sacred can be interpreted in a secular as well as in a
     religious way is that, for purposes of his characterization of the
     abortion controversy, he wants to be able to attribute the idea (in
     its secular version) to secular folks as well as (in its religious
     version) to religious ones. His principal incentive to claim that the
     issue of why and how human life is sacred is essentially religious
     is is that, for purposes of his argument about the (un)con-
     stitutionality of restrictive abortion legislation, Dworkin wants to
     be able to rely on a constitutional premise according to which
     government may not take coercive action predicated on nothing
     more than a contested position on an essentially religious issue;
     see ibid., 160-68. (That there is such a constitutional premise is
     open to question; Cf. Michael Perry, "Religious Morality and
     Political Choice: Further Thoughts — and Second Thoughts on
     Love and Power," *San Diego Law Review* 30 (1993): 703.)

72. Dworkin, "Life is Sacred," 36 (emphasis added).

73. Dworkin, *Life's Dominion*, 69-71.

74. A. W. Price, "Varieties of Objectivity and Values," *Proceedings of the
     Aristotelian Society* 83 (1983): 103, 106. See David Hume, *A
     Treatise of Human Nature*, ed. L. Selby-Bigge (Oxford: Clarendon
     Press, 1973): 469, "Vice and virtue, therefore, may be compar'd to
     sounds, colours, heat and cold, which, according to modern
     philosophy, are not qualities in objects, but perceptions in the
     mind: And this discovery in morals, like that other in physics, is
     to be regarded as a considerable advancement of the speculative
     sciences; tho', like that, too, it has little or no influence on practice."
     See also Anthony Kronman, "A Comment on Dean Clark,"
     Columbia Law Review 89 (1989): 1748, 1755. "[The view] that there
     are goods which are not the goods of any human beings at all, is
     likely to appear . . . wholly unintelligible, for it conflicts with what
     is perhaps the deepest and most widely shared orthodoxy of
     modern moral thought— the assumption that only the goods of
     human beings (or perhaps sentient beings) count in assessing
     different practices and institutions;" see Robin Lovin, "Empiricism

and Christian Social Thought," *Annual of Society of Christian Ethics* (1992): 25, 41: "Ethics will never be like physics, chemistry, or certain types of sociology, because it understands the moral reality to be about an interaction between persons and the world which can only be known from the reports of those who experience that interaction."

Does Dworkin disagree? It's difficult to tell; see Dworkin, *Life's Dominion*, 248 n. 1: "I do not mean to take any position on a further, very abstract philosophical issue not pertinent to this discussion: whether great paintings would still be valuable if intelligent life were altogether destroyed forever so that no one could ever have the experience of regarding paintings again. There is no inconsistency in denying that they would have value then, because the value of a painting lies in the kind of experience it makes available, while still insisting that this value is intrinsic because it does not depend on any creatures' actually wanting that kind of experience."

At one point in his discussion of "intrinsic" value, Dworkin writes: "David Hume and many other philosophers insisted that objects or events can be valuable only when and because they serve someone's or something's interests. On this view, nothing is valuable unless someone wants it or unless it helps someone get what he does want;" ibid., 69. The second sentence here is a glaring non sequitur. It does not follow, from the Humean view, that nothing is valuable unless someone wants it or unless it helps someone get what he does want. It follows only that nothing is valuable unless it serves someone's or something's interests. That something serves my interests does not entail that I want it (or that it helps me get what I do want). After all, I may not know that something serves my interests, or I may not know what my real interests are. Indeed, that I want something (or that it helps me get what I do want) does not entail that it serves my interests: I may want things that are not good for me— indeed, that are bad for me.

75. To say that something has *merely* subjective value for someone is to say that she believes it to have value for her even though it does not. Considered in isolation something may have (objective and/or subjective) value for someone even if considered in context it does not: One thing that has value for someone may crowd out or preclude another thing that has even greater value for her.

76. Dworkin, *Life's Dominion*, 78.

77. Ibid., 82, 81-84.

78. Ibid., 82.

79. Ibid., 83.

80. Ibid., 84.

81. Ibid., 82.

82. Ibid., 83.
83. Ibid., 78.
84. Ibid., 71.
85. Robert Grant, "Abortion and the Idea of the Sacred," *Times Literary Supplement*, 18 June 1993, 11.
86. There are, of course, others. (See n. 95 (mentioning the work of John Finnis and that of Jürgen Habermas).) A prominent secular argument for human rights— that is, a prominent argument that does not rely on the possibly ineliminably religious idea of human rights— is Alan Gewirth's. See Alan Gewirth, *Reason and Morality* (Chicago: Il.: University of Chicago Press, 1978), ch. 1-2; Alan Gewirth, *Human Rights: Essays on Justification and Applications* 41-78 (Chicago: University of Chicago Press, 1982); Alan Gewirth, "The Epistemology of Human Rights," *Social Philosophy and Policy* (1984): 1. For Gewirth's most recent statement, see Gewirth, "Human Dignity as the Basis of Rights," in Michael Meyer and William Parent, eds., *The Constitution of Rights: Human Dignity and American Values* (Ithaca, N.Y.: Cornell University Press, 1992), 10. Gewirth's argument has been extremely controversial, to say the least. Indeed, I am tempted to say that there is as close to a consensus as one gets in moral philosophy that Gewirth's argument simply doesn't work. See, e.g., Edward Regis, ed., *Gewirth's Ethical Rationalism* (Chicago: University of Chicago Press, 1984); Brian M. Barry, *Theories of Justice* (Berkeley, Cal.: University of California Press, 1989), 285-88. For a careful restatement and defense of Gewirth's argument, see Derek Beyleveld, *The Dialectical Necessity of Morality: An Analysis and Defense of Alan Gewirth's Argument for the Principle of Generic Consistency* (Chicago, Il.: University of Chicago Press, 1991). For a skeptical review of Beyleveld's book, see Nick Fotion, *Ethics* 101 (1993): 579.
87. Arthur Leff, "Economic Analysis of Law: Some Realism about Nominalism," *Virginia Law Review* 60 (1974): 451, 454 (emphasis added).
88. James Griffin, *Well-Being* (Oxford: The Clarendon Press, 1987): 239.
89. David Tracy, "Theology, Critical Social Theory, and the Public Realm," in Browning and Fiorenza, *Habermas, Modernity, and Public Theology*, 19, 37.
90. James Nickel, *Making Sense of Human Rights: Philosophical Reflections on the Universal Declaration of Human Rights* (Berkeley, Calif.: University of California Press, 1987), 97.
91. See Stephen Scott, "Motive and Justification," *Journal Philosophy* 85 (1988): 479, 499: "When he was deliberating about how to live, St. Augustine asked, 'What does anything matter, if it does not have to do with happiness?' His question requires explanation, because he is not advising selfishness nor the reduction of other people to utilities, and even qualification, because other things can have

THE IDEA OF HUMAN RIGHTS

some weight. All the same, the answer he expects is obviously right: only a happy life matters conclusively. If I had a clear view of it, I could have no motive to decline it, I could regret nothing by accepting it, I would have nothing about which to deliberate further;" see Richard Taylor, "Ancient Wisdom and Modern Folly," *Midwest Studies in Philosophy* 13 (1988): 54, 57, 58: "The Greek *eudaimonia* is always translated 'happiness,' which is unfortunate, for the meaning we attach to the word *happiness* is thin indeed compared to what the ancients meant by *eudaimonia. Fulfillment* might be a better term, though this, too, fails to capture the richness of the original term. . . . The concept of happiness in modern philosophy, as well as in popular thinking, is superficial indeed in comparison." For an extended discussion of the "Why be moral?" problem from a neo-Aristotelian perspective, see Rudolph Bittner, *What Reason Demands* (New York: Cambridge University Press, 1989).

92. Nickel, *Making Sense of Human Rights*, 91.
93. Nathan Stoltzfus, "Dissent in Nazi Germany," *Atlantic*, September 1992, at 87, 94.
94. Taylor, *Sources of the Self*, 87; ibid., 3: "Much contemporary moral philosophy, particularly but not only in the English-speaking world, has given such a narrow focus to morality . . . This moral philosophy has tended to focus on what it is right to do rather than on what it is good to be, on defining the content of obligation rather than the nature of the good life . . . This philosophy has accredited a cramped and truncated view of morality in a narrow sense, as well as of the whole range of issues involved in the attempt to live the best possible life, and this not only among professional philosophers, but with a wider public." (Taylor's book is, among other things, a powerful argument for a different, larger understanding of "moral," an Aristotelian rather than a Kantian understanding; see ibid., 4, 14-15, 63-64, 79, 87.)
The effort to evade the why-be-moral question by distinguishing between "reasons" and "motives" is unavailing— as, indeed, is implicit in Taylor's comments; see Henry Veatch, "Modern Ethics, Teleology, and Love of Self," *Monist* 75 (1992): 52, 60.
The stock answer given to this question has long been one of trying to distinguish between a *reason* and a *motive* for being moral. For surely, it is argued, if I recognize something to be my duty, then surely I have a reason to perform the required action, even though I have no motive for performing it. In fact, even to ask for a motive for doing something, when one already has a reason for doing it, would seem to be at once gratuitous and unnecessary— at least so it is argued. Unhappily, though, the argument has a dubious air about it at best. For does it amount to anything more than trying to prove a point by first attempting to

make a distinction, implying that the distinction is no mere distinction, but a distinction with a difference— viz. the distinction between a reason and a motive. But then, having exploited the distinction, and yet at the same time insinuating that one might conceivably have a reason for doing something, but no motive for doing it, the argument draws to its conclusion by surreptitiously taking advantage of the fact that there possibly is no real distinction between a reason and a motive after all, so that if one has a reason for doing a thing, then one has a motive for doing it as well. In other words, it's as if the argument only succeeds by taking back with its left hand what it had originally given with its right.

95.   John Finnis's argument in defense of a requirement "of fundamental impartiality among the human subjects who are or may be partakers of [basic human goods]" is simply unavailing. For the argument, see John Finnis, *Natural Law and Natural Rights* (New York: Oxford University Press, 1980), 106-08. "[John] Finnis has tried to do in two pages what . . . others have devoted entire books to: . . . show that egoism is inherently self-contradictory or irrational. All of these attempts have failed. It is surprising that Finnis deals with such a problematic and contentious issue in such a brief and casual fashion." J. D. Goldsworthy, "God or Mackie: The Dilemma of Secular Moral Philosophy," *American Journal Jurisprudence* (1985): 43, 75; see ibid., 73-77. One of Finnis' most recent writings fares no better: John Finnis, "Natural Law and Legal Reasoning," in *Natural Law Theory: Contemporary Essays*, ed. Robert George (Cambridge: Clarendon Press, 1992), 134.
Given the current prominence in some circles of Habermasian "discourse ethics," this recent statement by Jürgen Habermas is worth reporting— a statement that should be very sobering for anyone who thinks that discourse ethics is an effective secular argument for human rights: "It is true that a philosophy that thinks postmetaphysically cannot answer the question that [David] Tracy . . . calls attention to: why be moral at all?" Habermas, "Transcendence from Within," 239. What Habermas then goes on to say is really quite remarkable, if not incredible: "At the same time, however, this philosophy can show why this question does not arise meaningfully for communicatively socialized individuals. We acquire our moral intuitions in our parents' home, not in school. And moral insights tell us that we do not have any good reasons for behaving otherwise: for this, no self-surpassing of morality is necessary. It is true that we often behave otherwise, but we do so with a bad conscience. The first half of the sentence attests to the weakness of the motivational power of good reasons; the second half attests that rational motivation by reasons is more than nothing [*auch nicht nichts ist*].

— moral convictions do not allow themselves to be overridden without resistance;" ibid. Put aside the fact that "we" acquire our moral "intuitions" in many places besides (or in addition to) our parents' home— in the streets, for example. The more important point, for present purposes, is that we do not all acquire the same moral intuitions. Some of us acquire moral intuitions that enable us to ignore, and perhaps even to brutalize, the Other without any pangs of "conscience." It is incredible that in the waning days of this unbearably brutal century, Habermas— writing in Germany of all places— could suggest otherwise. We need not even look at the oppressors themselves; we need look only at those whose passivity makes them complicitors— as the quote in the text accompanying the preceding note confirms.

96. See Williams, *Ethics and the Limits of Philosophy*, 103-04.
97. David Gauthier, "Rational Constraint: Some Last Words," in *Contractarianism and Rational Choice: Essays on David Gautier's "Morals by Agreement,"*, ed. Peter Vallentyne (New York: Oxford University Press, 1991), 323, 330.
98. See Vallentyne, "Gauthier's Three Projects," in ibid., 1, 2.
99. Friedrich W. Nietzsche, "All Too Human," in *Basic Writings of Nietzsche,* ed. and trans. Walter Kaufmann (New York: Modern Library, 1973), 148; see n.121 and accompanying text.
100. See Henry Kissinger, "Continuity and Change in American Foreign Policy," *Society* 15 (1977): 97, 99 : One of the basic challenges of foreign policy [is] the perennial tension between morality and pragmatism. Whenever it has been forced to wield its great power, the United States has also been driven to search its conscience. How does our foreign policy serve moral ends? How can the United States carry out its role as human example and champion of justice in a world in a world in which power is still often the final arbiter? How do we reconcile ends and means, principle and survival? How do we keep secure both our existence *and* our values? These have been the moral and intellectual dilemmas of the United States for two hundred years."
101. See Jerome Shestack, "An Unsteady Focus: The Vulnerabilities of the Reagan Administration's Human Rights Policy," *Harvard Human Rights Yearbook* 2 (1989): 25, 49-50 (footnotes omitted). What reasons should motivate an administration to afford human rights a central role in United States foreign policy as a matter of national interest? I believe that there are at least the following compelling motivations:
1. Human rights values advance national security. Nations that accept human rights are likely to be more stable and make better allies. Repression of human rights invites interventions and endangers stability. Conversely, human rights include

responsiveness to the will of the people and restraints on aggressive action.

2. Human rights and world peace are interrelated. Peace and stability cannot be maintained in a world in which people are repressed and impelled to rise up against their oppressors. Afghanistan, Armenia, Burundi, Bangladesh, Haiti, the Philippines and many other places are stark examples.

3. Human rights are premised on the observance of rules of international law. Acceptance of the rule of law is a condition for a system of world order which, in turn, promotes world peace.

4. Human rights have become a central item on the global agenda, appealing to the expectations of people on every continent. The United States is perceived as having an immense potential to further human dignity and freedom. Championing human rights affords the United States the opportunity to be relevant to that agenda and responsive to the aspirations of peoples around the world.

5. Advancing economic and social human rights removes causes of tension and instability among less developed nations and promotes an equitable world order.

6. Human rights endeavors offer the United States the opportunity to act in concert with other nations to generate "coalitions of shared purposes."

7. Human rights address one of the world's most pressing problems: the enormous increase of refugees. The plight of refugees contributes to international tensions, and refugees impose huge burdens on nations to which they flee. Enforcing human rights will alleviate the suffering and number of refugees.

8. Including human rights in foreign policy formulation is favored by Congress. Without accommodation to this concern, the executive branch faces a polarized foreign policy marked by continuing disputes with Congress. A consensus with Congress on human rights issues advances the effectiveness and reliability of United States foreign policy initiatives.

9. Human rights policies command respect and support from this nation's citizenry. Conversely, foreign policies which ignore human rights are likely to be self-defeating by failing to sustain popular support.

10. Finally, advancing human rights reinforces this nation's own cohesion, its moral purpose and its appreciation of its own domestic liberties. Human rights have long been a focus for shared purpose in this nation's tradition, and a sense of shared purpose among its people is in the national interest.

102.   See Richard Bilder, "Rethinking International Human Rights: Some Basic Questions," *Wisconsin Law Review* (1969): 171, 187-

91 (commenting on "the difficulties in constructing a wholly selfish rationale for major national commitments to the human rights of foreigners").

103. Ibid.
104. See Richard Bilder, "Human Rights and U.S. Foreign Policy: Short-Term Prospects," *Virginia Journal of International Law* 14 (1974): 597, 608–09: "Moral compromises . . . may have real costs in terms of the way Americans view their own country and its role in the world. We are coming to see that national pride, self-respect, cohesion, and purpose are meaningful elements of both national power and domestic tranquility. It is true that there are practical limits to what the United States can reasonably attempt to accomplish in promoting the human rights of other peoples. But, in a period following Vietnam and Watergate, it may be worth some foreign policy risks to reassert historic American commitments to human worth and dignity."
105. In his review of *Love and Power*, Ned Foley thought that I was denying that one can be moral without being religious. See Edmund Foley, "Tillich and Camus, Talking Politics," *Columbia Law Review* 92 (1992): 954, 964-77.
106. See ibid.
107. See Kristen Monroe, Michael Barton, and Ute Klingeman, "Altruism and the Theory of Rational Action: Rescuers of Jews in Nazi Europe," *Ethics* 101 (1990): 103; Neera Badhwar, "Altruism v. Self-Interest: Sometimes a False Dichotomy," *Social Philosophy and Policy* 10 (1993): 90.
108. Leszek Kolakowski, *Religion, if There Is no God* (New York: Oxford University Press, 1982), 191; emphasis added.
109. But see Jackson, "The Disconsolation of Theology," 9, ("Promethean self-creation and utterly gratuitous care for others risks collapsing into its (putative) opposite, a self-destructive and domineering hubris."); Fred Dallmayr, "Critical Theory and Reconciliation," in *Habermas, Modernity, and Public Theology*, 119, 139: "If the world is totally corrupt and perverse, then this world must be destroyed and replaced by a completely new one through some kind of *creatio ex nihilo*; moreover, given the removal of absolutes, such creation can only be the work of human agents or producers. In this manner, reconciliation and redemption become the targets of goal-directed activity, that is, or purposive fabrication. . . . At the same time, being themselves part of the corrupt world, human agents can only perpetuate or re-create the state of corruption; thus, instrumentalism becomes inescapable and self-destructive.
110. Matthew 25:40.
111. For a series of meditations on Camus's work by one of the most important Christian (Catholic) writers of the late twentieth

century— a writer who did not pretend that Camus was in any way an "anonymous" Christian— see Thomas Merton, "Seven Essays on Albert Camus (1966-68)," in *The Literary Essays of Thomas Merton*, ed. Patrick Hart (New York: New Directions Publishing Co., 1981), 179-301.

112. Foley suggests that it would not have have arisen as between Paul Tillich and Albert Camus. He also explains that it need not arise as between someone who is "pro-choice" on the issue of abortion and someone who is "pro-life." See Foley, "Tillich and Camus," 973-75.

113. See n. 118 [Waldron on Locke].

114. Foley thinks that Camus' nonreligious response to the question of validity, no less than a religious response, works. See Foley, "Tillich and Camus," 965-66. Pace Tinder (and Nietzsche), this author is skeptical. I am inclined to say of any nonreligious response much the same thing Tim Jackson has said of anti-realism: [T]he loss of realism . . . means the loss of any and all realities independent of or transcendent to inquiry. In this respect, God must suffer the same fate as any other transcendent subject or object. Because faith makes sense only when accompanied by the possibility of doubt, Rorty's distancing of scepticism means a concomitant distancing of belief in "things unseen." He, unlike Kant, denies both knowledge and faith; but for what, if anything, is this supposed to make room? Faith may perhaps be given a purely dispositional reading, being seen as a tendency to act in a certain way, but any propositional content will be completely lost. The pull toward religious faith is at best a residue of metaphysical realism and of the craving for metaphysical comfort. The taste for the transcendent usually associated with a religious personality will find little place in a Rortian world. Similarly, hope and love, if thought to have a supernatural object or source, lose their point. The deconstruction of God must leave the pious individual feeling like F. Scott Fitzgerald after his crackup: "a feeling that I was standing at twilight on a deserted range, with an empty rifle in my hand and the targets down." The deconstructed heart is ever restless, yet the theological virtues stand only as perpetual temptations to rest in inauthenticity. We live in a world without inherent *telos*; so there simply is no rest as Christianity has traditionally conceived it; Timothy Jackson, "The Theory and Practice of Discomfort: Richard Rorty and Pragmatism," *Thomist* 51 (1987): 270, 284-85.

115. See Kolakowski, *Religion* and accompanying text.

116. Habermas, "Transcendence from Within," 239.

117. Jackson, "The Theory and Practice of Discomfort," 289.

118. See Jeremy Waldron, "Religious Contributions in Public

Deliberation," *San Diego Law Review* 30 (1992): 817, 844-45.

Consider, for example, the issue of whether property owners are obliged by natural law to share their wealth with the poor. Locke's position on this is well known:

[W]e know God hath not left one Man so to the Mercy of another, that he may starve him if he please: God the Lord and Father of all, has given no one of his Children such a Property, in his peculiar Portion of the things of this World, but that he has given his needy Brother a Right to the Surplusage of his Goods; so that it cannot justly be denied him, when his pressings Wants call for it.

We could presumably rephrase this as follows: "A needy person has a right to the surplus goods of a rich person if they are necessary to keep him from perishing." But if we do, someone is likely to ask us for an *argument* to support this controversial proposition. In Locke, the argument is based on the seminal fact of God's creating the world for the sustenance of all men:

God made Man, and planted in him, as in all other Animals, a strong desire of Self-preservation, and furnished the World with things fit for Food and Rayment and other Necessaries of Life, Subservient to his design, that Man should live and abide for some time upon the Face of the Earth, and not that so curious and wonderful a piece of Workmanship by its own Negligence, or want of Necessaries, should perish again presently after a few moments continuance. . . .

Once again, we could at a pinch translate *that* into secular language: "It is common sense that people have a right to make use of the goods that may help them to survive." But it loses a little in the translation. It is hard to keep hold of the idea that we were *meant* to survive, and that there is something offensive *to the fact of our existence* in our being denied access to the naturally available resources that we need.

See also Rachel Mariner, "Burdens Hard to Bear: A Theology of Civil Rights," *Harvard Civil Rights-Civil Liberties Law Review* 27 (1992): 657.

119. Simone Weil, *Waiting for God*, trans. Emma Crauford (New York: Capricorn Books, 1973), 139, 143 (quoted at the beginning of Jackson, n. 48).

120. See n. 117 and accompanying text.

121. Nietzsche, *The Will to Power*, 159-60; see n. 99 and accompanying text. David Gauthier's "morality" seems quite Nietzschean; see n. 97-99 and accompanying text.

122. See Bernard Williams, "Auto-da-Fé," *New York Review*, 28 April 1983, 33: "Rorty is so insistent that we cannot, in philosophy, simply be talking about human beings, as opposed to human beings at a given time. . . . Rorty . . . contrasts the approach of

taking some philosophical problem and asking . . . 'What does it show us about *being human*?' and asking, on the other hand, 'What does the persistence of such problems show us about *being twentieth-century Europeans*?" (Emphasis in original.) This author recalls Alasdair MacIntyre saying to Rorty, at a meeting years ago (circa 1984), that all Rorty could say to Soviet Communists is: "You're un-American."

123. See Thomas Nagel, "A Faith of the Enlightenment," *Times Literary Supplement*, 14 December 1990, ("a religious answer stands as much in need of defense and explanation as does a secular one").

124. Kent Greenawalt, *Religious Convictions and Political Choice* (New York: Oxford University Press, 1988), 6; see Perry, *Love and Power*, 67 and 173, n. 1; see Richard Neuhaus, *The Naked Public Square: Religion and Democracy in America* (Grand Rapids, Mich.: W.B. Eerdmanns Publishing Co.,1984), 86: "In the minds of some secularists the naked public square [i.e., neutral/impartial political discourse] is a desirable goal. They subscribe to the dogma of the secular Enlightenment that, as people become more enlightened (educated), religion will wither away; or, if it does not wither away, it can be safely sealed off from public consideration, reduced to a private eccentricity."

125. See Goldsworthy, "God or Mackie;" Leff, "Unspeakable Ethics, Unnatural Law," 1979 *Duke Law Journal* (1979): 1229; see also Philip Johnson, "Nihilism and the End of Law," *First Things* (March 1993): 19.

126. Nietzsche, *The Will to Power*, 157.

127. Leff, "Unspeakable Ethics," 1249.

4

The Regulatory Dilemma Concerning Pornography

DOLF ZILLMANN

Pornography is a multi-billion-dollar business across the Western world.[1] In the United States alone, pornography sales have been in the billions each year since its de facto legalization. In 1984, for example, pornography grossed a conservatively estimated $8 billion,[2] which is said to be more than the revenue of the national music and movie industries combined.

The enormity of the pornography market makes two things very clear. First, there are plenty of takers, especially among men. The interest in pornography is not limited to particular social groups, although stark differences in the frequency of consumption of sexually explicit materials may exist.[3] Pornography's appeal is universal and apparently permeates all social strata. The pornography issue, then, does not—as some appear to believe—pertain only to minorities that are characterized by excessive libido or the like; it concerns the population at large.

Second, those who reap the economic benefits of such massive consumption will understandably resist any effort at curtailing the free distribution of pornography. Their vested interest is likely to inspire actions and counteractions, legal and otherwise, that aim at keeping the market open.

The legal defense of an open market for sexually explicit material of any kind is primarily based on the freedom of expression guarantees of the First Amendment to the United

States Constitution. Although legal interpretations on this point differ sharply,[4] sexual imagery tends to be regarded as freedom of speech; therefore, regardless of the consequences it might produce, it is entitled to protection. The fact that some may take offense at displays of sexual activities is generally deemed insufficient for regulatory intervention. Marjorie Hines of the ACLU[5] stated this position emphatically: "There should be no law punishing or suppressing sexually explicit expression, no matter how tasteless, offensive, or . . . vile." Being offended by pornography, irrespective of the emotional intensity of this reaction, is thus considered trivial and immaterial.

Such global contentions, it should be noted, are actually inconsistent with present legislation concerning community standards. If a communal majority is, or claims to be, offended by explicit sexual material and elects to act to prevent exposure, distribution of the offensive material may be legally curtailed. Given the universal appeal of pornography, however, concerted majority action of this kind is utterly unlikely.

The apparent reluctance to organize against at least the vilest forms of pornography derives in large measure from our commitment to free speech. Freedom of expression is a fundamental American value; and everything that smacks of curtailment of that freedom is deemed censorship, the perpetration of which is something akin to a crime against culture. Academicians, in particular, are acutely apprehensive about the commission of such a crime. Even the mere impression of promoting censorship is avoided. On occasion, this leads to unusual titles of legal publications: "Legislating Against Pornography Without Censorship."[6] It also spawns legislative proposals that attempt to curtail the distribution of pornography on the basis of women's victimization that resulted from the availability of pornography. It is ironic that devoted feminists take pains to avoid tackling directly the apparent roots of presumed consequences that they condemn—as this would amount to advocating censorship—and prefer to accept an approach to curtailment that requires the demonstrable suffering, and its public display, of potentially many women.

Notwithstanding the paradox of seeking curtailment of pornography (which is, of course, an attempt at censorship) without endorsing the censorship concept, feminist theory of the power of pornography[7] has greatly helped to bring into focus numerous forms of potential victimization and the need to demonstrate harm in order to effect legislation.

In particular, the conceptualization of pornography-inspired harm has been extended and now reaches far beyond "being offended" (i.e., emotionally upset during and shortly after exposure). It incorporates the exercise of undue social power and privileges in the sexual realm, the abusive domination of others by sexual means, and the plain forcible violation of others' sexual expectations. Feminists see pornography as the central societal force that perpetuates gender inequality: men's domination over women. They consider it a violation of women's civil rights when men enact nonegalitarian pornographic scripts, and they seek to remedy the situation through the introduction of civil-rights legislation sensitive to such violations. In operational terms, punitive actions against pornographers are attempted[8] by documenting, in a court of law, (a) that civil-rights violations have occurred and (b) that they were caused by consumption of pornographic material. Both portions of this process, especially the latter, should prove difficult to establish beyond reasonable doubt. Regardless of these rather formidable problems, it should be clear that feminist objections to pornography are motivated by equal-rights concerns, and that the sexual nature of existing inequalities is secondary, if not immaterial. In fact, the display of power-balanced, egalitarian sexual behavior has been sanctioned as enlightening erotica, in contrast to deplorable pornography.[9]

A more open approach to harm that can be traced to pornography consumption is pursued in social-science explorations. Harm to the consumer can be anything from the compulsive, unmanageable consumption of erotica to the erroneous, self-serving perception of others' willingness to partake in specific sexual ventures and the adoption of callous attitudes about coercive sexual practices. Social harm pertains to the victimization of others by those whose attitudes and behaviors may be influenced by pornography consumption. It concerns, primarily, coercive sexual behaviors.

Unlike in a court of law, where the determination of inflicted harm usually concerns a single individual and is handled by a judge who acts on personal experience and the advice of a few experts who give their impressions of both the magnitude and the causation of distress, the social-science approach requires the collection of information from potentially large numbers of respondents in agreement with procedures that are open to inspection by anyone. Most importantly, in order to evaluate causal relations, it requires that equally constituted groups of respondents are subjected or not subjected to treatments presumed to bring about particular consequences. For presumed effects of pornography, this experimental paradigm calls for pornography exposure in one group and none in the so-called control group. Differences in perceptions, attitudes, or overt behaviors between the groups may then be attributed, with a high degree of confidence, to the treatment — consumption of pornography in this case.

It is increasingly recognized that social-scientifically generated knowledge about consequences of particular actions constitutes a more veridical and reliable basis for public policy than alternative approaches. Granted that research demonstrations may be less than perfect on occasion, the fact that a consensually validated canon of principles is followed, that all procedures are open to scrutiny, that replications can be undertaken, that findings can be compared and inconsistencies addressed, and that implications can be freely debated, makes research superior to considered opinions about harm and its causes.

Research demonstrations of effects of pornography consumption, especially of asocial effects, thus define an essential source of information in the formation of public policy. Such policy, it should be noticed, need not focus on curtailment and censorship. It might concentrate on educational efforts that aim at correcting inappropriate sex-related perceptions and dispositions.[10] However, those who contemplate to serve public health by curtailing the distribution of some forms of pornography through legislation also have to rely on social-science demonstrations of harm as their most compelling evidence.[11] Social-science research on pornography effects, then, is vital in establishing the foundation on which policy in the service of public health is built.

Given a controversial, volatile issue such as pornography and its potential regulation, the building process is by no means an easy one. This is best illustrated by the governmental commissions that have been formed to determine the impact of pornography on society and, if necessary, to recommend remedial regulation. A first Commission on Obscenity and Pornography was constituted in 1970. Based on eclectic research findings as well as hastily commissioned investigations, the commission eventually concluded that there was insufficient evidence to consider pornography implicated in the causation of asocial effects, and it refrained from recommending more stringent regulation of pornography.[12] The press, which with few exceptions has dealt with pornography legislation as if any sanction of curtailment would place the freedom of the press itself at risk, liberally (and erroneously) interpreted "insufficient evidence" as proof of no or negligible effects.

Concerns about pornography's societal impact did not vanish, however; and in light of much new research[13] a second commission, the Attorney General's Commission on Pornography, was created in 1985. It was to be assisted by a committee of the Surgeon General. This committee, known as the Surgeon General's Workshop on Pornography and Public Health, met in 1986. Oddly, its advisory report[14] was issued about one month after the concluding report of the Attorney General[15] and, hence, was without appreciable consequence for the legislative process.

There were problems with all these committees. The selection of commissioners proved controversial, culminating in allegations that "potentially difficult" leading scholars had been ostracized.[16] Regarding social-science research, the fact that most commissioners were ill-prepared to evaluate the merits of particular demonstrations led to conclusions that had little, if anything, to do with the available research.[17] Foremost in this outcome is the generalization that violent pornography has asocial consequences, but that nonviolent pornography does not. We shall see that such generalization is not warranted on the basis of pertinent findings. The generalization is best explained as a politically safe concession to appease those who wanted to see an indictment of pornography. The concession is actually rather meaningless, because violent pornography to date constitutes only a trivial portion of available pornography.[18]

In addition, there has been a considerable amount of quibbling among social scientists themselves. Some started on the premise that, regarding the societal impact of pornography, "nothing ain't broke" and questioned the need for examination of the issue by cautioning, "don't fix it."[19] Others exploited immaterial, explainable inconsistencies in findings to sweepingly propose that none of the findings are to be trusted.[20] As a result, the social sciences failed again to provide a secure, agreed-upon knowledge base that could meaningfully guide public-policy decisions.[21]

Difficulties of this kind are not specific to the pornography issue. They are to be found in the policy process concerning essentially all controversial issues (e.g., media violence, public smoking, nuclear energy). But they seem to have been particularly severe regarding pornography regulation.[22] The heated and not entirely reasonable debate may have had a positive consequence, however. Numerous fallacies in the hitherto employed procedures to base public policy on social-science research have been identified, and superior procedures have been proposed.[23] It may be hoped that in future deliberations the generation and utilization of science information will be less plagued by the scientists' own political and moral convictions than it has been in the past.

Attention now needs to turn to research demonstrations that are pertinent to the debate of possible regulation of forms of pornography. The research is excerpted, for the most part, from the author's paper on societal effects of pornography that was commissioned by Surgeon General C. Everett Koop.

DEMONSTRATED CONSEQUENCES OF PROLONGED
PORNOGRAPHY CONSUMPTION

Most experimental investigations of the behavioral consequences of exposure to graphic portrayals of sexual activities have employed a research paradigm in which (a) respondents consume pornographic stimuli just once, and (b) any effects are ascertained more or less immediately thereafter.[24] This paradigm has much to recommend itself and is particularly suited to the testing of specific proposals concerning the psychological and physiological mediation of known consequences. However, as a means of establishing perceptual, attitudinal, and behavioral *changes*, especially lasting ones, the paradigm can rightly be questioned. First, many effects of interest may manifest themselves only after repeated exposure to critical stimuli. Second, and equally important, effects may be transient[25] and without consequence for later behavior. In establishing perceptual, attitudinal, and behavioral consequences of the consumption of pornography, then, it would seem imperative to employ experimental designs that accomplish (a) repeated exposure with between-exposure intervals that simulate characteristic consumption patterns and (b) delayed assessments of effects with an interval between consumption and effects that rules out that the effects are of trivial duration. Effect demonstrations that use the indicated prolonged-exposure, delayed-measurement design quite obviously have greater ecological validity than those generated by the one-session experiment, and we shall consequently focus on investigations employing the superior type of design.

The prolonged-exposure paradigm has been pioneered in two investigations that were initially presented in the Technical Report of the Commission on Obscenity and Pornography. Mann, Sidman, and Starr (1971) explored the effect of repeated exposure to pornography on sexual behavior, and Howard, Reifler, and Liptzin (1971) probed consequences for excitation and cognition in the later consumption of pornographic materials.

The Mann team exposed married couples in four consecutive weekly sessions to sexually explicit films or, in a control condition, to nonerotic films. During the treatment period, respondents recorded their sexual activities in diaries. Exposure to erotica was found to stimulate sexual behavior only shortly. Sexual activities were more frequent on exposure days than on the days thereafter. The transitory, sex-stimulating effect diminished over the weeks and became negligible in the fourth week. Their findings emphasized that this stimulating effect was rather nonspecific, manifesting itself in a variety of sexual activities with which the couples were familiar. The investigators concluded that the couples did not adopt depicted sexual practices that were not already part of their behavioral repertoire. Exposure to pornography merely seemed to revive well-established but dormant sexual practices.

The conclusion that pornography does not entice consumers to try out novel sexual practices is compromised by the fact that the investigation was conducted with couples who were married for at least ten years. Couples with such sexual histories presumably could detect little, if anything, in the erotic materials that was not already part of their sexual repertoire. The conclusion also clashes with more recent findings which show that sexually inexperienced persons readily accept and are willing to practice particular sexual behaviors that they have witnessed on the screen.[26] Most importantly, however, the findings reported by the Mann team seem of little consequence for considerations of public health because effects of pornography on sexual behaviors are, in general, not feared to produce socially undesirable effects. The instigation of sexual interest and desire, as well as the likely expansion of repertoires of sexual techniques through modeling, are usually treated as inconsequential, if not positive, effects of pornography. The notable exception is the use of pornography in the enticement of prepubertal girls and boys to take part in sexual activities with adults.[27] However, these uses have not been subjected to systematic effects research.

In the Howard group's investigation of the effects of pornography consumption on later reactions to pornography, male college students were given access to pornographic films, photographs, and readings, or they were not given such access in a control condition. This was done in fifteen sessions that were distributed over a three-week period. The experimental respondents were free to choose from among these materials and from among nonerotic ones in the first ten sessions. In the following three sessions, the original pornographic materials were replaced by new ones. In the last two sessions, the nonerotic materials were removed. Each session lasted ninety minutes, and during this time respondents recorded their activities at regular intervals. Both experimental and control respondents were shown an explicitly sexual film prior to and following the extended exposure treatment. Eight weeks after the treatment, the experimental respondents were once more shown an explicitly sexual film. Numerous measures of sexual arousal were taken during and after exposure to the films, and a battery of self-perception and attitudinal measures was recorded following exposure.

The findings show, first of all, that the young men initially had a strong interest in pornographic films. However, this interest faded rapidly with repeated consumption. Pornographic photographs and readings received comparatively little attention, but this attention was sustained. The eventual introduction of novel pornographic materials failed to return interest to the initial high levels. Following the unrestricted consumption of pornography in the experimental condition, respondents characterized their reactions to pornography as boredom. Although interest in pornography was maintained to some degree, the findings give no indication that frequent consumption of the materials in question fosters or facilitates favorable reactions such as enjoyment.

The analysis of the physiological data yielded results that are consistent with increased boredom. It revealed a loss of responsiveness as the result of frequent consumption. Exposure to an explicitly sexual film immediately after the conclusion of the longitudinal treatment produced diminished reactions of sexual excitedness. On the most direct measure of sexual arousal, penile tumescence, reduced responsiveness was obtrusively evident. Erections were less pronounced and more poorly maintained than prior to frequent exposure to pornography. Complementary measures, such as release of acid phosphatase, showed redundant changes. Sympathetic activity, a vital concomitant of sexual excitedness, also underwent parallel changes. Heart rate, respiration rate, and skin temperature indicated reduced responsiveness. Finally, the remeasurement of physiological reactions to pornography after a period of eight weeks, during which respondents were not treated in any particular way, revealed some degree of recovery from the loss of responsiveness. But more importantly, this responsiveness, primarily concerning erection, remained markedly suppressed.

The investigation reported by the Howard team is not without problems. In the ten initial exposure sessions, respondents' choice of pornography was severely limited. What appeared to be a loss of interest in pornographic films is more likely the result of tiring familiarity with all available films. Because the respondents themselves had to record their consumption choices, it is additionally likely that they experienced evaluation apprehension and avoided giving the impression of excessive erotic interest and eagerness by not watching the films repeatedly. At any rate, the conclusion about rapidly growing disinterest in and boredom with pornography that was drawn from the findings, together with the authors' assertion that interest in pornography is self-corrective, proved to be premature. More recent research, yet to be detailed, leads to very different generalizations about erotic interest. Additionally, the projection of growing boredom with pornography is obviously incompatible with the continued commercial success of pornography as a genre of entertainment. What the study does show, with some degree of rigor, is that consumers of pornography grow tired of watching the same materials repeatedly.

The observation of diminished excitatory responding, in terms of both specific sexual arousal and accompanying sympathetic activity, is not compromised by these procedural difficulties, however. In the later sessions, the respondents were enticed to consume pornography; and the intended, strong difference in pornography consumption between the experimental and control groups was accomplished. The demonstration of substantial, enduring habituation effects of prolonged pornography consumption, then, is not in doubt. The consequences for public health are not immediately apparent, however. Habituation of excitatory reactivity might be specific to erotic entertainment and merely reduce enjoyment of the material. Pornographic materials might also start to fail as convenient arousers for sexual activities. On the other hand, the lessened excitatory reaction to erotic entertainment might generalize, to some degree, to erotic stimuli employed as arousers in actual, intimate, sexual settings. But these possible consequences have not been explored systematically.

A point to be made in this connection is that the enduring physiological changes that result from prolonged exposure to pornography are, in all probability, not modifiable by intervention techniques of "mere talk" (that is, by cautioning respondents to be on guard, by making them aware of the behavioral changes that occurred, and by debriefing them in the sense of telling them how they should undo and correct influences). Abstinence from pornography offers itself as a viable behavior-modification strategy for the regaining of the lost responsiveness—if such regaining of sensitivity to pornographic materials is deemed desirable. However, strategies of this kind also have gone unexplored.

The excitatory, attitudinal, and perceptual consequences of prolonged consumption of pornography were further explored in an investigation by Zillmann and Bryant.[28] In contrast to the experiment conducted by the Howard team, both male and female respondents were employed and exposure to pornography was strictly controlled. Respondents came to six exposure sessions in consecutive weeks. In each session, they saw (a) six pornographic films, (b) three pornographic and three innocuous films, or (c) six innocuous films. The pornographic films focused on the exhibition of heterosexual activities in all conceivable manifestations. Only consenting adults participated in these activities. None of the activities involved sadomasochistic acts or anything, such as bondage, that could be construed as nonvoluntary or coercive behavior on someone's part.

One week after the last exposure session, respondents' excitatory and evaluative reactions to three additional films were ascertained. The films featured (a) sexual activities in a suggestive fashion (as characteristic of R-rated material), (b) common sexual activities in graphic detail (X-rated), and (c) uncommon sexual activities in graphic detail (X-rated sadomasochistic ventures and bestiality). Similar assessments were made two weeks after the exposure treatment. Finally, in the third week after the treatment, the respondents participated in a purportedly independent study said to be conducted for the American Bar Association. The respondents dealt with a case in which a female hitchhiker was raped. They recommended the prison term, in years and months, that they thought was fair and most appropriate under the circumstances. Eventually, respondents estimated the popularity of sexual practices among all sexually active American adults and reported their concerns about the impact of pornography.

The findings regarding excitatory and evaluative changes are summarized in Figures 1, 2, and 3.

Figure 1: Habituation of the Excitatory Response to Pornography as the Result of Prolonged Consumption

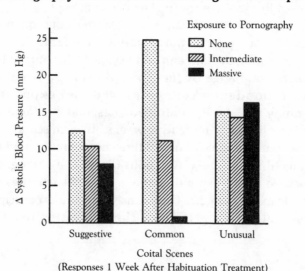

Coital Scenes
(Responses 1 Week After Habituation Treatment)

**Figure 2: Diminution of Repulsion from Pornography
as the Result of Prolonged Consumption**

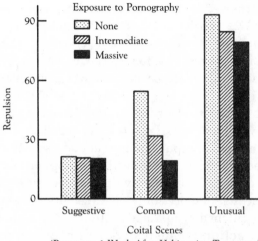

Coital Scenes
(Responses 1 Week After Habituation Treatment)

**Figure 3: Changing Enjoyment of Pornography
as the Result of Prolonged Consumption**

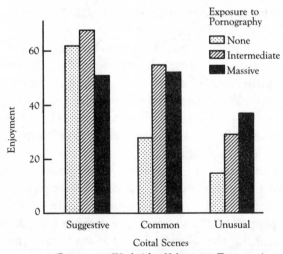

Coital Scenes
(Responses 1 Week After Habituation Treatment)

Figure 1 shows the habituation of excitatory responding in terms of systolic blood pressure. Other measures of sympathetic activity proved redundant. Predictably, the strongest habituation occurred for stimuli that had been consumed most frequently. Also predictably, habituation generalized to less explicit portrayals of common sexual activities. The lack of generalization in the response to material featuring uncommon, and presumably unfamiliar, sexual practices was not expected, however.

Figure 2 shows that prolonged exposure to common pornography reduces initial reactions of repulsion. Figure 3 shows that this loss of repulsion does not necessarily translate into increased enjoyment. Prolonged consumption of common fare fostered more favorable evaluations of portrayals of uncommon sexual practices only. Because intense enjoyment hinges on heightened sympathetic activity,[29] the diminished excitatory reaction to suggestive and common material presumably resulted in flat pleasurable reactions, if not in disappointment.

The same response patterns were observed in the second week after the initial exposure treatment. As the findings reported by the Howard team had suggested, the duration of excitatory habituation is indeed substantial. Related evaluative consequences appear to be similarly enduring.

The rape case, presented three weeks after the habituation treatment, produced remarkably strong and partly unexpected effects. As can be seen from Figure 4, prolonged consumption of common, nonviolent pornography trivialized rape as a criminal offense. After prolonged exposure to messages that depict women as sexually insatiable, as socially nondiscriminating in the sense that they seem eager to accommodate the sexual desires of any man in the vicinity, and as hypereuphoric about any kind of sexual stimulation, men apparently find exaggeration in the trauma of rape and consider lesser prison terms appropriate. This outcome was expected. Unexpected was the finding that women become similarly lenient with rapists, although they treat them altogether more punitively than do men. The public-health implications of these findings, then, do not only concern the evaluation of rape as a most fundamental violation of human rights, but also the self-concept of women as victims.

Figure 4: Incarceration Recommendations for Rape as a Function of Prolonged Consumption of Pornography

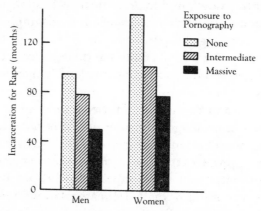

(Responses 3 Weeks After Habituation Treatment)

Regarding the perception of sexuality in general, respondents with prolonged exposure to pornography, as Figure 5 shows, overestimated the popularity of all less common sexual practices.

Figure 5: Perceived Popularity of Various Sexual Behaviors as a Function of Prolonged Consumption of Pornography

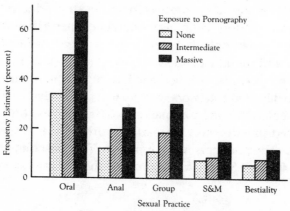

(Responses 3 Weeks After Habituation Treatment)

This shift in the perceived normalcy of sexual behaviors can be expected to promote tolerance toward behaviors deemed "deviant" by others. However, specific evaluations that could validate such a proposal were not collected. The investigation entailed, instead, measures of callousness toward women generally, as well as measures of respondents' concern about the impact of pornography on society. Prolonged consumption of pornography was found to promote men's callousness toward women and to diminish concerns about pornography's impact in both genders (e.g., respondents came to believe that minors would not suffer undue emotional distress from exposure to pornography and that restrictions are largely inappropriate and unnecessary).

Zillmann and Bryant[30] conducted a series of investigations into effects of prolonged consumption of pornography that go beyond sexual callousness in connection with rape and its victims. Specifically, these investigators explored the implications of such consumption for (a) perceptions and attitudes concerning sexually intimate relationships, especially marriage and the family as essential societal institutions, (b) personal happiness and sexual satisfaction, and (c) possible shifts in erotic appetite.

The experimental paradigm was essentially that employed in the earlier work of Zillmann and Bryant.[31] Both male and female respondents consumed either nonviolent pornography or innocuous materials in hourly sessions in six consecutive weeks. In an effort to expand the generalizability of findings, nonstudent respondents were involved in addition to student respondents. Nonstudents were recruited in strict adherence to procedures of random sampling. Another change concerns the pornographic materials that were used. Instead of films, the latest color and sound videocassettes were acquired from rental stores. The materials were screened, as before, to assure that none of the depicted behaviors were violent or coercive.

One week after the exposure treatment, respondents participated in ostensibly unrelated work on the American family and aspects of personal happiness. They responded to a Value-of-Marriage Survey and completed the Indiana Inventory of Personal Happiness. Shifts in pornographic preferences were ascertained in the second week after the exposure treatment.

The impact of prolonged consumption of pornography on the evaluation and desirability of marriage, family, and children was explored for its apparent implications for public health.[32] The nuclear family is generally considered vital for societal welfare.[33] It is said to be the optimal child-rearing structure. Although the family concept has undergone considerable change in recent years,[34] in its basic form it seems universally endorsed. Educational efforts are usually directed at the promotion of the value of this social institution. Yet the values expressed in pornography clash so obviously with the family concept, and they potentially undermine the traditional values that favor marriage, family, and children.

Even a cursory look at pornography makes this very clear. Pornographic scripts dwell on sexual engagements of parties who have just met, who are in no way attached or committed to one another, and who will part shortly, never to meet again. Not by accident, the parties involved accept no curtailing rules for their social and sexual conduct, enjoy sexual stimulation for what it is, and do so at no social or emotional expense. Sexual gratification in pornography is not a function of emotional attachment, of kindness, of caring, and especially not of continuance of the relationship, as such continuance would translate into responsibilities, curtailments, and costs. Irrespective of the merits or demerits of the projection that much gratification is accessible from sexual activities involving unattached others, the projection is diametrically opposed to the values that promote enduring social aggregations, especially those that are to serve reproduction. Enduring intimate relationships curtail personal freedoms to some degree. Relationships that provide economic and emotional security are based on responsibility, if not on sacrifice. And where, in such a relationship, sexuality is vital and valued, partners tend to lay claim to exclusive sexual access. Finally, the decision to have a child or children, whether by a married couple or by persons otherwise aggregated, is probably the greatest responsibility that human beings accept. It amounts to restricted freedom, servitude, and to enormous expenditures for a good portion of adult life. If sexuality is considered part and parcel of such enduring relationships, there can be no question that it comes at a forbidding price. In terms of sheer recreational sexual joy, these relationships compare poorly with the short-lived ones that are continually exhibited in pornography—those that invariably show that great pleasures can be had at next to no cost. Prolonged consumption of entertainment with clear messages of this kind thus must be expected to impact profoundly the perception and evaluation of sexuality and its social institutions and arrangements.

Strong perceptual and attitudinal changes were indeed observed. The perception of the very nature of sexuality changed. Promiscuity in both men and women was deemed more natural after prolonged consumption of pornography than without such consumption. Beliefs in the faithfulness of sexual partners predictably declined with the greater acceptance of promiscuity. Additionally, prolonged consumption of pornography fostered greater acceptance of pre- and extramarital sexual relations for self and intimate partners. Along with that, it fostered acceptance of sexually nonexclusive relations with partners. Prolonged consumption also led to greater acceptance of the myth of health risks from sexual repression. Pornography apparently conveys the idea that unrestrained sexuality is wholesome and healthy, and that any restraint poses risks. All these effects are uniform for men and women, students and nonstudents. Moreover, prolonged consumption of pornography was found to counteract gender equality. For intimate relationships, male dominance was favored over egalitarianism. This effect was also uniform for the various groups. Overall, however, females embraced egalitarianism more than did males, and students embraced it more than did nonstudents.

Pornography consumption had a most powerful effect on evaluations of the desirability and viability of marriage. Endorsement of marriage as an essential institution dropped from 60.0 percent in the control groups to 38.8 percent in the treatment groups. The effect was again parallel for males and females, students and nonstudents.

A most astonishing effect of prolonged pornography consumption on family values concerns the desire to have children. As can be seen from Figure 6, exposure to pornography reduced the desire to have children.

**Figure 6: Desire for Progeny as a Function
of Prolonged Consumption of Pornography**

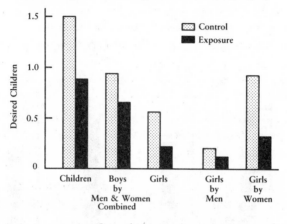

(One week after exposure treatment)

Male and female respondents, students and nonstudents alike, wanted fewer children. The desire to have male offspring dropped 31 percent. The desire for female offspring, being lower overall, dropped by about twice that margin: 61 percent. This reduction proved specific to gender. Male respondents expressed little desire for female offspring altogether. It is the desire of females for offspring of their own kind that, after consumption of pornography, shrank to one-third of its normal strength (see right-hand side of the graph in Figure 6).

These findings suggest that prolonged consumption of pornography, presumably because it continually projects the attainment of sexual joy without acceptance of social confinements and obligations, indeed makes having a family and raising children appear an unnecessary inconvenience. But such reasoning explains only the overall reduction in reproductive desire. It leaves unexplained the discrimination against female offspring by women. Exactly what, within pornography, inspires this own-gender discrimination remains unclear.

The Indiana Inventory of Personal Happiness generated clear-cut findings.[35] None of the items unrelated to sexuality showed differences in happiness or satisfaction. In stark contrast, all items pertaining to sexuality were affected. In Figure 7, prolonged consumption of pornography reduced sexual satisfaction and sex-related personal happiness markedly.

Figure 7: Sexual Satisfaction as a Function of Prolonged Consumption of Pornography

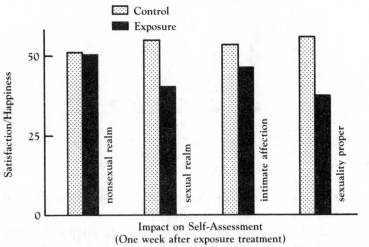

This effect was uniform for gender and students/nonstudents. The separation of elements of sexual satisfaction and happiness into an affective component (i.e., loving, caring), on the one hand, and into sexual activities as such, on the other, made it clear that satisfaction with sexual specifics (i.e., the looks of intimate partners, their sexual performance, and their willingness to engage in novel sexual activities) had suffered the most.

The findings point to a paradox. Presumably, pornography is initially consumed in hopes of increasing sexual satisfaction. But consumers eventually compare appearance and performance of pornographic models with that of their intimate partners, and this comparison rarely favors their intimate partners. The result is the realization that, in sexual matters, others may attain greater satisfaction. Dissatisfaction with intimate partners seems the inevitable result.

The final study in this series concerned shifting preferences for pornography.[36] Two weeks after the exposure treatment, respondents returned once more to the laboratory. An unavoidable delay was announced, and they were ushered into the office of a research assistant that was equipped with a monitor, a cassette player, and numerous cassettes. They were encouraged to watch cassettes from his collection while waiting in solitude. The cassettes contained movies that were G- and R-rated. However, some cassettes were X-rated and featured common nonviolent pornography, bondage, sadomasochism, or bestiality. The respondents' consumption of the various cassettes was unobtrusively monitored.

As Figure 8 shows, respondents with prolonged exposure to common pornography expressed virtually no interest in this common form of pornography.

Figure 8: Shifting Erotic Preferences as a Function of Prolonged Consumption of Pornography

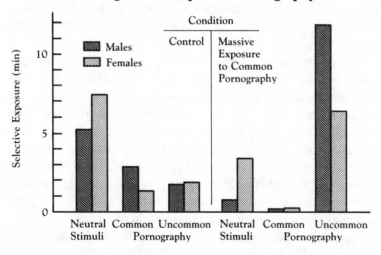

(Consumption 2 weeks after exposure treatment)

The males moved almost exclusively into pornography depicting less common sexual practices. Females showed the same preference, but to a markedly lesser degree.

The findings show that the consumers of pornography depicting the more common forms of sexuality did not limit themselves to these forms when given the opportunity to consume material featuring less common sexual practices, including sadomasochistic and violent sexual behaviors. This shift in preference can be expected on the basis of satisfied curiosity about common sexuality, as well as on the basis of excitatory habituation to frequently consumed fare. The research thus projects that, as a rule, consumers will advance to extreme material before, perhaps, reaching dead end and returning to whatever erotica in their recollection fostered the most gratifying sensations. Regarding young consumers, it can only be speculated at this point that they are likely to be more strongly motivated by curiosity than by excitatory habituation. This does not detract from the fact, however, that they are also inclined to go beyond the common and seek exposure to the less common sexual expressions, including aberrations—violent ones, in particular. For older consumers, a preference shift toward violent erotica, specifically, is to be expected, because witnessed violence is sympathetically arousing and, hence, well suited to supplement fading excitement (owing to habituation) with pure erotica.[37]

Bryant conducted an investigation to show that prolonged consumption of common pornography influences moral judgment concerning sexual behaviors specifically. Male and female respondents consumed pornography or innocuous material in one-hour sessions in five consecutive days. Two days later they participated in an ostensibly unrelated study in which they evaluated the moral indefensibility of numerous nonsexual and sexual improprieties and transgressions. Respondents indicated the degree to which they thought a particular social behavior was morally right or wrong.

Exposure to pornography proved to be without consequence for the moral judgment of nonsexual behaviors (e.g., drunken driving, shoplifting). In contrast, it greatly influenced the judgment of improprieties in the sexual realm (e.g., self-advancement through sexual favors, cover-up of homosexual relations to a heterosexual lover). Specifically, prolonged exposure to pornography consistently relaxed the moral verdict on behaviors that were deemed dishonest or immoral by those without the exposure in question. Presumably because the perception of greater prevalence of particular sexual behaviors grants them greater moral legitimacy, the morality manifest in pornography eventually enters into the moral judgment of sexual conduct generally.

An investigation by Buchman extended many of the reported effects of prolonged exposure to nonviolent pornography to the sexual abuse of children.[38] In this investigation, male and female students were repeatedly exposed to explicit sexual films or nonsexual films, among others. None of the films featured violence. Respondents attended hourly sessions on four consecutive days, watching recently released video movies. On the fifth day, a visiting investigator came to conduct an ostensibly unrelated study in criminal justice. He presented a series of brief case descriptions of a wide variety of crimes and noncriminal transgressions. The descriptions contained both sexual and nonsexual transgressions. Respondents judged the severity of the particular transgressions, the degree of suffering endured by the victims, and the punishment deemed appropriate for the transgressors. Punitive recommendations were assessed in terms of rated magnitude, monetary fine, and time of incarceration.

The sexual transgressions of interest victimized female children (pedophilia, incest) or female adults (date rape, stranger rape). These transgressions varied in the amount of physical force employed. Nonsexual transgressions varied analogously. Effects of exposure, being uniform for both respondent genders, were observed on all these measures.

The effects were specific to sexual transgressions. Exposure was without consequence for nonsexual ones. Specifically, prolonged exposure to pornography was found to trivialize sexual transgressions associated with comparatively low levels of coercive violence, but not those linked with brutalities. Evaluations of victim suffering produced the same pattern of effects. The corresponding effects on punitive recommendations are displayed in Table 1.

Table 1

Punitive Recommendations for Sexual and Nonsexual Offenses as a Function of Prolonged Prior Consumption of Nonviolent Pornography

Transgression	Victim	Prolonged consumption of	
		Innocuous material	Nonviolent pornography
Sexual	Child	.32[a]	-.35[b]
Sexual	Adult	.26[a]	-.52[b]
Nonsexual	Child	-.05[a]	-.08[a]
Nonsexual	Adult	.11[a]	-.08[a]

Note. Measures are combined standardized scores of recommended punishment (magnitude), monetary fine (dollars), and incarceration sentence (years, months). Comparisons between means are across consumption conditions only (horizontal). Means associated with different letter superscript differ significantly. Adapted from Buchman (1989).

As can be seen, prolonged exposure to explicit, nonviolent pornography fostered recommendations consistent with the perception of diminished suffering by victims and the judgment of diminished transgressive severity of sexual coercion. After extended consumption of pornography, sexual coercion is apparently deemed a lesser crime that calls for lesser punishment. The findings show very clearly that this effect applies to the sexual abuse of children as well as to that of adults. Buchman's findings thus replicate the trivialization of rape by prolonged exposure to nonviolent pornography that has been reported earlier.[39] Most importantly, however, they extend this trivialization effect to the usually rather nonviolent sexual abuse of children.

A most informative investigation[40] was conducted in connection with the Fraser Committee on Pornography and

Prostitution in Canada. Unlike other studies that employed horror films featuring episodes of R-rated sex and that purport to explore the effects of pornography proper,[41] this investigation determined consequences of prolonged exposure to graphic sexual and violent-sexual behaviors. It is, in fact, the only investigation to date that allows a direct comparison of the effects of violent and nonviolent pornography on dispositions toward rape.

Actually, three classes of explicit portrayals of sexual behavior were distinguished: nonviolent erotica (defined as material devoid of "objectionable elements"), nonviolent pornography (defined as material "demeaning" to women, in particular), and violent pornography. The nonviolent erotica featured ideal sexual activities. The material was taken from sex-education and sex-therapy programs. Nonviolent pornography featured what pornography commonly shows, namely, any conceivable form of sexual intercourse and related activities consented to by all parties involved. Violent pornography featured events such as torturous gang rape and rape with an oversize plastic penis while the victim screamed in pain—unmistakably so.

Male students and nonstudents attended three exposure sessions that were scheduled within one week or two weeks. These respondents consumed a thirty-minute tape of one of the three kinds of pornography each session. On average four to five days later, they participated in a test session in which the impact was ascertained. A control group participated in this test session only. The effects of interest were sexually aggressive attitudes, the inclination to coerce and force women into unwanted sexual acts, and the proclivity for rape. Prolonged exposure to nonviolent pornography influenced both the reported likelihood of coercing women into unwanted sexual acts and, more importantly, the reported likelihood of committing rape. As can be seen from Table 2, the likelihood of forced sexual acts increased significantly after prolonged consumption of such commonly available pornography.

Table 2

Proclivity for Coercive Sexual Behavior as a Function of Prolonged Prior Consumption of Nonviolent and Violent Forms of Pornography

Coercive sexual behavior	Prolonged consumption of			
	No pornography	Nonviolent erotica	Nonviolent pornography	Violent pornography
Rape	3.5[a]	7.8[ab]	11.0[b]	10.8[b]
Forced acts	11.8[a]	14.0[ab]	19.0[b]	16.0[ab]

Note. Pornography classes are explained in the text. Measures are self-reported likelihoods, in percent, of committing rape or coercion to attain cooperation with particular sexual actions. Comparisons between means are across consumption conditions only (horizontal). Means not sharing a letter superscript differ significantly. Adapted from Check and Guloien (1989).

Increases after consumption of nonviolent erotica as well as after consumption of violent pornography are apparent, but were not reliable. The effect pattern for rape proclivity proved to be similar, yet different. Both nonviolent and violent pornography increased the reported likelihood of committing rape significantly and to the same degree. The apparent increase from consumption of nonviolent erotica again failed to be reliable.

The investigation has obvious implications for public health. It shows that, on the whole, commonly available nonviolent pornography has the strongest influence on men's self-proclaimed willingness to force intimate partners into forms of sexuality that are not to their partners' liking and on the self-acknowledged propensity for forcing sexual access altogether. Violent pornography, according to this pivotal research, has the same impact as nonviolent pornography on rape proclivity, but its influence on the proclivity for coercion of specific sexual acts is limited— weaker, at any rate. Erotica featuring sensitive, egalitarian, ideal sexual behaviors are the only form of pornography without clear-cut effects on the readiness for sexual coercion and on rape proclivity. But even here caution is indicated, because the effect is consistently intermediate and clearly in the same direction as that from the other forms of pornography.

LEGISLATIVE PROSPECTS

Our exposition of pertinent research is merely a sampling of existing research. More complete summaries are offered elsewhere.[42] Meta-analyses of the published experimental research reveal that the large majority of these investigations has indeed demonstrated asocial effects of pornography consumption.[43] Correlational studies give further evidence to the effects, showing a clear relationship between pornography consumption and the trivialization of rape, among other things.[44]

Enough proof? Not in the eyes of numerous academicians and lawyers of the pornography industry, who offered a variety of arguments, some exceedingly contrived, to call the research into question.[45] Ignoring much piddling to undermine the merits of particular investigations, essentially two strategies are used to discredit the validity of the research demonstrations. First, the fact that not all studies produced positive results is used to allege irreconcilable inconsistencies. Those with research expertise should know that "finding nothing" in experimentation can result from a host of ineptitudes. Poorly conducted research is likely to come up with nothing. Nonetheless, those who want to see the research discredited, by using a cooperative press and speaking to lay persons, have managed to cast considerable doubt on research demonstrations by pointing to rather trivial, sometimes readily explainable inconsistencies in the findings.

Second, it has been argued, validly so, that the research demonstrations show changes in perceptions and attitudes concerning rape, not changes in the commission of rape itself; and, furthermore, that dispositions do not by necessity convert to actions. Implicit in this argument is that only a direct demonstration of a causal relationship between pornography consumption and actual rape is acceptable proof. Such proof can, of course, not be furnished. No experimenter can consider setting up conditions that would place women at risk of being raped—not to mention, that would allow rape to occur. Observational data will have to suffice in complementing dispositional changes (regarding rape and related coercive behaviors) that are known to be caused by prolonged exposure to pornography. Policy decisions will have to be made on the basis of these dispositional changes along with supporting correlational observations, clinical observations included.[46] This is to say that such decisions will have to be made in the face of some remaining uncertainty. But the fact that compelling, definitive proof of a causal relation between pornography consumption and sexually coercive overt behaviors cannot be provided is sure to be used, and effectively so, to thwart any legislative effort at restricting pornography.

It should not be forgotten, however, that science information concerning a significant social issue is only one factor in the formation of public policy. The ultimate decisional power rests with the people. If the people were in uproar about pornography, curtailing legislation would come about swiftly. But a grass-roots movement of this kind does not exist, and it is increasingly unlikely in the future. If our findings on habituation and changing erotic appetites are any indication, the erotica-saturated youths of today will hardly see anything objectionable in the sexual displays of tomorrow. Adolescents naturally will continue to press their right of access to erotic fare. A majority favoring erotic entertainment thus seems assured. Could educational efforts about the asocial effects of pornography make a difference under these circumstances? Eventually perhaps, after many more people than presently are offended by the pornographic brutalization of human sexuality— offended to a point where their civic responsibilities are revived and they feel compelled to take action.

NOTES

1. David Hebditch and Nick Anning, *Porn Gold: Inside the Porn Business* (London: Faber and Faber, 1988).

2. Catherine Itzin, "Entertainment For Men: What It Is and What It Means," in *Pornography: Women, Violence, and Civil Liberties,* ed. Catherine Itzin (Oxford: Oxford University Press, 1992), 27-53.

3. Jennings Bryant and Dan Brown, "Uses of Pornography," in *Pornography: Research Advances and Policy Considerations,* eds. Dolf Zillmann and Jennings Bryant (Hillsdale, N.J.: Erlbaum, 1989), 25-55.

4. William A. Linsley, "The Case Against Censorship of Pornography," in *Pornography: Research Advances and Policy Considerations,* 343-59; Alan E. Sears, "The Legal Case For Restricting Pornography," in ibid., 323-42.

5. Dan Rather, "Porn in the USA," on *CBS News: 48 Hours,* 18 November 1992.

6. Catherine Itzin, "Legislating Against Pornography Without Censorship," in *Pornography: Women, Violence, and Civil Liberties,,* 401-34.

7. Susan Brownmiller, *Against Our Will: Men Women, and Rape* (New York: Simon and Schuster, 1975); Andrea Dworkin, "Against the Male Flood: Censorship, Pornography, and Equality," in *Pornography: Women, Violence, and Civil Liberties,* 515-35; Catherine A. MacKinnon, "Pornography, Civil Rights, and Speech," in ibid., 456-511; Diana E. H. Russell, "Pornography and Rape: A Causal Model," *Political Psychology* 9 (1988): 41-73.

8. Dworkin, "Against the Male Flood," 515-35.

9. Gloria Steinem, "Erotica and Pornography: A Clear and Present Difference," in *Take Back the Night: Women on Pornography,* ed. Laura Lederer (New York: William Morrow, 1980), 35-39.

10. William A. Fisher and Azy Barak, "Sex Education as a Corrective: Immunizing Against the Possible Effects of Pornography," in *Pornography: Research Advances and Policy Implications,* eds. Dolf Zillmann and Jennings Bryant (Hillsdale, N.J.: Erlbaum, 1989), 289-320; Daniel Linz and Edward Donnerstein, "The Effects of Counter Information on the Acceptance of Rape Myths," in ibid., 259-88.

11. Robert Showers, "Research, Public Policy and Law: Combination for Change," in *Media, Family, and Children: Social Scientific, Psychodynamic, and Clinical Perspectives,* eds. Dolf Zillmann, Jennings Bryant, and Aletha C. Huston (Hillsdale, N.J.: Erlbaum, 1994), 327-39.

12. "Report of the Commission on Pornography," (Washington, D.C.: U.S. Government Printing Office, 1970).

13. Edward Donnerstein, "Aggressive Erotica and Violence Against Women," *Journal of Personality and Social Psychology* 39: 269-77; "Erotica and Human Aggression," in *Aggression: Theoretical and Empirical Reviews, vol. 2: Issues in Research,* eds. Russell G. Geen and Edward I. Donnerstein (New York: Academic Press, 1983), 127-54; Neil M. Malamuth, "Rape Fantasies as a Function of Repeated Exposure to Sexual Violence," in *Archives of Sexual Behavior* 10:33-44; Malamuth, "Aggression Against Women:

Cultural and Individual Causes," in *Pornography and Sexual Aggression*, eds. Neil M. Malamuth and Edward Donnerstein (Orlando, Fl.: Academic Press, 1984), 19-52; Dolf Zillmann and Jennings Bryant, "Pornography, Sexual Callousness, and the Trivialization of Rape," in *Journal of Communication* 32 (Autumn 1992): 10-21.

14.   E. P. Mulvey and J. L. Haugaard, "Report of the Surgeon General's Workshop on Pornography and Public Health," (Washington, D.C.: U.S. Department of Health and Human Services, Office of the Surgeon General, 4 August 1984).

15.   "Attorney General's Commission on Pornography: Final Report" (Washington D.C.: U.S. Department of Justice, July, 1986.

16.   Victor B. Cline, ed., *Where Do You Draw the Line?* (Salt Lake City: Brigham Young University Press, 1974).

17.   Dolf Zillmann, "Pornography Research, Social Advocacy, and Public Policy," in *Psychology and Social Policy*, eds. Peter Suedfeld and Philip E. Tetlock (New York: Hemisphere, 1992), 165-78.

18.   Hans-Bernd Brosius, "Sex and Pornographie in den Massenmedien: Eine Analyse ihrer Nutzung und ihrer Wirkung," in *Der andere Blick: Aktuelles zur Massenkommunikation aus weiblicher Sicht*, ed. Ruth Frolich (Bochum: Brockmeyer, 1992), 139-58; T. S. Palys, "A Content Analysis of Sexually Explicit Videos in British Columbia: Working Papers On Pornography and Prostitution, Research Report No. 15" (Ottowa, Canada: Department of Justice, June, 1984); Stephen Prince, "Power and Pain: Content Analysis and the Ideology of Pornography," *Journal of Film and Video* 42 (1990): 31-41; Ni Yang and Daniel Linz, "Sex and Violence in Adult Videos," *Journal Of Communication* 40 (Winter 1990): 28-42.

19.   David Byrne and Kathryn Kelly, "Basing Legislative Action on Research Data: Prejudice, Prudence, and Empirical Limitations," in *Pornography: Research Advances and Policy Considerations*, eds. Dolf Zillmann and Jennings Bryant, 363-85.

20.   Edward Donnerstein, Daniel Linz, Stephen Penrod, *The Question of Pornography: Research Findings and Policy Implications* (New York: Free Press, 1987).

21.   Edna F. Einsiedel, "The British, Canadian, and U.S. Pornography Commissions and Their Use of Social Science Research," *Journal of Communication* 38 (Winter 1988): 108-21.

22.   Dolf Zillmann, "Pornography Research, Social Advocacy, and Public Policy," in *Psychology and Social Policy*, eds. Peter Suedfeld and Philip E. Tetlock (New York: Hemisphere, 1992), 165-78.

23.   Ibid.

24.   Neil M. Malamuth, "Aggression Against Women: Cultural and Individual Causes," in *Pornography and Sexual Aggression*, eds. Neil M. Malamuth and Edward Donnerstein (Orlando, Fl.: Academic Press, 1984), 19-52.

25. Leonard Berkowitz and Karen Heimer Rogers, "A Primary Effect Analysis of Media Influences," in *Perspectives On Media Effects*, eds. Jennings Bryant and Dolf Zillmann (Hillsdale, N.J.: Erlbaum, 1986), 57-81.

26. Jennings Bryant, "Effects of Pornography: Research Findings." (Testimony to the U.S. Attorney General's Commission On Pornography, Houston, Tex., September 1985); Ruth Wishnoff, "Modeling Effects of Explicit and Nonexplicit Sexual Stimuli on the Sexual Anxiety and Behavior of Women," *Archives of Sexual Behavior* 7 (1978): 455-61.

27. Kenneth V. Lanning and Ann Burgess, "Child Pornography and Sex Rings," in *Federal Bureau of Investigation Law Enforcement Bulletin* 53: 10-16.

28. Zillmann and Bryant, "Pornography, Sexual Callousness, and the Trivialization of Rape," 10-21; Dolf Zillmann and Jennings Bryant, "Effects of Massive Exposure to Pornography," in *Pornography and Sexual Aggression*, eds. Neil M. Malamuth and Edward Donnerstein (Orlando, Fl.: Academic Press, 1984), 115-38.

29. Dolf Zillmann, *Connections Between Sex and Agression* (Hillsdale, N.J.: Erlbaum, 1984).

30. Dolf Zillmann, "Erotica and Family Values," in *Media, Family, and Children: Social Scientific, Psychodynamic, and Clinical Perspectives*, eds. Dolf Zillmann, Jennings Bryant, and Aletha Huston, (Hillsdale, N.J.: Erlbaum, 1994), 199-213; Dolf Zillmann and Jennings Bryant, "Pornography's Impact On Sexual Satisfaction," *Journal of Applied Social Psychology* 18 (1988): 438-53. Dolf Zillmann and Jennings Bryant, "Shifting Preferences in Pornography Consumption," *Communications Research* 13 (1982): 560-78.

31. Dolf Zillmann and Jennings Bryant, "Effects of Massive Exposure to Pornography," in *Pornography and Sexual Aggression*, eds. Neil M. Malamuth and Edward Donnerstein (Orlando, Fla.: Academic Press, 1984), 115-38.

32. Dolf Zillmann, "Erotica and Family Values," in *Media, Family, and Children: Social Scientific, Psychodynamic, and Clinical Perspectives*, 199-213.

33. Select Committee On Children, Youths, and Families. "U.S. Children and Their Families: Current Conditions and Recent Trends." (Washington, D.C.: Government Printing Office, 1983).

34. Constance R. Ahrons and Roy Rogers, *Divorced Families: A Multidisciplinary View* (New York: Norton, 1987).

35. Dolf Zillmann and Jennings Bryant, "Effects of Prolonged Consumption of Pornography on Family Values," *Journal of Family Issues* 9 (1988): 518-44.

36. Dolf Zillmann and Jennings Bryant, "Shifting Preferences in Pornography Consumption," *Communication Research* 18 (1986): 560-78.

37.   Dolf Zillmann and Jennings Bryant, "Effects of Massive Exposure to Pornography," 115-38.

38.   Joseph G. Buchman, "Effects of Repeated Exposure to Nonviolent Erotica on Attitudes toward Sexual Child Abuse," Ph.D. diss., Indiana University, Bloomington, Ind., 1989.

39.   Zillmann and Bryant, "Pornography, Sexual Callousness, and the Trivialization of Rape," 10-21.

40.   James V. P. Check, *The Effects of Violent and Nonviolent Pornography*. (Ottowa: Department of Justice of Canada, 1985); James V. P. Check and Ted H. Guloien, "Reported Proclivity of Coercive Sex Following Repeated Exposure To Sexually Violent Pornography, Nonviolent Dehumanizing Pornography, and Erotica," in *Pornography: Research Advances and Policy Considerations*, eds. Dolf Zillmann and Jennings Bryant.

41.   Daniel Linz, "Sexual Violence in the Media: Effects On Male Viewers and Implications For Society," Ph.D. diss., University of Wisconsin, Madison, 1985; Catherine Krafka, "Sexually Explicit, Sexually Violent, and Violent Media: Effects of Multiple Naturalistic Exposures and Debriefing on Female Viewers," Ph.D. diss., University of Wisconsin, Madison, 1985.

42.   James Weaver, "The Social Science and Psychological Research Evidence: Perceptual and Behavioral Consequences of Exposure to Pornography," in Catherine Itzin, *Pornography: Women, Violence, and Civil Liberties*, 284-309; Dolf Zillmann, "Effects of Prolonged Consumption of Pornography," in *Pornography: Research Advances and Policy Considerations*, eds. Dolf Zillmann and Jennings Bryant (Hillsdale, N.J.: Erlbaum, 1989), 127-57.

43.   Mike J. Allen, Tara Emmers, Louis Gephardt, and Mary A. Giery, "Exposure to Pornography and Acceptance of Rape Myths: A Summary of Research Using Meta-Analysis"; paper presented at the Meeting of the Speech Communication Association, Chicago, Ill., November 1992; John S. Lyons, Rachel L. Anderson, and David B. Larson, "A Systematic Review of the Effects of Aggressive and Nonaggressive Pornography," in Zillmann and Bryant, *Media, Family, and Children*, 273-312.

44.   Elisabeth H. Preston, "Pornography and the Construction of Gender," in *Cultivation Analysis: New Directions In Media Effects Research*, eds. Nancy Signorielli and Michael Morgan (Newberry Park, Cal.: Sage Publications, 1990), 107-22.

45.   For a detailed discussion, see Dolf Zillmann, "Pornography Research, Social Advocacy, and Public Policy" in *Psychology and Social Policy*, eds. Peter Shedfeld and Philip E. Tetlock (New York: Hemisphere, 1992), 165-78.

46.   Victor B. Kline, "Pornography Effects: Empirical and Clinical Evidence," in *Media, Family, and Children*, 229-47.

5

Notes on the Marginalization of Marriage in America: Altered States in Constitutional Law

WILLIAM W. VAN ALSTYNE

Marriage is a term that appears in the most ordinary dictionary,[1] but does not appear in the Constitution or in the Bill of Rights.[2]   Unlike the Constitution's treatment of "the freedom of speech," or "the freedom of the press,"[3] there is no provision addressing or establishing "the freedom to marry," or the "right to have a family," or even the right "to have children within marriage." Indeed, there are no provisions addressed to distinguish any rights for those who do marry from any rights of those who do not. Necessarily, since even the very word "marriage" does not appear in the Constitution, neither is it given any definitional boundaries constraining either Congress or the states.[4]

Even so, over the course of two centuries of judicial review, the United States Supreme Court has considered the status of marriage in many decisions testing the permissible scope of state and federal laws that deal with marriage. On the whole, moreover, at least until quite recently, these decisions have treated marriage as a special relationship more vital and more foundational within our constitutional culture than nearly any other. More than a century ago, the Supreme Court described the centrality of marriage in society in the following way: "Upon it [the institution of marriage] society may be said to be built, and out of its fruits spring social relations and social obligations and duties, with which government is necessarily required to deal."[5] And so, quite naturally, the institution of marriage, and its regulation, have been recurring subjects of constitutional review.

The principal sources of the judicial decisions sheltering rights within marriage have been the two "due process of law" clauses in the Constitution. The immediate pertinence of these clauses springs from their express protection of liberty.[6] The earlier of these identically-framed clauses appears in the Fifth Amendment of the Bill of Rights;[7] but this clause is binding only on Congress and not on the states.[8] The other, enacted in 1868, appears in the Fourteenth Amendment; it expressly does bind the states.[9] Taken together, these clauses have been understood to limit the national government and the state governments from enacting arbitrary laws infringing on private liberty within marriage.[10] They have likewise been applied to provide for the equal protection of husbands and wives within marriage.[11] For the greater part of the twentieth century, the pattern of judicial decisions of both kinds — the special protection of marriage and equality of interests within marriage — tended to be of a piece. Overall, they very strongly sheltered marriage and the mutual interests of married persons in their children as some reflection of themselves. Perhaps the remembrance of a fairly early case, decided nearly seventy years ago, affords a suitable example of this sort.

Immediately following World War I, several states enacted laws forbidding any language instruction other than English to be furnished in any school to any child prior to the eighth grade. These laws were ostensibly enacted to insure that the children of first or second generation immigrant families would become fluent in English. Rather than taking care merely to do so, however, they went much further. That is, they forbade any language instruction in any other language at all until a child was in the eighth grade regardless of the degree of English literacy a child might already have or be able to demonstrate according to such tests, written or oral, the state might require.

The effect of these laws was particularly grim on immigrant families.[12] They effectively deprived these families of any lawful means whatever to enable their own children to receive any instruction in any school of the language spoken and written by their parents, however well they might already understand English as well. The statutory prohibition was sweeping and absolute: no school in the state could lawfully permit any teacher to teach any language other than English to any child until he or she was thirteen years old (that is, until the child was in the eighth grade).

In *Meyer v. Nebraska*,[13] the Supreme Court held this restriction to be a violation of the Fourteenth Amendment's Due Process Clause. The principal emphasis was on the central role of interests in one's own children within marriage. The Court's opinion treated as "fundamental"[14] the "freedom . . . to marry," and the "right . . . to bring up children."[15] Protecting the interests of parents in the education of their own children meant that the state could not forbid them from learning their own language as well as English, in schools with teachers willing to provide such instruction. The opinion pointedly contrasted Plato's visionary Republic in which, it observed, "[n]o parent [was] to know his own child nor any child his parent," but all were to be impersonally commingled and assigned according to some designated social utility and role. While acknowledging that such forms of social organization have been commended by writers of great capacity, the Court simply observed that their premises are "wholly different from those upon which our institutions rest."[16] The state laws at issue did not seek literally to enact this vision, but they were cut from the same ideological cloth. There was no sufficient justification for this form of state ideology, in the Court's view. Accordingly, on due process grounds, the restrictive state laws were struck down.

II

The enduring pertinence of *Meyer* and of a number of similar, subsequent decisions[17] by the Supreme Court, lay in their treatment of family aspirations, of shared interests within marriage as a special commitment, and in the protection of the family from being undermined by the state. In more recent years, however, there has been a marked shift in respect to marriage. In certain respects, what it once was it no longer is.[18] Formerly the distinctions of marriage as a special estate were indeed such that in some measure society itself could be said virtually to be "built upon it," because of how much it mattered. More recently, the emphasis has shifted to something else: to marriage substantially diminished and in some measure constitutionally reduced. In 1972 the Supreme Court itself broke the boundary separating intimacy within marriage. It did so in *Eisenstadt v. Baird*.[19]

In quite ringing terms, in *Eisenstadt*, Justice William J. Brennan, Jr. dismissed prior emphases on the institution of marriage. Perhaps the most significant sentence in the Court's opinion was this: "If the right to privacy means anything, it is the right of the *individual*, married or single, to be free from unwarranted intrusion into matters so fundamentally affecting a person as the decision whether to bear or beget a child."[20] The departure in *Eisenstadt*, the emphasis on the "the right of the *individual*" to decide "whether to bear or beget a child" whether one was married or not, as the very essence of a special personal right ("privacy"), was altogether startling. It had never previously been thought to be so, that is, that marriage mattered so little on matters of this kind.[21] Still, the proposition was hardly but a casual dictum given the deliberate stress — the italics — added by Justice Brennan with obvious feeling for his view. *Eisenstadt v. Baird* provisionally effaced marriage as a significant distinction in measuring "unwarranted intrusion(s)" into such decisions as "whether to bear or beget a child." One is left to struggle for ways to mark the potential consequence of this view in its startling suggestion that there is little that may matter about marriage after all. Still, one may quickly see what a difference this view may tend to make in one's own thinking, in the following brief review of the further marginalization of marriage by the Supreme Court.

III

Consider the constitutionality of a state statute that does attach a cricual value to marriage in the strength of the state's interest in the birth of a child. In brief, consider the following specific act:

Minn. Civ. Code Sec. 241: *Absent any compelling medical necessity, no physician shall undertake any act to destroy any child in gestation, conceived willingly within marriage, and wanted as the lawful child by either parent.*

How might an Opinion be framed reviewing this sort of law, tested against a claim that the act should be held to offend the Constitution (on grounds that it lacks the quality of "due process of law")?[22]   One may not be quite certain, of course, but something like the following Opinion would have been an unexceptionable report, at least consistent with *Griswold v. Connecticut*, though perhaps not after *Eisenstadt v. Baird*:

It is startling to think there may be any substantial constitutional question raised by this statute. We do not think that there is. That marriage, the most personal and sheltered estate known to the law, should come accompanied by no recognition of mutually protected parental interests in children willingly conceived within that marriage[23]— that a law might in fact license a physician to proceed to destroy that offspring without regard for both parents (rather than merely the sole choice of one)— might more reasonably itself be thought to raise the more substantial constitutional question than the reverse. Insofar as it licensed any physician to proceed with an abortion calculated to kill and destroy a four-month developing child without regard to its place in the life and the feelings of its lawful father as well as its mother— to hold such a physician harmless against any and all anguish and suffering the father may then endure as a consequence of the physician's terminal act— it would be hard to say that so partisan a law meets the requirements of due process at all. Within marriage, at least, a gestating child need not be regarded by the law as but one person's "separate property." Not since *Dred Scott v. Sanford*[24] has this Court taken so distanced a view of what passes for due process of law. We decline to take that view here.

As Justice Douglas acknowledged for this Court in *Griswold v. Connecticut*, 381 U.S. 479 (1965) at 486: "Marriage is a coming together . . . intimate to the degree of being sacred. It is an association that promotes a way of life, not causes . . . a *bilateral* loyalty . . . an association for as noble a purpose as any involved in our prior decisions" (emphasis added). We think the state has so regarded it, in the protection this law provides. This Court noted more than a half-century ago, "We are dealing here with legislation which involved one of the basic civil rights of man. Marriage and procreation are fundamental to the very existence and survival of the race." *Skinner v. Oklahoma* , 316 U.S. 535 (1942) at 541. Nor were these observations (in *Skinner*) the least bit novel or wanting in precedent. Twenty years earlier, in *Meyer v. Nebraska*, 262 U.S. 390 (1923) at 399, we had already observed: "While this Court has not attempted to define with exactness the liberty thus guaranteed [by the Fourteenth Amendment] . . . [w]ithout doubt, it denotes not merely freedom from bodily restraint but also the right of the individual . . . to marry, establish a home and bring up children." Marriage is a relationship the state may foster by the security it intends that relationship to provide.

Human life in gestation may be subject to much debate and differences of opinion, but not such that a state's resolve to protect the desire of either parent to cherish it, regardless of how little the other may value it, can be put aside with the ease of any physician's licensed craft. Accordingly, we find no ground to invalidate a law that merely provides that absent any compelling medical necessity, no physician shall undertake any act to destroy any child in gestation, conceived willingly within marriage, and wanted as the lawful child by either parent. Rather, we find it difficult to grasp an argument grounded in the Constitution sufficient to maintain the opposite conclusion— that a law of this protective sort could somehow be regarded as at odds with some clause, or some principle, derived from the Constitution of the United States. We are quite convinced that it is not.

But consider, also hypothetically, that instead of the preceding statute, a state legislature enacted its opposite, i.e. a statute that would read in the following way:

Minn. Civ. Code Sec. 48: *"Marriage" shall be deemed in this jurisdiction to confer no interest whatever that one not married lacks in regard to each woman's reproductive autonomy either to bear a child or not free of unwarranted intrusions into her choice. Accordingly, no physician providing any abortion service need concern himself with any alleged interest any husband may claim to hold in securing the life of the child, it being the policy of this state that he has none sufficient to count.*

How might an Opinion from the Supreme Court respond to this development? Perhaps as a mere extrapolation of the dicta in *Eisenstadt,* the following opinion would provide a plausible account:

It is startling to think that there could be any constitutional question raised by this statute. We do not think that there is. It scarcely does more than to report in statutory form what our own decisions have already declared to be the controlling law. In recent decisions decided since *Eisenstadt v. Baird*, 405 U.S. 438 (1972), this Court has held that there is nothing whatever sufficient in marriage to permit a state to impose any restriction on the right of any woman, whether or not married and regardless of with whom she conceived a child, to secure the abortion of any fetus she does not deem worthwhile to carry to term, so long as she acts within the first six months. See *Planned Parenthood of Southeastern Pennsylvania v. Casey*, 112 S.Ct. 2791 (1992); *Roe v. Wade*, 410 U.S. 113 (1973). We have already held that not even notice to her husband of her intention need be provided if she is not inclined so to advise him— whether or not the child is his; for indeed, we have ourselves most recently held that the imposition of any such obligation imposed by law is void on its face. *Planned Parenthood of Southeastern Pennsylvania v. Casey;* see also *Planned Parenthood of Missouri v. Danforth*, 528 U.S. 52 (1976).

The statute before us merely carries these dispositive holdings of ours into suitable provisions of statutory law; so it plainly raises no constitutional issue at all. To the contrary, it merely helps to make the real meaning of our own prior decisions more publicly accessible and clear. The interest in the lives of children in gestation stands on no higher footing, constitutionally speaking, for husbands in marriage than the interest of those who eschew marriage and have made no commitment at all of this kind. And a state statute that merely advises them that this is so (which in effect is just what this statute does), is an unexceptionable law in keeping with our own prior expressions affecting this subject since 1972.

Which of these sets of strikingly different statutes and opinions finds stronger support in the precedents of the Supreme Court? The answer will not long detain us, for it but reports what has become of the law during the past two decades of judicial review. The answer is that prior to *Eisenstadt*, and prior to 1972, the first opinion would find the far greater support. Up until roughly 1972, virtually *every* opinion from the Supreme Court dealing with marriage had treated it as exceedingly special— as a cornerstone of social organization in the United States, emphasizing its bilateral loyalties, its mutuality, its sheltered community, and offering it an encouragement pursuant to the Constitution and the Bill of Rights. In fact, the opinion hypothesized for the Court (i.e., the imaginary opinion sustaining the first statute) was itself a mere construction of existing Supreme Court views evolved during a century of principal cases touching this field. The first opinion treats the relationship as quite special, indeed. The second opinion, however— in tone as well as in substance— m o r e nearly reveals the current constitutional status of marriage in the decisions of the Supreme Court. Indeed, in light of the Court's most recent opinion on this particular subject,[25] the first opinion would not be consistent with its current view and it is only an opinion of this second sort that would, with rough accuracy, describe the current state of our constitutional law.

IV

"Marriage" is in fact presently an institution in moral and legal transition. It is easily entered, and almost as easily exited. The majority of states have long since switched to "no fault" divorce, and, in keeping with this trend, decisions to marry may be more lightly made insofar as they are also virtually cancelable at will. So also is marriage a mere alternative arrangement, not notably preferable (and in some ways less preferable)[26] than some other arrangements available in a number of states where "Marvin" agreements (private contracts of cohabitation) are legal alternatives to marriage itself.[27] Not only has marriage been reduced overall in terms of any legal specialness, moreover, marriage is itself discouraged by some other features of our law. It is commonly supposed that marriage is encouraged at least in the structure of the federal income tax (i.e., the advantage of filing a joint return), but even this notion is substantially false. For many couples, marriage comes accompanied by a tax penalty. Such a couple may pay several thousand dollars *more* each year into the federal treasury than had they not married but simply stayed single and filed separate returns.[28] Likewise, marriage may also be discouraged for the same reason for the working poor as well; they, too, may likewise be penalized by the federal tax tables by marrying.[29] In another country (Germany), to be sure, the tax act of the national legislature that discriminated in this fashion (subjecting married couples to higher taxes) was held to be inconsistent with the Constitution's protection of marriage.[30] But of course there has been no similar successful challenge entertained by our Supreme Court, nor could there likely be such a successful challenge in light of the manner in which marriage has been diminished in its overall constitutional standing by the Court itself. In a larger sense, in short, the second opinion modeled in this brief review merely reflects these trends in the marginalizing of marriage in the social (dis)organization of the United States. The particular statute we have modeled and briefly reviewed here merely reports these vagaries and this sense of anomie of much of modern life.

Perhaps these developments are nonetheless, on balance, progressive developments, as many evidently believe to be true. Even so, there may be some reason to think this is not entirely so, or at least that they have not come without some real costs and possible real losses as well. As the idea of the centrality of marriage appears to be on the wane, the idea of one's family is in some disarray as well. The two are not, after all, entirely easy to distinguish as one tries to think these matters through. In a widely reported article recently appearing in *The Atlantic*, for example, author Barbara Whitehead noted these disquieting facts:[31]

Survey after survey shows that Americans are less inclined than they were a generation ago to value sexual fidelity, lifelong marriage, and parenthood as worthwhile personal goals. *** The out-of-wedlock birth rate . . . went from five percent in 1960 to 27 percent in 1990.*** Fewer than half of all adult Americans today regard the idea of sacrifice for others as a positive moral virtue. More than half of the increase in child poverty in the 1980s is attributable to changes in family structure, according to David Eggebeen and Daniel Lichter, of Pennsylvania State University. In fact, if family structure in the United States had remained relatively constant since 1960, the rate of child poverty would be a third lower than it is today.

To be sure, as noted earlier in this essay, the Constitution does not expressly address "marriage," "family," or "children," so perhaps it is altogether pointless to presume to relate any of these things to developments in constitutional law, as I have sought in some mild way to relate them here. Yet, in the end, it is difficult to believe that they are wholly disconnected insofar as the Supreme Court itself has historically participated in this cultural debate, first specially treating these interests with the utmost solicitude and protection under the Due Process Clause, and now treating them from quite a different point of view. And whether one believes that the Court merely reflects public attitudes in its various constitutional decisions or, rather, does not merely reflect but acts also to influence public attitude in its various occasions for interpreting and applying the Constitution (as certainly seems likely), it does appear that we now find ourselves in an altered state that has left some important values too much out of account. If even so much as this is true, moreover, then perhaps we should worry a good deal more than we or the Court have seemed to have done, as we see what we have now become. Things change, as William Yeats reminded us, and now things also fall apart: "And what rough beast, its hour come round at last, slouches toward Bethlehem, to be born?"[32]

NOTES

1. See *The American Heritage Dictionary* (1971), 801 ("marriage," n. [Middle English *mariage*, from Old French, from *marier*, to marry]: **1a**. The state of being husband and wife; wedlock. **1b**. The legal union of a man and woman as husband and wife. . . ." But see also ibid. at 3. [marriage defined more loosely "any close union (e.g., a marriage of minds)" or even "a union of inanimate objects (as music and drama in opera)."]

2. In contrast, it does appear expressly in some other recent constitutions, e.g., the Constitution ("The Basic Law") of Germany. (Article 6(1): "Marriage and the family shall enjoy the special protection of the state.") See also *The Universal Declaration of Human Rights*, Art. 16 (Men and women . . . have the right to marry and to found a family. They are entitled to equal rights as to marriage, during marriage, and at its dissolution."); *International Covenant on Civil and Political Rights*, Srt. 23 ("The family is the natural and fundamental group unit of society and is entitled to protection by society and the State.*** The right of men and women . . . to marry and to found a family shall be recognized."); *American Convention on Human Rights*, Art. 17 ("The right of men and women . . . to marry and raise a family shall be recognized. . . The States Parties shall take appropriate steps to ensure the equality of rights . . . during marriage. . . .").

3. U.S. Constitution, First Amendment (1791): "Congress shall make no law . . . abridging the freedom of speech, or of the press. . . ."

4. Note that a last-listed definition of marriage in a modern dictionary (n.1 herein) acknowledges a usage of "marriage" as the mere "union of inanimate objects (as music and drama in opera)." Does it follow that a legislature might treat marriage as such a relationship, i.e., as a relationship merely between inanimate objects? The very idea seems startling, so far removed is it from one's natural intuitions on what marriage between two people must surely mean. Still, in certain respects, it is arguable that the modern treatment of marriage

sometimes amounts to little more. Moreover, as it will be argued briefly in this essay and its notes, the Supreme Court may itself have contributed to the diminishing significance of marriage in the United States.

5. *Reynolds v. United States*, 98 U.S. 145 (1878) at 165. The question before the Court in *Reynolds* was whether polygamous marriage (one husband and several wives) must be accepted by law as "marriage" (rather than disallowed as a form of bigamy or criminal cohabitation), for persons claiming under the free exercise of religion clause in the First Amendment. The answer was "no." That a free exercise claim may nonetheless provide some degree of family exemption from otherwise compulsory state statutes (e.g., mandatory enrollment of one's children in some accredited school), however, see *Wisconsin v. Yoder*, 406 U.S. 205 (1972) (Amish withdrawal of children from any further accredited schooling at the eighth grade). (But see *Employment Division of Oregon Dept. of Human Resources v. Smith*, 494 U.S. 872 (1990) (recharacterizing *Yoder* as a family-liberty-parental rights due process case).

6. The use of the Due Process Clause (protecting life, liberty, and property) as a source of substantive limits on state power traces its lineage in legal history to chapter 39 of Magna Carta, at Runnymede, in 1215: "No free man shall be . . . stripped of his rights or possessions . . . except by lawful judgment of his equals or by the law of the land." The latter phrase ("the law of the land") was accepted into American practice to mean laws "consistent with right and with reason," i.e., not arbitrary in the treatment of personal liberty; see Edward C. Corwin, "The Higher Law Background of American Constitutional Law," *Harvard Law Review* 42 (1928): 149; Edward C. Corwin, "The Doctrine of Due Process of Law Before the Civil War," *Harvard Law Review* 24 (1911): 366.

7. U.S. Constitution, Fifth Amendment (1791): "No person . . . shall be . . . deprived of life, liberty, or property, without due process of law. . . ."

8. Note that unlike the First Amendment (see n.3 herein), the Fifth Amendment has no language expressly confining its application only to acts of Congress. Nevertheless, it was understood solely to be meant to limit the national government, and to leave the state governments to be limited only in such manner, and according to such restrictions, as their own respective state constitutions might provide. The Supreme Court accepted this understanding of the Fifth Amendment. Accordingly, it held the amendment to have no applicability to the states (see *Barron v. Baltimore*, 32 U.S. 243 (1833).

9. U.S. Constitution, Fourteenth Amendment (1868): "No State shall . . . deprive any person of life, liberty, or property, without due process of law. . . ." In the aftermath of the Civil War (1860-1865), in the course of proposing new constitutional limits on the states,

Congress was unwilling any longer to trust the states not to "deprive any person of life, liberty, or property, without due process of law," as was previously the case under the Fifth Amendment (see discussion in n.8 herein). Accordingly, the 39th Congress (the Reconstruction Congress of 1866) proposed to extend the Fifth Amendment provision in a new form to make it equally controlling in every state; as the national government was not empowered to deprive any person of life, liberty, or property, without due process of law (but, rather, had at all times since 1791 been forbidden to do so), so, too, the states were likewise thereafter to be subject to the same restraint. With the ratification of the Fourteenth Amendment in 1868, therefore, the anomaly of exempting state legislatures from due process standards previously applicable only to Congress, finally came to an end.

10. No doubt the single strongest modern example is *Griswold v. Connecticut*, 381 U.S. 479 (1965), where the Court held that consensual expressions of sexual intimacy within marriage are generally reserved from state authority by the Due Process Clause. The Court expressly distinguished "marital privacy" from sexual liberty claims without regard to marriage, stressing the special commitment reflected within marriage and describing marriage as a "bilateral loyalty," a relationship traditionally sheltered and ordinarily protected by the law. See also *Michael H. v. Gerald D.*, 109 S.Ct. 2333 (1989) (where the Court stated once again that "our traditions have protected the marital family"); *Moore v. City of East Cleveland*, 431 U.S. 494 (1977); *Poe v. Ullman*, 367 U.S. 497 (1961) (Harlan, J., dissenting); *Boddie v. Connecticut*, 401 U.S. 371 (1971); and *Meyer v. Nebraska*, 262 U.S. 390 (1923). And, for contrast, compare *Bowers v. Hardwicke*, 478 U.S. 186 (1986).

11. See, e.g., *Califano v. Goldfarb*, 430 U.S. 199 (1977); *Weinberger v. Wiesenfeld*, 429 U.S. 636 (1975); *Frontiero v. Richardson*, 411 U.S. 677 (1973) (disparities in treatment under federal law of spousal benefits received by husbands and by wives struck down as inconsistent with Fifth Amendment due process clause requirements of equality of treatment of spouses within marriage). In cases arising under state laws rather than under federal laws, the Court has tended more often to rely on the Equal Protection Clause — rather than the Due Process Clause — to provide equality of treatment of spouses within marriage; see, e.g., *Orr v. Orr*, 440 U.S. 268 (1979) (one-way alimony rights held invalid as denying equal protection within marriage); see also *Loving v. Virginia*, 398 U.S. 1 (1967) (state law restrictions on interracial marriage held void pursuant to the Equal Protection Clause of the Fourteenth Amendment); and *Zablocki v. Redhail*, 434 U.S. 3174 (1978).

12. There was evidence in these cases strongly suggesting that these

laws were enacted out of anti-German animus following World
War I.

13.   *Meyer v. Nebraska*, 262 U.S. 390 (1923); see also *Bartels v. Iowa*, 262
      U.S. 408 (1923) (same issue, same result); *Farrington v. Tokushige*,
      273 U.S. 284 (1927) (same case arising under federal statute
      applicable to the federal territory of Hawaii, same result on Fifth
      Amendment due process grounds).

14.   *Meyer* at 401.

15.   Ibid. at 399.

16.   Ibid. at 402.

17.   See n.10 herein for references to cases, and see especially *Griswold
      v. Connecticut*, 381 U.S. 479 (1965).

18.   See generally, Mary Ann Glendon, "Marriage and the State: The
      Withering Away of Marriage," *Virginia Law Review* 62 (1976):
      1663.

19.   *Eisenstadt v. Baird*, 405 U.S. 438 (1972) (right of access to
      contraceptive devices of unmarried persons held to be equal to
      those within marriage).

20.   Ibid. at 453.

21.   The *Eisenstadt* decision was most significant because the Court
      decided it on equal protection grounds, holding that since the law
      in question did not forbid retail sale of contraceptive devices to
      married couples, the restriction of sales to unmarried persons was
      arbitrary. The equation, however, between married couples and
      unmarried persons managed in a single decision to turn the
      Court's holding in *Griswold v. Connecticut* (see n.10 herein) upside
      down. (It was the special protection of marriage that was the
      foundation of *Griswold*.) For clear statements on both *Griswold v.
      Connecticut* and *Eisenstadt v. Baird*, see Michael Sandel, "Moral
      Argument and Liberal Toleration: Abortion and Homosexuality,"
      California Law Review 77 (1989): 521, 526-28, and H. Jefferson
      Powell, "The Moral Tradition of American Constitutionalism," in
      California Law Review (1993): 174-77.

22.   I.e., that it is unconstitutional for a state to treat marriage as in any
      way affecting one's liberty to terminate an unwanted developing
      child in gestation, regardless of whose child it is, insofar as the
      decision to do so is exercised within six months of its development
      and is accomplished by medical procedures posing no undue
      complications to one's own health.

23.   Which is all that this statute purports to reach. (Cf. *Planned
      Parenthood of Missouri v. Danforth*, 428 U.S. 52 (1976).) We express
      no opinion respecting the validity of any law purporting to do
      anything more. This act reaches no claim by anyone outside of
      marriage. Equally clearly, it makes no claim other than in respect
      to children conceived within marriage willingly, that is, by mutual
      choice. That a child thus conceived could be protected from

abortion only by the will of one parent but not saved by the conscience of the other parent, is to devalue its life indeed. We know of no principle requiring such a result, and certainly none to be found in the Fourteenth Amendment of the Constitution of the United States (Cf. *Roe v. Wade*, 410 U.S. 113 (1973).) (Note by the Court.)

24. Cf. *Dred Scott v. Sandford*, 60 U.S. 393 (1857) (the slave decision by Chief Justice Roger Taney of this Court). (Note by the Court.)

25. *Planned Parenthood of Southeastern Pennsylvania v. Casey*, 112 S.Ct. 2791 (1992).

26. A man who marries— and only one who does marry (as distinct from the single unmarried man)— may become liable for the support of such offspring his wife chooses to bear adulterously during the marriage, as well as liable also for the support of such offspring she has with him (whether he desired them or not). On the other hand, there is no symmetry in this liability for the wife is not liable for the support of any children she did not bear— not for children the husband conceived adulterously with another. (For a brief review of the general topic, see Ira Ellman, Paul Kurtz, and Katherine Bartlett, *Family Law: Cases, Text, Problems*, 2nd ed. (Charlottesville, Va.: Michie Co., 1991), 888-97.

27. See *Marvin v. Marvin*, 134 Cal. Rptr: 815 (1976). Such agreements were formerly void on public policy grounds (akin to contracts of prostitution or meretricious criminal cohabitation). But nonmarital cohabitation is currently not merely lawful in most jurisdictions, rather, it is on its way to becoming a civil right (e.g., in California, a refusal to rent to unmarried "cohabitants" is actionable in state court).

28. See *Wall St. Journal*, 28 July 1993, A1, col. 5 (reporting that for 1994, it may cost a given professional married couple $6,300 more each year, as a tax purely on their marriage).

29. So also according to the *Wall Street Journal*, 26 March 1993, A10, col. 1, under the current proposed tax bill: "A couple earning $12,000 each and planning three kids . . . will pay $2,744 in taxes if they get married, but collect refunds totaling $831 if they stay single."

30. In Germany, where marriage (and the family) is expressly protected in The Basic Law (see n.2 herein), the Constitutional Court has struck down tax provisions putting those who marry at a tax rate disadvantage of the kind reflected in our own current tax laws. See, e.g., BVerfGE 6 (1957): 55, 70-84.

31. *The Atlantic* 271 (April 1993):47. See also Mary Ann Glendon, "Marriage and the State: The Withering Away of Marriage," n.18 herein.

32. William Butler Yeats (1865-1939), *The Second Coming* (any edition).

6

Compassion: The Liberal Virtue

ROSEMARIE TONG

FEMINIST CHALLENGES TO THE TRADITION

What is the relation between law and morality? Or, more specifically, should law control morality? The traditional debate on this issue focuses almost exclusively on so-called sexual morality. Should society criminalize, or otherwise legally regulate, pornography, prostitution, homosexuality— o r indeed, any sexual behavior that is widely regarded as "immoral," as "against the rule of a higher authority" (God) or "against a societal taboo?"[1] Liberals give priority to individual freedom, claiming that the law has no business governing private sexual behavior, peeping under the covers of citizens' beds to see what is or what is not occurring there. Conservatives emphasize the good of society, insisting that the law must see to it that individuals do not sin, be it under their covers or on the street— since a society without an enforced, as well as shared, moral code is in danger of crumbling, fragmenting, splintering.

These liberal and conservative positions are crystallized in the now classic debate between Lord Patrick Devlin and H.L.A. Hart on the appropriate reach of the criminal law. In its 1954 report on homosexuality, prostitution, and other sex crimes, the Wolfenden Committee of the British Parliament recommended that such "offenses" be decriminalized.[2] Lord Devlin, the conservative, responded most negatively to the committee's recommendations seeing in them the seeds of the British Empire's final fall:

The Report finds it (the division of crime and sin) in the principle that the criminal law exists for the protection of individuals;. . . *but the true principle is that the law exists for the protection of society.* It does not discharge its function by protecting the individual from injury, annoyance, corruption, and exploitation; the law must protect also the institutions and the community of ideas, political and moral, without which people cannot live together. Society cannot ignore the morality of the individual any more than it can his loyalty; it flourishes in both and without either it dies.[3]

Without a common morality, insisted Devlin, a society cannot survive, let alone thrive.

Hart, the liberal, challenged Devlin's analysis. He questioned the *morality* of any view that would force the status quo value system down the throats of a minority unwilling to swallow its contents: "Is the fact that certain conduct is by common standards immoral sufficient to justify making that conduct punishable by law? Is it morally permissible to enforce morality as such?"[4] In raising his objections, Hart was largely reiterating John Stuart Mill's nineteenth-century belief that the law may limit individual freedom only when the failure to do so results in harm to others. If a person's actions cause no harm to others, they are his or her own business. The majority does not have the right to make their moral opinions law and force dissenters to follow them.

The Hart-Devlin debate is a very substantial one. For years, this author regarded it as a nearly perfect summary of all the basic arguments on the relationship between law and morality. In general, I was on the liberal side— what I perceived as the enlightened side when it came to questions of private sexual morality. Not wanting to force my "enlightened" views upon my students, however, I tried as best as I could to give the "unenlightened" conservatives enough floor space. Thus, for the first ten years of my teaching career, I used a debate format to structure my philosophy of law course, always reserving a week or so for the annual obscenity and censorship debate. The cultural conservatives would sit on one side of the room brandishing the sword of public morality. The civil libertarians would sit on the other side of the room waving the flag of individual liberty.

Relying on the principles of legal moralism and legal paternalism, the cultural conservatives would argue: first, that good sex is always heterosexual, usually takes place in marriage, and is, if at all possible, oriented towards procreation; second, that sexually explicit material activates all those polymorphous perverse snakes deep within us that threaten to undo civilization in general, and each of us in particular; third, that sexually explicit material either does not qualify as real speech (since it is a noncognitive mode of expression appealing not to brains but to hormonal urges and the like), or, if it qualifies as real speech, it is low-value speech undeserving of First Amendment protection; and, finally, that the law ought to serve as morality's handmaiden, protecting it from the forces of the flesh that would, if they only could, devour it.

Relying on the harm principle, and to a lesser extent on the offense principle, the civil libertarians would argue: first, that good sex is a matter of aesthetics not ethics, of taste not virtue; second, that sexually explicit material invites us to try out a variety of sexual experiences and to overcome any number of our unhealthy Puritanical and Victorian sexual inhibitions; third, that sexually explicit material is real speech with a socially valuable message— "Cast off your old, tired, and repressive sexual mores and celebrate your body"; and, finally, that the law ought to serve simply as a system of green and red lights that permits each of us to get our sexual satisfaction whenever, wherever, however, and with whomever or whatever we please, provided that no one, with the possible exception of ourselves, is either harmed or egregiously offended in the process.[5]

Around 1978 or 1979, just when I thought I had all the moves down, a different voice— a woman's voice— shattered the predictable format of the annual obscenity and censorship debate. This voice sang neither the conservative praises of public morality nor the libertarian praises of individual freedom; rather it pleaded for equality for women. As feminist antipornographers saw it— and here I am referring primarily to those radical feminists who believe that the main cause of women's subordination is female sexuality— pornography was "not a *moral* issue"[6] but a *political* issue. Feminist lawyer Catharine A. MacKinnon adamantly declared:

Obscenity law is concerned with morality, specifically morals from the male point of view, meaning the standpoint of male dominance. The feminist critique of pornography is a politics, specifically politics from women's point of view, meaning the standpoint of the subordination of women to men. Morality here means good and evil; politics means power and powerlessness. Obscenity is a moral idea; pornography is a political practice. Obscenity is abstract; pornography is concrete. The two concepts represent two entirely different things. Nudity, explicitness, excess of candor, arousal or excitement, prurience, unnaturalness— these qualities bother obscenity law when sex is depicted or portrayed. Abortion, birth control information, and treatments for "restoring sexual virility" (whose, do you suppose?) have also been included. Sex forced on real women so that it can be sold at a profit to be forced on other real women; women's bodies trussed and maimed and raped and made into things to be hurt and obtained and accessed, and this presented as the nature of women; the coercion that is visible and the coercion that has become invisible— this and more bothers feminists about pornography. Obscenity, as such, probably does little harm; pornography causes attitudes and behaviors of violence and discrimination that define the treatment and status of half of the population.[7]

To the extent that pornography represents women as things, objects, instruments, or willing victims for men to selfishly use for their own pleasure, MacKinnon claimed that it leads men (and to some degree women) not only to think less of women, but to treat women as second-class citizens in the academy and workplace. If the law has managed to recognize that sexual harassment on a college campus or along a corporate corridor is not so much an outrage to an individual woman's sensibilities, or to society's notions about how gentlemen should treat ladies, as an instance of women generally being burdened with physical and psychological pressures that men escape, then the law can also recognize that pornography is not so much an affront to an individual woman's feelings, or to society's values about "proper" sex, as a matter of women generally being represented as creatures worthy of less respect and consideration than men. MacKinnon reasoned that if women spend their workdays or study hours fending off their male employers' or professors' unwanted sexual advances, they may find it difficult to perform their required tasks as well as their relatively unbothered male counterparts do. Similarly, if the imaginations of women's male employers and professors are "pornographic," if they are filled with representations of men giving women "what they're asking for," then these employers and professors may not be able to see their female subordinates in the same professional light that they see their male subordinates.[8]

As this author reflected upon MacKinnon's thoughts, the conclusion was reached that feminists' understanding of the relationship between law and morality simply did not fit the contours of the traditional Hart-Devlin debate. Only later when I became better schooled in feminist thought did I realize that MacKinnon's views were not necessarily the views of all feminists. Although most radical feminists shared her approach to law and morality, liberal and cultural feminists tended to diverge from her path. Nevertheless, all of these feminists—liberal, radical, and cultural— maintained, to a greater or lesser degree, that the real law and morality debate may lie in deciding just how "moral" the law itself is; for if the law itself contributes to immoral practices of male domination and female subordination, then it, rather than morality, is what needs to be disciplined, chastised, reformed.

This essay explores the different ways in which liberal, radical, and cultural feminists approach the relationship between morality and law, highlighting how these gynocentric approaches differ from the traditional conservative and liberal approaches of Devlin and Hart respectively. In order to make this task manageable, surrogate motherhood will be focused upon as a typical "women's issue" that has generated legal and moral consternation inside as well as outside the feminist community. The conclusions reached will be straightforward ones: First, *liberal* feminists do not sufficiently challenge the fundamental assumptions that support the law as it is now known. On the contrary. With respect to what harms and benefits women, their goal is simply to ensure that the law offers the same opportunities, protections, and rights to women as it does to men. Second, *radical* feminists reject the notion that women should want what men have had. Because everything men have had is the product of a legal system and a moral tradition that maintain themselves by enabling some people to oppress, repress, and suppress other people, women should think twice before they adopt men's desires as their own. With respect to what harms and benefits women, radical feminists want to make certain that the law, either by its sins of commission or by its sins of omission, does not maintain systems, structures, policies, institutions, and attitudes of male domination and female subordination. Third, *cultural* feminists insist that the deconstructive projects of radical feminists need to be accompanied by some constructive projects, however visionary and experimental. With respect to what harms and benefits women, cultural feminists want to use the law, even in its present, flawed state, to support those relational systems and networks that contribute to women's well-being. Fourth, and finally, traditional jurisprudence and ethics should welcome rather than resist feminist challenges; for unless they learn how to accommodate difference, they will find themselves without an audience.

LIBERAL, RADICAL, and CULTURAL FEMINISTS: SOME ONTOLOGICAL and EPISTEMOLOGICAL ASSUMPTIONS

According to Mary C. Dunlap, contemporary feminist legal activity has clustered around four sets of issues: (1) the "physical health" cluster; (2) the "money" cluster; (3) the "violence-empowerment" cluster; and (4) the "creativity" cluster.[9] The physical health cluster covers issues relating to women's bodies and bodily health— that is, personal choices about sexuality and reproduction. The money cluster deals with the bread-and-butter issues of equal pay, benefits, ownership, comparable worth, divorce settlements, and so on. The violence cluster deals with the sexual harassment, rape and battery of women. The creativity cluster is a bit harder to define. It involves those areas where women are only beginning to express themselves— art, education, law, sports. Dunlap argues that underlying the physical health and violence clusters are two moral themes: namely, "the idea that harm and pain and hurt that are gender-correlated must end, must be prevented, must be remedied," and "the idea or notion of equalizing opportunity."[10] Harm is not just about physical bruises— it is also about the spiritual harm of oppression. Likewise, lost opportunity is not only about lack of freedom in sexual and reproductive relationships, but also about lack of freedom in pursuing a career and an education. Dunlap, it would seem, articulates what most feminists mean by a moral issue. For feminists, morality is about much more than what goes on in the bedroom— it is also about what goes on in the boardroom, in the classroom, in the examining room. A moral issue includes any harmful or disempowering act inflicted upon a woman *because* she is a woman.

Of course, the challenge for feminists— be they liberal, radical, or cultural feminists— is making the law address women's issues even though it has been designed to address men's issues. Feminist legal theorist Robin West emphasizes that the law was developed of, for, and by *men*. The "human" model the law serves is actually a "male" model that reflects the world as the "Great Thinkers" (almost exclusively men) have known it. West explains how what she terms the "separation thesis" informs virtually all aspects of legal, moral, and political life. According to this view, "a 'human being,' whatever else *he* is, is physically separate from all other human beings."[11] Human beings are autonomous, atomic, separate, and boundaried individuals, proceeding with their own private lives.

West goes on to describe what she regards as the two main strains of "masculine" or "male" jurisprudence: legal liberalism and critical legalism. While both espouse the separation thesis, the thesis manifests itself differently in each approach. Legal

liberalism believes that the natural human state of separation
brings with it both autonomy and freedom. Freedom, which
allows individuals the right to pursue their own separate ends, is
legal liberalism's official value.[12] However, the very separation
that makes an individual free also makes him vulnerable. Given
that human beings are all separate, their goals will not only be
different, but they might also conflict. The subsequent
competition might lead to suffering, injury, or even death:
"Annihilation by the other, we might say, is the official *harm* of
liberal theory, just as autonomy is its official value."[13]

Agreeing with legal liberalism that individuals' separation is
natural, critical legalism bemoans, rather than celebrates, the
loneliness of it all. Man's isolation haunts him. He craves
community. He wants to transcend the separation that is natural
to him. "Alienation," not "annihilation" by the other, is the real
harm to lament, just as "community" not "autonomy" is the real
value to cherish.[14] Separation is man's tragic destiny: the
"original sin" for which redemption is sought.

Paradoxically, separation may also be behind the
conservative worldview. Although West does not attempt to
describe how the "male" model is at work in the thought of
someone like Devlin, as well as someone like Hart, it is this
author's opinion that the kind of community Devlin lauds as
somehow "naturally" or "instinctually" in place is actually an
artificial structure meant to keep otherwise atomistic units from
going their own separate ways. After all, if morality is so
common, so shared, why does the law have to work so hard to
enforce it? Dissent is the official harm of conservatism, just as
conformity (not community) is its official value.

The male model is not the exclusive possession of men,
however. In their desire to secure for women the same
opportunities, occupations, rights, and privileges men have had,
liberal feminists adopt male metaphysics, especially the form
that values autonomy and fears annihilation (the power of
sisterhood apparently not withstanding). According to
philosopher Alison Jaggar, liberal feminists are "normative
dualists"— thinkers committed to the view that the functions
and activities of the mind are somehow better than those of the

body.[15] Eating, drinking, excreting, sleeping, and reproducing are not, according to this view, paradigmatic human activities because members of most other animal species also engage in them. Instead, human beings' capacity to wonder, imagine, and comprehend sets them apart from the rest of animal creation.[16]

Liberal feminists' adherence to normative dualism is problematic, according to Jaggar, not only because it leads to a devaluation of bodily activities and functions, but also because it usually leads to both solipsism and skepticism. (Solipsism is the belief that the rational, autonomous person is essentially isolated, with needs and interests separate from, and even in opposition to, those of every other individual. Skepticism is the belief that the fundamental questions of political philosophy—i n what does human well-being and fulfillment consist, and what are the means to attain it?— have no common answer.) Thus, the immediate result of privileging mind over body is a set of political attitudes and behaviors that put an extraordinary premium on liberty — on the rational, autonomous, independent, self-determining, isolated, separated, unique person being able to think, do, and be whatever he or she deems worthy.[17]

Radical and cultural feminists reject the "male" metaphysics that guides both liberal feminist and traditional thought— be it liberal or conservative. West points out that the central insight of most radical and cultural feminists is "that women are 'essentially connected,' not 'essentially separate,' from the rest of human life, both maternally, through pregnancy, intercourse, and breast-feeding, and existentially, through the moral and practical life."[18] In West's estimation a connection thesis, not a separation thesis, guides radical and cultural feminists, but takes them in two very different directions.

Following the lead of thinkers like Carol Gilligan[19] and Nel Noddings,[20] whose "feminine" approaches to ethics valorize the traits and behaviors traditionally associated with women—sharing, giving, empathy, sympathy, nurturance, and so on—cultural feminists stress women's different voice of caring. They believe that women value relationships and strive to create and maintain them. For women, connection *is* the

raison d'etre. Young girls, who supposedly do not experience the
"break" with the mother that boys do, experience connection
concomitantly with the formation of their identity. The
connection thesis, filtered through the lens of cultural feminism,
produces a completely different picture of morality than does
masculinist legal theory: As expressed by Robin West, "Intimacy
and the ethic of care constitute the entailed *values* of the
existential state of connection with others, just as autonomy and
freedom constitute the entailed values of the existential state of
separation from others for men."[21] Indeed, separation is cultural
feminism's *harm.*

Radical feminists paint the darker side of the connection
thesis. They agree with cultural feminists that connection is
women's fundamental reality, but they do not believe this
connection is a cause for celebration. They observe that
women's "connection" sets women up for exploitation and
misery: "Invasion and intrusion, rather than intimacy,
nurturance and care, is the unofficial story of women's subjective
experience of connection."[22] Women are connected to others,
most especially through the experience of heterosexual
intercourse and pregnancy. But when the sugar-coating is licked
off, these "connecting" experiences taste of women's violation.
This harm is unique to women; men cannot understand.
Whereas men fear annihilation, isolation, or disintegration of
their artificially constructed communities, women fear
occupation: "Both intercourse and pregnancy are literal, physical,
material invasions and occupations of the body. The fetus, like
the penis, literally occupies my body."[23] According to radical
feminists, women actually value and crave "individuation" —
the freedom to pursue their own ends and gain "solitude, self-
regard, self-esteem, linear thinking, legal rights, and principled
thoughts."[24] But this is the value they dare not express. In a
society that rewards self-sacrificial women and frowns upon
independent ones, self-expression may be dangerous. Men try
to control women through fear of violent retribution (rape) or
emotional revenge (divorce or spinsterhood). Thus, it may be
safer for women to acquiesce to men's wishes: to be "good girls."

Yet even as they diverge in their reaction to connection, both radical and cultural feminists hold connection to be fundamental to the female experience. Likewise, no matter how they interpret the reality of human beings' (that is, men's) separation, liberal legalism, critical legalism, traditional conservatism, and liberal feminism accept the reality of separation at the ontological level. Thus, because traditional jurisprudence is built upon the separation thesis, it cannot comprehend the connection thesis in either its positive or negative form. West comments that because "the laws we actually have are 'masculine' both in terms of their intended beneficiary and in authorship,"[25] they have difficulty recognizing and remedying what harms and disempowers women. If we accept West's critique, the implications for any discussion of the relationship between law and morality are powerful. When it comes to women's issues, the law cannot *see*, or see very clearly, what the actual *moral* problems are, let alone discuss or remedy them.

SURROGATE MOTHERHOOD: A CASE STUDY

Keeping the preceding analysis in mind, it is now appropriate to return to the Hart-Devlin debate with a specific women's issue in mind: surrogate motherhood. There are two types of surrogate mothers: those who gestate an embryo genetically related to them (partial surrogacy) and those who gestate an embryo genetically unrelated to them (full surrogacy).[26] In cases of partial surrogacy, a woman agrees (1) to be artificially inseminated with the sperm of a man who is not her husband; (2) to carry the subsequent pregnancy to term for a fee (commercial surrogacy); and to relinquish the child at birth to the people who have contracted to rear it. Although the contractual arrangements are the same in cases of full surrogacy, the medical ones are not, since the woman gestates an embryo that is not hers genetically. In an effort to minimize the complexities of surrogacy arrangements, the discussion to follow will focus, as much as possible, on commercial, partial surrogacy.

If someone asked Devlin about surrogacy arrangements, he would probably agree that although the House of Lords made a mistake in the 1960s when it decriminalized prostitution — selling one's sexual services— it acted correctly when it passed the Surrogacy Arrangements Act in 1985, criminalizing the practice of commercial surrogate motherhood— the selling of one's reproductive services. Lawyers, physicians, and social workers are subject to fines and/or imprisonment if they facilitate in any way a surrogacy arrangement.[27] In addition, publishers, directors, and managers of newspapers, periodicals, and telecommunications systems are subject to fines or imprisonment if they accept ads such as "womb for hire" or "couple willing to pay royally for host womb."[28]

The authors of the Surrogacy Arrangement Act apparently relied on the principle of legal moralism, according to which a person's liberty may be restricted to prevent immoral conduct on his or her part. In other words, they did not argue that commercial surrogate motherhood always or usually has *harmful* consequences. Rather, they proclaimed in the manner of Devlin, "Even in compelling medical circumstances the danger of exploitation of one human being by another appears to the majority of us far to outweigh the potential benefits, in almost every case. That people would treat others as a means to their own ends, however desirable the consequences, must always be liable to moral objection."[29] People should not sell either their sexual or their reproductive services. Certainly, they should not sell the children whom they have gestated; doing so undermines the institution of marriage and the biological family. Without marriage and the family as society has known them, society will crumble. The sins of prostitutes and surrogate mothers will be visited on us all, as sexuality and reproduction erupt from the structures society has so painstakingly constructed for them. The chaos we have come from will replace the order we have created. *Men* will stand naked and alone, stripped bare of the institutions they have devised to link themselves to women and children. Women must not destroy men's institutions, their artificial communities, for in doing so they will return humankind to its original state of nature.

In contrast to the conservative Devlin, the liberal Hart would reason that since it is not the law's business to prohibit unharmful commercial sex between consenting adults, neither is it the law's business to prohibit unharmful commercial reproduction between consenting adults. Just because the majority of a society may think it is morally wrong for women to sell their reproductive services does not mean that the law should ban commercial surrogacy arrangements. Unless it can be empirically proven that surrogate mothers, the persons who contract for their services, or the children born to them are significantly harmed by the contractual relationship that binds them together, there is no justification for the law to interfere with their right to procreate.

Liberals admit that there is some anecdotal evidence to support the claim that surrogacy arrangements can result in harm. Several surrogate mothers have blackmailed contracting couples, threatening to abort or keep the child unless more money is forthcoming.[30] Similarly, several contracting couples have bullied and badgered the surrogate mothers who serve them, treating them like mere fetal "containers."[31] Even worse, several of the children born of surrogate mothers have been rejected by all of their "parents" on the grounds that no one bargained for a defective child.[32] Yet, as liberals usually see it, most of these harms can be eliminated, or at least substantially ameliorated, with rigorous medical screening, sensitive psychological counselling, and carefully-crafted legal contracts. They maintain that surrogate motherhood is probably no more or less harmful than any other form of human reproduction that requires more than the energies, efforts, and endowments of one married couple.

Throughout the ages, says lawyer John A. Robertson, "collaborative reproduction" has assumed many forms: "Children have often been reared by genetically unrelated stepparents, wet-nurses, nannies, babysitters, and other surrogates."[33] If the law did not ban any of these past practices, it should not ban a practice such as surrogate motherhood simply because the majority of society reacts negatively to a "technological" variation on the collaborative reproduction theme. If it is not harmful to rear children to whom one is not genetically related, it cannot be somehow harmful to rear children to whom one is not gestationally related. If adoption is legally permitted, then surrogate motherhood should be legally permitted. Provided that the contracting couple and the surrogate mother enter into and conclude their negotiations freely, and provided that they fully intend to abide by the terms of their mutual contract, there is no particular reason to be concerned about their arrangement. On the contrary. With rare exception, their arrangement will produce more benefits than harms. The contracting couple will be overjoyed that their wish for a baby has finally come true; the surrogate mother will be glad to have served, admittedly for a fee, the contracting couple in their time of need; and the child will find himself or herself very much wanted and loved.[34] Thus, from the liberal perspective of a thinker like Hart, there is no reason for the law to ban the practice of commercial surrogate motherhood, especially because any such ban would encroach on individuals' rights to procreate.

Liberal feminists do not add anything essentially new to a Hart-inspired argument. However, they are much more attentive to how surrogacy arrangements affect *women* than classical liberals are. Typically, liberal feminists argue that (1) women should be permitted to use whatever reproduction-controlling or reproduction-aiding technologies they wish, provided that they do not harm anyone in the process; and (2) if women want to be treated as autonomous persons, then they must act like autonomous persons, living up to the terms of any contract to whose terms they have freely consented. Liberal feminist Lori B. Andrews observes that supporting a ban on surrogate motherhood equals inviting the government to dictate "the circumstances under which a woman should be allowed to have a child and under which families may be formed."[35] If such government intervention is anathema to women insofar as contraception, abortion, and sterilization are concerned, it should be anathema to women insofar as artificial insemination, in vitro fertilization, and surrogate motherhood are concerned. Andrews also believes that a woman's right to procreate includes her right to enter into a surrogacy arrangement. Andrews is quick to note, however, that any such decision must be a fully informed and consensual one, and that in order to be legally enforceable a surrogacy arrangement must not violate a woman's abortion rights.[36] Contracting couples may not require surrogate mothers to sacrifice their health or their life for the fetus's sake.

Radical feminists are deeply distressed that liberal feminists claim that choice is the moral issue in surrogacy arrangements. In radical feminists' estimation, *control*, not *choice*, is the moral issue for women. They argue that when a woman agrees to sell her reproductive services to an infertile couple, her "consent" is more often the product of economic coercion than of free choice. Like most prostitutes, most surrogate mothers are much poorer than their clients. Unable to get decent jobs, women are often driven to sell their bodies, the only possessions they have that anyone seems to want. Saying that a woman chooses to do this means saying that when forced to choose between being poor and being exploited, a woman may choose being exploited as the lesser of the two evils.[37] Radical feminists often note that although some surrogacy agencies refuse to accept indigent women into their program,[38] other agencies prefer poor women, especially Third-World women, reasoning that poor women, especially if they have children of their own, are unlikely to change their minds and want to keep the babies that they are gestating for profit.[39]

The fact that surrogacy arrangements may lead to women's exploitation certainly counts against them in the radical feminists' estimation; but the fact that they make women parties to their own *occupation* is unforgivable. Radical feminists suggest that the married woman who serves as a surrogate is doubly invaded when she sells her gestational services in order to provide her own children with some benefits they would otherwise not have. Under such circumstances, radical feminists see surrogate motherhood adding insult to injury. Having already sacrificed her own interests to those of their children, the surrogate mother surrenders her bodily integrity yet again: not to further her own interests, but those of her first invaders.

Radical feminists emphasize the fact that the siren call to self-sacrificial or voluntary invasion does not even have to include promises of money. Just as prostitutes are not born but made by a society that teaches girls that, if all else fails, they can always sell their bodies to men, surrogate mothers are not born but made by a society that teaches girls that they are *better* than boys because they are so willing to share all that they have, including their bodies. Society tries to trick girls/women into *enjoying* invasion, be it sexual invasion or reproductive invasion. Because *only* women can be mothers, surrogate motherhood often serves as a "compassion trap" for women.[40] An appeal is made to generous, loving, altruistic women to step forward and give the gift of a new life to a desperately lonely, unfulfilled infertile couple by surrendering their bodily integrity for nine months, typically in service of a strange *man's* genetic continuity. The fact that approximately one-third of all the women who answer this appeal have either had an abortion or given up a child for adoption strengthens the radical feminist suspicion that deep and dark forces are driving women to be surrogate mothers even when it may not be in their best interests to do so[41] — indeed, even when they appear to be punishing themselves for having failed to preserve some of their past connections.

The concerns of cultural feminists about surrogacy arrangements are quite different from those of radical feminists. They worry not so much about questions of occupation, but about questions of division. They fear that surrogacy arrangements, improperly handled by the law, might create even more splits and schisms among women than the ones that currently exist. The gap between economically privileged women and economically disadvantaged women is already large enough without encouraging relatively rich women to use— o r let their husbands use— relatively poor women to meet their reproductive needs, adding childbearing services to the childrearing services that poor women have traditionally provided to rich women.[42] For some well-to-do women paying, or letting their husbands pay, poorer women to be "invadees" may constitute escape from an invasion they themselves may fear. As reported a few years ago in *Time* magazine, it was not that Elizabeth Stern was infertile; it was that she feared the risks of pregnancy.[43]

Reflecting upon the ways in which the law facilitates the segmentation of reproduction as if it were simply a form of production, feminist Gena Corea sees the law as building *barriers* between childbegetters, childbearers, and childrearers. In the future, no one woman will beget, bear, and rear a child. Rather, genetically superior women will beget embryos in vitro; strong-bodied women will carry these test-tube babies to term; and sweet-tempered women will rear these newborns from infancy to adulthood.[44]

As a result of this undesirable division of labor, Corea fears that the fictional dystopia Margaret Atwood describes in her novel, *The Handmaid's Tale,* may yet become a reality. In the Republic of Gilead, Atwood's fictional dystopia, women are reduced to their respective functions. There are the Marthas, or domestics; the Wives, or social secretaries and functionaries; the Jezebels, or sex prostitutes; and the Handmaids, or reproductive prostitutes. One of the most degrading Gileadean practices, from a woman's perspective, consists of the so-called Commanders engaging in ritualistic sexual intercourse with their Wives. The Wife, who is infertile, lies down on a bed with her legs spread open. The Handmaid, one of the few fertile women in the environmentally-polluted and war-ravaged Gilead, then assumes this same position but with her head cradled between the spread legs of the wife, whereupon the Commander engages in sexual intercourse not with his Wife, but with the Handmaid. If the Handmaid becomes pregnant, the child she bears is regarded as that of the Commander— and as footnote to him, his Wife. On the day the Handmaid gives birth to the child, however, the Commander is absent from the picture. The Wife simulates labor pains, the Handmaid has labor pains, and all the Wives and Handmaids in Gilead gather around the laboring Wife and Handmaid, experiencing through them an ephemeral moment of female bonding— of women's pride, passion, and power.[45]

After one such birthday, the central character, a woman named Offred, thinks back to better times, and speaks in her mind to her mother, who had been a feminist leader: "Can you hear me? You wanted a woman's culture. Well, now there is one. It isn't what you meant, but it exists. Be thankful for small mercies."[46] And, of course, they are *very* small mercies, for with the exception of birthdays— those rare occasions when a Handmaid manages to produce a child— women have little contact with one another. The Marthas, Wives, Jezebels, and Handmaids are segregated by function; and what contact women do have— even within their own class— is largely silent, for they are permitted to speak to one another only when absolutely necessary. They lack connection.

Cultural feminists also fear that surrogacy arrangements, improperly handled by the law, may prevent a biological parent, in this case the surrogate mother, from maintaining appropriate connections with her child. Philosophers Hilde and James Nelson argue that when parents bring a child into existence, they "create a vulnerability"[47] for whom they are *personally* responsible. Having created a person with a set of basic needs, one parent may not let another parent, however willing, assume full childrearing responsibilities. Both parents owe a "debt" "to the child."[48] Mom may not mind if dad largely ignores their children, but the children may wonder why their dad bothered to procreate them if he had no intention of playing a role in their lives. Analogously, even if a contracting couple is willing to rear the child they contracted for by themselves, it is still the surrogate mother's responsibility to help rear her child, unless she is unfit to do so.[49] A surrogate mother may not absent herself from her child's life simply by offering the excuse that the contracting couple will probably discharge their parental responsibilities excellently.[50] For all she knows, the people who purchased her gestational services may turn out to be failures as parents, a misfortune she will be in no position to remedy, once she forsakes her parental rights over the child. Because the only person's actions she can control are her own, a surrogate mother owes it to her child to maintain a relationship with him or her.[51]

Despite their serious reservations about improperly handled surrogacy arrangements, cultural feminists nonetheless hold out hope for properly handled surrogacy arrangements. Sociologist

Barbara Rothman has urged contracting couples to treat their child's surrogate mother as if she were his or her aunt.[52] Other cultural feminists suggest that the law recognize, as family units, families in which a child has two mothers and one father. Still other cultural feminists insist that the law recognize that a parent's gestational relationship to a child supersedes any contractual or even genetic relationship a parent may have to a child.

Lawyer George Annas argues that there are at least two moral reasons why a gestational mother should be legally presumed to have the parental right and responsibility to rear the child. First, because the gestational mother has made such a large "biological and psychological" investment in the child, she deserves to maintain her relationship with the child unless she is an "unfit" person— a child abuser, for example.[53] Second, because the gestational mother "will of necessity be present at birth and immediately thereafter to care for the child," designating her the legal or "natural mother" of the child is more likely to protect his or her interests than any alternative arrangement.[54] Initially, what makes a person a parent is not the mere intention to be a parent, nor even the fact that without one's genetic material no child would have been conceived, but the fact that without one's lived commitment to that child during pregnancy no child would have been born.

CONCLUSION

Once their stances on the separation versus the connection thesis is understood, it is possible to predict with relative confidence what liberal, radical, or cultural feminists will say about any so-called "woman's issue" and how what they say will depart both from the liberal and conservative traditions. For liberal feminists, who want to play by men's rules and somehow win equality, the law-morality debate is largely a meaningful one. Liberal feminists understand the male rhetoric behind legal discourse. They accept the separation thesis because for them morality is about autonomy, about choice. As long as the law gives women their freedom, and preserves rather than interferes with their choices, women are well served. Admittedly, sometimes male liberals do not see the harms that female liberals see. But with a little guidance, they can be brought to see the light by casting "women's issues" in "male terms," like talking about surrogacy arrangements in terms of fair contracts. Basically, as far as liberal feminists are concerned, as long as we follow the standard liberal views of a John Stuart Mill or H.L.A. Hart, things will turn out all right for women in the end.

For radical feminists, the old law-morality debate is empty because the structure of the law harms women, that is, it keeps women subordinate and men dominate. As they see it, the same strategies that guide feminist approaches to ethics must guide feminist approaches to jurisprudence. According to philosopher Alison Jaggar, in order to count as a *feminist* approach to ethics, the approach must seek: (1) to articulate moral critiques of actions and practices that perpetuate women's subordination; (2) to prescribe morally justified ways of resisting such actions and practices; and (3) to envision morally desirable alternatives that will promote women's emancipation.[55] Jaggar's definition resonates with MacKinnon's point about what counts as a real moral issue for women. How can Devlin worry about prostitution or surrogacy unraveling the fabric of society without acknowledging the domination-subordination status quo that exploits women and drives them to such straits? How can Hart wax poetic about everything between two "consenting adults" being quite all right— as if women had the power to consent or choose within the confines of a patriarchal society? In short, how can the classic law-morality debate be moral when it is written by, for, and about males only?

Likewise, those "cultural feminists" who focus on a feminine ethics of care rather than a feminist ethics of power strongly feel the inadequacy of the present law-morality debate. Cultural feminists like Carol Gilligan add to the universal voice of justice the particular voice of care. They view themselves as playing "a new game whose parameters have not been spelled out, whose values are not well known, as at the beginning of the process of inquiry, in which the methods themselves will have to be re-

examined because the old methods are from the old game."[56]
The law-morality debate might be reframed as follows: What
would one say about regulating morality if the focus was on
caring, or the relationship between individuals and between
individuals and society? What would one say about the
prostitute if the focus was on her, not as a threat to the fabric of
society (Devlin), not as a free adult making a choice (Hart), not
as a subordinated victim of patriarchy (MacKinnon), but as a
human being with a possibly damaged network of relationships
and in need of caring? What would one say about the surrogate
mother if she was seen not as a baby seller, not as a woman
exploring her economic and reproductive options, not as a paid
victim of invasion, but as one human being trying to aid other
human beings in building a network of childcarers that included
herself?

Clearly, the questions that cultural feminists raise are ones
that the law should answer. But not quite yet. Any attempt to
answer the cultural feminist questions of *difference* would falter
to approximately the same degree that the law has failed in its
attempt to answer the liberal feminist questions of women's
sameness to men. The law cannot fully appreciate what
constitutes harm to women (or to minorities), or what constitutes
a good human relationship as opposed to a bad one for women
(or minorities), unless it is first willing to answer the questions of
power that radical feminists have posed— even if answering
these questions means that the law has to change fundamentally.

Our first task must be to explode the structures, systems,
lifestyles, and attitudes of domination and subordination that
tradition has permitted to flourish. Only when tradition
expresses a willingness to discard its debris of oppression,
repression, and suppression, will women (and minorities)— the
representatives of difference— find enough space to help
reconfigure a legal system that is better equipped to prevent not
only human beings' other-directed, caring actions from
continually mutating into acts of masochism, control, and/or
servility, but also their self-affirming, free actions from
continually mutating into acts of sadism, alienation, and/or
arrogance. Questions must be asked about power before

questions are asked about goodness. Devlin and Hart asked the wrong question. We need not worry about the relationship *between* law and morality. First, we must worry whether or not the law, and its structures, are moral themselves. The questions must be right, in order to get the answers right. Perhaps the new question should be "How can we restructure the law so that it is fully moral?" Then, when the law itself is not oppressive, one may ask whether the law should control morality. Until then, however, tradition may be unsafe for women (and minorities) either to honor or to obey, let alone love.

NOTES

1. Joel Feinberg, *Social Philosophy* (Englewood Cliffs, N.J.: Prentice-Hall, 1973), 36-54.
2. *The Wolfenden Report: Report of the Committee on Homosexual Offenses and Prostitution* (N.Y.: Stein and Day, 1963), 5, 19. The Wolfenden Report was prepared for British Parliament by the committee at the request of the Moral Welfare Council of the Church of England to consider "(a) the law and practice relating to homosexual offenses and the treatment of persons convicted of such offenses by the courts; and (b) the law and practice relating to offenses against the criminal law in connection with prostitution and solicitation for immoral purposes, and to report what changes, if any, are in our opinion desirable."
3. Quoted in Basil Mitchell, *Law, Morality and Religion in Secular Society* (London: Oxford University Press, 1967), 10 (my emphasis).
4. Ibid., 10-11.
5. Rosemarie Tong, "Women, Pornography, and the Law," *Academe* 73 (September-October 1987): 14.
6. Catharine A. MacKinnon, "Not a Moral Issue," in Catharine A. MacKinnon, *Feminism Unmodified: Discourses on Life and Law* (Cambridge, Mass.: Harvard University Press, 1987), 147-62.
7. Ibid., 147.
8. See Catharine A. MacKinnon, *Sexual Harassment of Working Women* (New Haven, Conn.: Yale University Press, 1979).
9. Isabel Marcus and Paul J. Spiegelman, "Feminist Discourse, Moral Values, and the Law— A Conversation," *Buffalo Law Review* 3 4 (Winter 1985): 13-14.
10. Ibid., p. 15.
11. Robin West, "Jurisprudence and Gender," 55(1) *The University of Chicago Law Review* (Winter 1988): 1.

12. Ibid., 6.
13. Ibid., 7.
14. Ibid., 12.
15. Alison M. Jaggar, *Feminist Politics and Human Nature* (Totowa, N.J.: Rowman & Allenheld, 1983), 28.
16. For someone who disputes the contention that only members of the human species can be persons, see Peter Singer, *Practical Ethics* (New York: Cambridge University Press, 1979).
17. Jaggar,*Feminist Politics*, 40-42.
18. West, *Jurisprudence and Gender*, 3.
19. Carol Gilligan, *In a Difference Voice: Psychology (Cambridge: Harvard University Press, 1982)*.
20. Nel Noddings, *Caring, A Feminine Approach to Ethics and Moral Education* (Berkeley, Cal.: University of California Press, 1984).
21. West, "Jurisprudence and Gender," 18.
22. Ibid., 29.
23. Ibid., 34-35.
24. Ibid., 35.
25. Ibid., 60.
26. Peter Singer and Deanne Wells, *Making Babies: The New Science and Ethics of Conception* (N.Y.: Charles Scribner's Sons, 1985), 96.
27. Department of Health and Social Security, United Kingdom, *Report of the Committee of Inquiry into Human Fertilization and Embryology* (London: HMSO, July 1984), 47.
28. Surrogacy Arrangements Act 1985, United Kingdom, Chapter 49, 2, (1) (a)-(c).
29. Ibid., 3, (1)-(5).
30. Linda M. Whiteford and Marilyn L. Poland, eds., *New Approaches to Human Reproduction: Social and Ethical Dimensions* (Boulder, Colo.: Westview Press, 1989), 174, 189.
31. Larry Gostin, ed., *Surrogate Motherhood* (Bloomington: Indiana University Press, 1990), 51.
32. Whiteford and Poland, *New Approaches*, 192.
33. John A. Robertson, "Embryos, Families, and Procreative Liberty: The Legal Structure of the New Reproduction," *Southern California Law Review* 59 (July, 1986): 1001.
34. Gostin, *Surrogate Motherhood*, 133, 156, 158.
35. Lori B. Andrews, "Alternative Modes of Reproduction," in *Reproductive Laws for the 1990s*, ed. Sherrill Cohen and Nadine Taub (Clifton, N.J.: Humana Press, 1989), 365.
36. Ibid., 366.
37. Rosemarie Tong, "The Overdue Death of a Feminist Chameleon: Taking a Stand on Surrogacy Arrangements," *Journal of Social Philosophy* 21 (Fall/Winter 1990): 45.
38. Gena Corea, *The Mother Machine* (New York: Harper & Row, 1985), 230.

39. Robert H. Miller, "Surrogate Parenting: An Infant Industry Presents Society with Legal, Ethical Questions," 18(3) *Ob. Gyn. News* , 1-14 February 1983), 3.
40. Quoted in Corea, *The Mother Machine*, 231.
41. Patricia A. Avery, "Surrogate Mothers: Center of a New Storm," *U.S. News and World Report,* 6 June 1983), 76.
42. Rosemarie Tong, "The Overdue Death of a Feminist Chameleon," 48.
43. Richard Lacayo, "Whose Child Is This?" *Time*, 19 January 1987, 58.
44. Corea, *The Mother Machine*, 276.
45. Margaret Atwood, *The Handmaid's Tale* (Boston, Mass.: Houghton Mifflin, 1986), 93, 123.
46. Ibid., 127.
47. Hilde Lindemann Nelson and James Lindemann Nelson, "Cutting Motherhood in Two: Some Suspicions Concerning Surrogacy," *Hypatia* 4 (Fall 1989): 91.
48. Ibid., 93.
49. Ibid.
50. Ibid.
51. Ibid.
52. Barbara Katz Rothman, *Recreating Motherhood Ideology and Technology in a Patriarchal Society* (New York: W. W. Norton & Company, 1989), 255.
53. Sherman Elias and George J. Annas, "Social Policy Considerations in Noncoital Reproduction," *JAMA* 255 (3 January 1986): 67.
54. George J. Annas, "Death Without Dignity for Commercial Surrogacy: The Case of Baby M," *Hastings Center Report* 18 (April-May 1988), 23-24.
55. Quoted in Rosemarie Tong, *Feminine and Feminist Ethics* (Belmont, Cal.: Wadsworth Publishing Company, 1993), 10-11.
56. Ellen Goodman, "Whose Child?" *Charlotte Observer*, 28 October 1990, 3c.

7

Is There a Right to Life at the End of Life?

KATHLEEN M. BOOZANG

Is there a "right to life at the end of life?" This question reflects the growing trend of physician challenges to patient *demands* for continued treatment that physicians contend is futile or not cost-beneficial because the patient is either dying or dead. Physicians in increasing numbers argue that unreasonable patient requests for treatment violates physician autonomy and medical ethical prerogatives of beneficence, stewardship, and justice.

It will be argued in this essay that the legal principles that establish a dying patient's right to refuse unwanted medical treatment also protect the chronically or terminally ill patient's right to request life-sustaining treatment. These protections should not extend, however, to a patient who is legally dead. Also, according legal protection to the right to request continued life-sustaining treatment does not resolve the separate issue of whether public or private third-party payers should pay for such treatment.

The discussion of these topics will consist of two parts: first, the current status of right-to-die jurisprudence and the evolution of brain death criteria as a medical and legal standard for determining death will be briefly explained. Second, four case studies will be presented and analyzed to demonstrate how the right-to-life conflict arises. This analysis will also show how the liberty interest in life and the right-to-die jurisprudence protect a dying, but not dead, patient's decision to continue life-sustaining treatment.

OVERVIEW

Right-To-Die Jurisprudence

The patient's right to refuse unwanted life-sustaining medical treatment arises out of two legal theories: (1) federal constitutional interests in liberty, and (2) the common law doctrine of informed consent. Both the constitutional liberty interest and the common law right to informed consent rest fundamentally on classical liberal theories of self-determination. The United States Supreme Court recently held that the Fourteenth Amendment's guarantee that no state shall "deprive any person of life, liberty, or property without due process of law" incorporates a liberty interest in refusing unwanted medical treatment.[1] The doctrine of informed consent promotes patient self-determination, privacy and integrity by requiring physicians to obtain informed consent before treating the patient. The Supreme Court recognized, however, that rights of self-determination and the liberty interest in refusing unwanted medical treatment are not absolute. Consequently, courts balance four state interests against the patient's common law and constitutional rights to refuse treatment. These state interests include preservation and sanctity of life, prevention of suicide, protection of innocent third parties, and maintenance of the integrity of medical ethics.[2] Courts have generally held, however, that none of these four state interests outweighs the patient's right to refuse treatment except, perhaps, when the patient is pregnant.[3] Two landmark cases in right-to-die jurisprudence demonstrate how the courts have applied this theoretical framework, *In re Quinlan*[4] and *Cruzan v. Missouri Department of Health*.[5] In *Quinlan*, one of the first in a long line of right-to-die cases, the father of an irretrievably brain-damaged woman sought the withdrawal of his daughter's artificial life support. The New Jersey Supreme Court held that neither the state's interest in preservation and sanctity of life, nor the physician's claim that withdrawal of treatment conflicted with his professional judgment, outweighed the patient's interest in refusing unwanted medical treatment. The court based this conclusion on a federal constitutional right to privacy. After *Quinlan*, virtually every state appellate court confronted with a right-to-die case determined that a patient may refuse life-sustaining treatment based upon rights arising out of federal or state constitutional rights of privacy,[6] the common law doctrine of informed consent,[7] or both.[8] Having resolved the fundamental issue of whether a patient has a legally protected right to refuse life-sustaining treatment, state courts struggled to define the parameters of this right. The most difficult and divisive of these defining issues has been whether and how the right to die should be exercised by surrogate decision-makers on behalf of incompetent patients. These cases generally involve minors,[9] retarded adults,[10] or chronically or terminally ill patients[11] who are presently incompetent, and who may or may not have previously expressed their opinions about death-prolonging treatment. Because of the patient's incompetence, a surrogate decision-maker must ultimately determine the appropriate treatment for the patient.

State judiciaries' handling of cases involving incompetent patients can be divided into two basic categories: those that direct the surrogate decision-maker to decide according to an objective determination of the patient's best interests,[12] and those that direct the surrogate decision-maker to engage in a subjective determination of substituted judgment— that is, the surrogate decision-maker must make the treatment decision that the patient would have made if competent.[13] Substituted judgment jurisdictions are split in how they apply this test. Some states allow substituted judgment to be used even if the patient never expressed an opinion about life-sustaining treatment. The most extreme example is the use of substituted judgment when the patient is a child[14] or a retarded adult.[15] Other states are much more strict. They only allow the surrogate to request treatment withdrawal if the surrogate presents clear and convincing evidence that a decision to discontinue treatment reflects the patient's previously expressed wishes. For example, some states require evidence that the patient, while competent, explicitly stated that she would want treatment discontinued given her present condition.[16] Obviously, this purely objective standard is extremely difficult to satisfy and can make it nearly impossible to withdraw life-sustaining treatment.[17]

Indeed, in the *Cruzan* case, decided in 1989,[18] the U. S. Supreme Court was asked to decide whether the standard of clear and convincing evidence violated the incompetent patient's constitutional rights. In this case, Nancy Cruzan had been living in a persistent vegetative state (PVS) for six years when her case reached the Supreme Court. Her brain was severely and permanently atrophied. She was a spastic quadriplegic, which caused contraction of her extremities, and led to permanent muscle and tendon damage. Nancy possessed no cognitive or reflexive ability to swallow food, and would never regain these functions. She felt no pain and had no cognitive functioning. She was able to breathe on her own, and with continued feeding, had a life expectancy of thirty years. Significantly, Nancy's condition did not meet the statutory definition of death in Missouri; nor was she terminally ill.

Prior to her accident, Nancy had never memorialized her opinions about life-sustaining treatment. She had, however, expressed to a relative that she would only want to survive a serious injury or illness if she could, in her words, live halfway normally. In addition, family members testified that based on who Nancy was and how she lived her life, they felt certain that she would never have wanted to live in her present condition.

Nancy's parents filed a declaratory judgment action seeking authority to request discontinuation of Nancy's artificially provided nutrition and hydration. The trial court granted their request, holding that the state's refusal to comply with Nancy's parents' request violated Nancy's right to liberty under the Missouri and federal constitutions. The trial court found that Nancy's prior expressions indicated that she would not have wanted continued nutrition and hydration, and that no state interest outweighed her right to liberty. Both the state of Missouri and Nancy's appointed guardian *ad litem* appealed, although the guardian ad litem believed that withdrawal was in Nancy's best interests.

Reversing the lower court, the Missouri Supreme Court held that no unfettered right to privacy existed under the state constitution.[19] Turning to the federal constitution, the Missouri court concluded that the right to privacy did not encompass a right to terminate the provision of food and water to an incompetent patient. The court further stated that even if such a right did exist, Missouri's interest in sustaining life, particularly the life of someone who is not terminally ill, outweighed any privacy interest. Likewise, the court determined that the state's interest in preserving life outweighed any common law right under the doctrine of informed consent that Nancy may have to refuse treatment.

Subsequently, the U. S. Supreme Court agreed to accept Cruzan's case. In a plurality decision, the Supreme Court upheld the constitutionality of Missouri's clear and convincing evidence standard. This heightened evidentiary requirement, Chief Justice William Rehnquist reasoned, constituted a permissible means by which the state may protect patients against abuses by surrogate decision-makers, ensure the accuracy of substituted judgments, and protect against quality of life decisions being made for patients who would not have chosen to die. In sum, Rehnquist concluded that a state may "assert an unqualified interest in the preservation of human life to be weighed against the constitutionally protected interests of the individual."[20] Although the Cruzans lost their bid to withdraw Nancy's treatment, the case is important to the viability of the right to die because eight justices recognized a *competent* patient's liberty interest in refusing lifesaving treatment, including, presumably, nutrition and hydration.

Brain Death

Although issues arising out of the treatment of dying patients have captured the most attention over the last two decades, the concept of death has not escaped medical and legal attention. A conception of death consists of four elements: (1) a definition of what it means to die; (2) criteria for determining that death has occurred; (3) specific medical tests showing whether or not the criteria have been fulfilled;[21] and (4) the legal and social consequences of death. Although death is a process of deterioration, society has traditionally chosen a particular biological event to signify the moment of death. This moment is significant in that it not only establishes the time at which a person's existence has ended, but also radically alters his or her legal and moral relationship in society.[22] For example, death ends the decedent's marriage, shifts the financial responsibility for any unpaid hospital bills to the decedent's estate, triggers the payment of life insurance benefits, and causes the transfer of the decedent's property.[23]

The traditional biological event signifying death was, and continues to be, the permanent cessation of heart and lung functioning.[24] Before mechanical ventilators existed, the cessation of breathing, heartbeat, circulation, and brain functioning were interdependent and occurred relatively simultaneously,[25] thereby precluding a need to enunciate specifically whether the definition of death was brain-centered or heart-centered. Technological advancements in medicine interfered with the relative simultaneity of heart and brain functioning, however, and gave rise to calls for alternative criteria by which physicians could determine that the patient had died.[26] In addition, the advent of medicine's ability to transplant organs required the adoption of whole brain death so that viable, intact organs could be ethically and legally harvested from patients on artificial life support.[27] As a result, medicine proposed and the law adopted the whole brain standard as an alternative means of determining death.

Whole brain death refers to the permanent cessation of brain functioning at all levels, including the brain stem,[28] although isolated nests of neurons may continue to operate.[29] The majority of physicians, philosophers, and lawyers agree that determining death according to whole brain death criteria is medically, ethically, and legally acceptable. Today, most states recognize the concept of brain death either through its common law or statutes.[30]

Despite general acceptance of brain death, a growing body of physicians, philosophers, and lawyers urge that the whole-brain death standard should be replaced with higher-brain criteria[31] or neocortical death.[32] Neocortical death would occur when a person irretrievably loses consciousness. Neocortical theorists generally base their argument on two main theses. First, they believe that an irretrievable loss of consciousness or the capacity for social interaction should be considered the point of death.[33] Second, many neocortical theorists argue that adoption of whole- brain death standards signaled a *redefinition* of death from heart-centered to brain-centered criterion[34] and that a move to neocortical-death criterion maintains the concepts underlying whole brain death, which have already been adopted.[35]

Adoption of higher-brain criteria would expand the number of patients who are considered dead. For example, patients in persistent vegetative states[36] and anencephalic infants[37] would be classified as dead. Neocortical theorists believe that adoption of higher-brain criteria would resolve the medical, ethical, and legal struggles over discontinuing treatment of permanently unconscious patients. If neocortical death becomes the standard, physicians, families, and judges would no longer be required to engage in guessing games as to whether a PVS patient would want life-sustaining technologies to be withdrawn; the patient would be dead and treatment would terminate.[38] The inclusion of anencephalics within the definition of death would also alleviate the critical shortage of organs for neonates and infants. Current definitions of death prevent physicians from retrieving much needed organs from anencephalics while these infants are still breathing and their hearts are beating.

THE PATIENT'S RIGHT TO DEMAND
NON-BENEFICIAL TREATMENT: CASE STUDIES

Twenty years of right-to-die jurisprudence and the transition to brain death signifies only the beginning of society's struggle with the appropriate use of technology at the end of life. Having accepted that compelling dying patients to receive medical treatment violates their dignity, physicians now argue that dying patients should be affirmatively discouraged from receiving life-sustaining treatment. The following four cases illustrate whether there is a right to life at the end of life.

Case One

In re Wanglie,[39] a 1991 Minnesota case, represents one of the first cases involving physician attempts to discontinue end-of-life treatment against family wishes. Mrs. Helga Wanglie was an eighty-six-year-old woman in a persistent vegetative state (PVS) who was being kept alive by a respirator, tube feedings, and a myriad of other life-sustaining technologies. It appeared that Mrs. Wanglie had never expressed her preferences about life-sustaining treatment.[40] Mrs. Wanglie's $700,000 bill for her care was being paid for by Medicare and a private insurer.[41] In the summer of 1990, the physicians suggested to the Wanglie family that the respirator should be withdrawn since it was not benefiting Mrs. Wanglie. According to Dr. Miles, the petitioning physician, "the grieving husband was simply mistaken about whether the respirator was benefiting his wife."[42] The family rejected the physician's advice, stating "that physicians should not play God, that the patient would not be better off dead, that removing life support showed moral decay in our civilization, and that a miracle could occur."[43] After months of disagreement between family and physicians, Mrs. Wanglie's physicians sought the appointment of a conservator in lieu of Mrs. Wanglie's husband to make medical decisions on her behalf. The probate court refused the physicians' request for a conservator. The court found that "[o]ther than proving that Oliver Wanglie does not accept the advice and counsel of the physicians treating Helga Wanglie and refuses to consent to remove the ventilator which breathes for her, [Dr.] Miles has offered no evidence that Oliver Wanglie is incompetent to discharge the trust as Conservator of the Person of his wife."[44] After nineteen months on the respirator, Mrs. Wanglie died.

Dr. Miles justified the court action that he sought on two bases: physician autonomy and stewardship. First, Dr. Miles argued that respect for patient autonomy does not allow patients to require physicians to prescribe fruitless or inappropriate treatments.[45] He did not argue that Mrs. Wanglie's treatment was futile because it was, of course, keeping her alive.[46] However, by deciding that maintaining Mrs. Wanglie on a respirator for nineteen months was fruitless, the physicians implicitly concluded that Mrs. Wanglie's continued life had no value. In other words, the physicians appear to contend that at some point (to be determined by the treating physician) the state interest in protecting physician autonomy has more value than the patient's life. This conclusion necessarily involves a quality of life assessment which neither physicians nor society should make. Until the physicians declare that a patient is dead, she retains her rights to liberty and self-determination.

Two commentators have rejected the argument that protection of self-determination and patient autonomy embrace the right to continued life-sustaining treatment.[47] They contend that because the legal right to refuse treatment is premised on the law of battery, it is illogical to extend the doctrine to incorporate a right to demand treatment. This argument ignores the values of patient dignity and self-determination sought to be protected by the doctrine of informed consent. In cases in which the federal constitution is implicated, the argument overlooks the patient's constitutionally protected liberty interest in life,[48] which was a primary focus of the Supreme Court's holding in *Cruzan*.[49] In addition, the liberty interest in refusing medical care recognized by the *Cruzan* court to protect patient self-determination is much broader than merely being free from unconsented bodily interference. According to Justice O'Connor, it protects the patient's "freedom to determine the course of her treatment."[50] Together, the liberty interests recognized by the Supreme Court in *Cruzan* should allow a patient to determine the extent to which she will pursue treatment that sustains her life.

Wanglie's physicians also sought the appointment of an alternative decision-maker on the basis of the "ethic of 'stewardship'."[51] This notion of stewardship, according to Dr. Miles, rests on fairness to people who have pooled their resources to ensure access to care and invests in physicians a

responsibility to counsel against or deny inappropriate care.[52]
The physician's exercise of the ethic of stewardship in this
manner raises several concerns. The patient-physician
relationship is widely understood as a fiduciary one in which the
physician's loyalty and duty are owed exclusively to his
patient.[53] By exercising an ethic of stewardship as described by
Wanglie's physicians, the physician deviates from his loyalty to
the patient he is treating and arguably breaches his fiduciary
responsibilities to that patient. If the patient-physician
relationship operates pursuant to this ethic of stewardship, the
doctrine of informed consent should require the physician to
inform the patient that his refusal to adhere to her treatment
request arises out of concerns about resource allocation, thereby
allowing the patient to obtain another health-care provider, if
she so desires.

Of greatest concern is the failure to distinguish between the
issues of whether a patient has a right to request life-sustaining
treatment and whether and who should pay for such treatment.
Neither the law nor societal consensus has accorded physicians
the authority to deny treatment out of concerns for resource
allocation to a patient whose health care bills are being paid. In
addition, no standards exist to guide physicians who assume this
responsibility of bedside rationing. Without such consensus or
standards, physicians' assumption of power to make unilateral
decisions that a particular treatment is not cost-beneficial
potentially subjects the patient to her physician's subconscious
biases.[54] Consequently, physicians should continue to respect
the patient's constitutional and common law rights to request or
refuse life-sustaining treatment and leave the decisions as to
whether such care will be paid for to third-party payers and
state or federal legislatures.

In sum, the premise underlying informed consent is that a
patient may independently accept or reject medical care.
Allowing physicians to override decisions to continue the
patient's life would strip the patient of her individual autonomy
and self-determination. Courts should protect a medical
decision in favor of life just as strongly as they protect the right
to die. The patient's liberty interest in refusing unwanted

treatment should also protect the patient's decision to choose life-sustaining treatment. It is this author's belief that the right to continue life is stronger than the right to die because the Fourteenth Amendment also guarantees a liberty interest in life. This conclusion does not dictate, however, that any third party payer must pay for the continued provision of life-sustaining treatment.

Case Two

A second case, which did not ultimately involve court resolution, further exemplifies patient-physician conflicts over appropriate care for dying patients. This situation arose out of the treatment of a five-year-old girl with minimal neurological functions and a seizure disorder. The child was admitted to the hospital for respiratory distress that required maximum ventilator support. The child's parents demanded that everything be done to prolong their child's life, including any experimental treatment. The treating physicians believed that the child would never be removed from the ventilator, her chances of survival were about 10 percent, and her neurological impairments were untreatable. Based on this prognosis, the attending health care providers concluded that continuing maximum therapy was medically inappropriate, and that the child should be allowed to die. The parents, who were Catholic, rejected any suggestions that treatment should be discontinued, based upon their religious beliefs that suffering is a blessing from God and results in the saving of souls. The physicians ultimately sought legal advice to determine whether the parents had the legal authority to require that the child be subjected to continued treatment and a prolonged life.

This case implicates at least three issues not presented in *Wanglie*. First, whether parents' fundamental liberty interest in making decisions regarding their child's welfare protects a parental decision to continue life-sustaining treatment for their child; second, whether the substituted judgment or best interest standard set forth in right-to-die cases applies to minors; and third, whether the First Amendment Free Exercise Clause protects a religiously-based parental decision to continue their child's life-sustaining treatment. One could interpret *Cruzan* as allowing a state to preclude the withholding of life-sustaining treatment from any infant or immature minor since it would be impossible for a child to satisfy the standard of clear and convincing evidence. However, notwithstanding *Cruzan*, it would seem that the parents' constitutionally protected interests in determining their child's well-being, particularly when supported by the Free Exercise Clause, provide them with the legal authority to decide whether it is in their child's best interest to continue to receive life-sustaining treatment. It is important to note that the federal constitutional arguments discussed here are inapplicable if the state is not exercising authority over the parents and hospital. In such a situation, a court might rely on its state constitution or common law, which sometimes reflects some of the protections afforded by the federal constitution.

The several courts that have confronted withdrawal of treatment decisions involving minors appear to agree that the parents, if involved in the child's care,[55] are presumed to be in the best position to determine what is in their child's best interest.[56] Relying on a long line of U. S. Supreme Court cases according constitutional protection to parental autonomy over their children, the Supreme Court of Georgia observed in *In re L.H.R.* that the "right of the parent to speak for the minor child is so imbedded in our tradition and common law that it has been suggested that the constitution requires that the state respect the parent's decision in some areas."[57] Engaging in similar analysis, the Michigan Supreme Court in *Rosebush v. Oakland County Prosecutor*[58] also concluded that "[i]t is well established that parents speak for their minor children in matters of medical treatment [citations omitted]. Because medical treatment includes the decision to decline lifesaving intervention, it follows that parents are empowered to make decisions regarding withdrawal or withholding of lifesaving or life-prolonging measures on behalf of their children."[59] Thus, it appears that precedent exists to support either or both common law and constitutional rights of parents to make medical decisions on behalf of their children.

Having established that in most cases parents are the appropriate decision-makers for their children, the question remains as to how the parents should best effectuate the decision about withdrawing or continuing life-sustaining medical care. As with incompetent adults, some courts commend parents to utilize a best interests test;[60] others prefer a substituted judgment approach;[61] and still others endorse substituted judgment if evidence exists of the child's preferences but allow best interests if such preferences are unknown.[62] Even those courts that extend substituted judgment to children recognize, however, that they are essentially engaging in a best interest analysis that takes into account the particular circumstances of the individual child.[63]

No reason exists to engage in a different analysis when parents desire to continue rather than terminate life-sustaining treatment for their child. The two cases in which physicians disagreed with parental decisions to continue treatment of their minor children appear to support this conclusion. *In re Jane Doe*[64] is a 1992 case which arose out of a disagreement between the parents of a thirteen-year-old child about discontinuing the child's treatment. The child suffered from a degenerative neurological disease from which she was apparently dying at the time the dispute arose. The child's mother concurred with the physicians' suggestion to discontinue life-sustaining treatment but her father did not. As a result of the parents' continued disagreement, the hospital filed a declaratory judgment action seeking guidance as to which of the parent's wishes it should follow. The hospital did not allege child abuse but did allege that continued aggressive treatment of the child constituted medical abuse. By the time of the hearing, the mother no longer supported termination of treatment. Consequently, the trial court entered an order enjoining the hospital from terminating treatment without both parents' concurrence. The state appealed, claiming that the child was not eligible for withdrawal of life support in any event and that a hospital does not have standing to advocate an alternative course of treatment when the parents agree about the course of care for their child.

Although the child died several weeks after the trial court's order, the appellate court considered the case and held that the Doe parents could legally refuse treatment on their child's behalf without seeking prior court approval. The court stated that continued treatment was prolonging her death, rather than her life, and that there existed no state interest in maintaining life support systems. The court further stated, however, that the parents also could have consented to continued treatment for the child. The court declined to resolve the state's claim that the hospital had no standing to challenge a parental decision to continue treatment.

In *In re Baby K*,[65] two federal courts in Virginia were forced to address the situation where a child's parents disagreed with each other and the hospital about their child's case. Baby K suffers from anencephaly.[66] She cannot hear or see and is permanently unconscious. No treatment exists for anencephaly and the child's physicians believe that continued treatment, including ventilator care, serves no therapeutic or palliative purpose.[67] Baby K's mother opposes the discontiuation of ventilator treatment because she believes that her Christian faith requires the protection of all life, that God should decide when her daughter should die, and that a miracle is possible.[68] The child's physicians, father,[69] and guardian ad litem[70] believe that ventilator treatment is futile and should be discontinued. As a result of continuing disagreement among the parents and physicians, the hospital sought a declaration that it would not be violating a variety of federal and state laws[71] if it failed to adhere to the mother's wishes.

The trial and appellate courts concurred in their refusal to allow the hospital to override the wishes of Baby K's mother. The trial court decision is most relevant to our discussion. The lower court explicitly concluded that a parent's Fourteenth Amendment right to raise children and First Amendment right to free exercise protect parental decisions regarding their child's medical care.[72] The court also held that when a conflict arises between the constitutional right to life and the liberty interest in refusing medical treatment, the right to life must prevail.[73] The appellate court agreed with the lower court's ultimate conclusion, but did not discuss the parents' constitutional rights.

In re Jane Doe and, to a lesser extent, *In re Baby K* indicate that a court confronted with a conflict between physicians seeking to terminate life-sustaining treatment and parents seeking to continue treatment defer to the parents' decision. The constitution's protection of parental autonomy and common law recognition of parents' rights to make health care decisions for their children require such deference. A conflict about whether to continue life-sustaining treatment ultimately involves value judgments about what is in the child's best interest. As long as the parents are not demanding treatment that would have no plausible benefit for their child (e.g., laetrile for cancer or renal dialysis for a healthy child),[74] neither physicians nor courts should seek to override the parental decision to continue treatment that sustains their child's life.

Case Three

The third case is a composite of a debate which has been raging among physicians for approximately two years — whether physicians must obtain consent to Do Not Resuscitate Orders when they conclude that CPR would be futile. A DNR order means that if the patient arrests, she will not be resuscitated. In compliance with state law and accreditation standards, hospital policy requires that the physician obtain the consent of the patient, family member, or legal guardian before placing such an order in the patient's chart.

In this instance, the physician decides that a Do Not Resuscitate Order is medically appropriate for his incompetent patient who is dying of cancer. The few extant family members have not had a relationship with the patient for years, and have visited her only once since her admission to the hospital. The physician believes that resuscitation would be futile in this patient's case. It might add a few hours or days to the patient's life, but would not improve the patient's condition sufficiently to enable the patient to leave the hospital. In fact, the physician believes that successful resuscitation would cruelly prolong an already unacceptable quality of life. The physician has no idea what course his patient would choose in this situation; he had no relationship with her prior to her admission to the hospital. He never discussed end-of-life treatment with her before she became incompetent. Nonetheless, despite hospital policy, the physician and many of his colleagues believe that the requirement for consent to the Do Not Resuscitate Order should be unnecessary when resuscitation constitutes futile treatment. Accordingly, he unilaterally enters a DNR order on the patient's chart. When the patient arrests a few days later, the hospital staff complies with the DNR order and allows the patient to die without any intervention.

This case evolves out of the so-called futility debate which has been the focus of much recent attention by medical ethicists and physicians in medical journals and is now being incorporated into some hospitals' policies. Succinctly, futility proponents argue that an exception to the informed consent requirement to Do Not Resuscitate orders should be recognized when the physician believes that resuscitation would be futile. Although futility exception proposals are currently confined to Do Not Resuscitate policies, its implications are far-reaching and could extend to many other kinds of treatment decisions.

The futility debate is not limited to but is most specifically being debated in the context of the over-use of resuscitation, particularly in hospitals, and the low success rates of resuscitation, especially for certain patients. For example, studies indicate that cancer patients who are successfully resuscitated have virtually no hope of surviving to hospital discharge.[75] Consequently, futility proponents argue that CPR should not be offered as a treatment option to patients for whom it has no medical benefit.[76] In addition, supporters of the futility exception argue that physicians should have the authority to refuse to comply with a patient request for CPR that the physician deems futile. Futility proponents identify two principles in support of the futility exception: first, the physician's judgment that a treatment is futile absolves doctors from the moral obligation to provide care and absolves patients from the obligation to seek care,[77] and second, the principle of patient autonomy does not allow patients to demand nonbeneficial and potentially harmful procedures.[78]

Critics of the proposed futility exception raise several objections, beginning with the problem of defining the exception.[79] One commentator presents five possible definitions of futility that may be encompassed by the exception: (1) CPR will not reestablish spontaneous heartbeat; (2) additional treatment may fail to postpone death for even a few minutes; (3) the patient may live a week, but will die before hospital discharge; (4) the patient's quality of life before or after CPR is unacceptable; and (5) it is highly unlikely, but not impossible, that life will be extended or that quality of life will be improved.[80] Another commentator offers a more generic but similar set of understandings of futility: implausible, unlikely to work, non-beneficial or non-validated.[81] Critics of the futility exception argue that all of these possible definitions, except for physiological futility and absolute inability to postpone death, involve value judgments that belong solely to the patient.[82] Futility critics further argue that physiological futility and absolute inability to postpone death are also problematic in that they require physicians to predict whether and how long a patient will survive after CPR, a determination that may potentially be made without sufficient medical reliability, certainty, and consistency.[83] In addition, many of the statistics upon which futility proponents rely are based on live discharge from the hospital, thereby ignoring the value to the patient of the additional days or hours lived.[84]

The question of whether a patient can demand treatment deemed futile by her physician has not been explicitly addressed by any court. The question of what decisions belong exclusively to the physician as medical judgments and what decisions belong solely to the patient as value judgments lies at the heart of the quest by physicians for a futility exception to DNR orders. Unless the physician is certain that resuscitation will not restore spontaneous heartbeat in his patient, the decision as to whether CPR is futile falls outside the realm of medical judgment and into the realm of patient self-determination.[85] The patient's evaluation of whether CPR is worthwhile involves value judgments, a cost-benefit analysis, or assessments of risk-taking. The protections afforded to patients by the common law doctrine of informed consent and the constitutionally protected liberty interest in life are not limited to patient decisions that physicians deem rational; decisions that reflect the physician's valuative process, culture, and values; or decisions that are statistically defensible. In fact, courts affirming patient decisions to refuse treatment have stated that if the right to informed consent is to have any meaning at all, it must be accorded respect even when it conflicts with the advice of the doctor or the values of the medical profession as a whole.[86] Medical choices should be free from societal standards of reasonableness or normalcy.[87]

Case Four

This final case is also a hypothetical one arising out of a more obscure, yet still controversial, issue confronting patients and health care providers. In this situation, the physician advises the parents of an eighteen-year-old motorcycle accident victim that their son is brain dead. The physician offers the parents an opportunity to see their son before his body is removed from the trauma unit. When the parents visit their son, they find him still connected to the respirator and breathing. Dazed and confused, they contact the physician and ask how their son could be dead; he is breathing and his body is warm. Despite the physician's repeated attempts to explain brain death, the parents refuse to accept that their son is dead and demand that the physician continue doing everything possible to save him. The physician believes that it is illogical, a waste of resources, and contrary to medical ethics to continue treating a dead body. Consequently, the physician consults the hospital attorney to determine whether he must accede to the parents' demands.

The purpose of this case is to demonstrate that continued and persistent misconceptions about brain death sometimes cause families of brain- dead patients to object to termination of life-support systems.[88] A determination of death is a medical decision that belongs solely to the physician and requires no patient or family consent. Consequently, physicians should not offer families the opportunity to object to the termination of life support. The physicians should declare the patient dead, terminate any life support systems, advise the family that the patient has died and allow them to visit the body if they so desire.[89] Such an approach should avoid any misconceptions by the family that the patient is somehow not really dead.

At least one commentator, Charlotte Goldberg, argues that this situation should be analyzed as a right-to-die case. Accordingly, she argues that respect for the patient's right of self-determination requires continued treatment even after the patient is considered legally dead.[90] The obvious retort to this argument is that once a patient is dead, his legal rights extinguish and he no longer has the right to demand continued medical treatment. Goldberg has two responses: first, she argues that if the patient's moral or religious beliefs conflict with brain death, the patient should not be considered legally dead; therefore, his rights remain intact. Alternatively, she argues that the right to prospectively control the disposition of one's body should encompass the ability to require continued life support. Thus, just as one may direct whether his or her body may be used for organ transplants or whether an autopsy should be performed, an individual should be able to require continued life support.[91]

It is this author's belief that several state interests outweigh any right a patient (or family) may have to demand continued medical support after death. First, the myriad of legal and social effects of death necessitate a uniform standard for determining the time of death. For example, allowing families to opt out of the legal definition of death would confuse the application of the legal and social consequences of death. Presumably, life insurance payments would not be paid until the alternative point of death occurred; health insurance benefits would continue for the treatment of a dead body.[92] If it is accepted that a patient or his next-of-kin may reject the legal definition of death in favor of a more restrictive definition, the next-of-kin logically should also be allowed to choose a more permissive definition, e.g., senility or mental illness.[93] Removing determination of death decisions from the realm of medical judgment into the arena of patient or family discretion threatens to resurrect society's still tenuous understanding of brain death and to bring chaos to clinical practice.

CONCLUSION

The question of whether there exists a right to demand continued life at the end of life remains unresolved. Significantly, debate about patient or family end-of-life demands for marginal treatment has occurred almost exclusively among physicians and medical ethicists, thereby naturally focusing upon their views, values, and diagnoses. As a result, the various cultural, religious, and other human factors that impact the patient's treatment decisions are sometimes undervalued. In addition, physicians and medical ethicists frequently overlook the legal implications of refusing to provide treatment requested by or on behalf of patients.

Failure to consider whether the law protects patient requests for marginal treatment has already resulted in emotion-laden legal battles in which judges and lawyers have had little guidance as to whether and how two decades of right-to-die jurisprudence applies to the question of whether "there is a right to life at the end of life." Although, optimally, patients, families, and physicians should implement end-of-life treatment decisions independent of judicial intervention, it is inevitable that many of these issues will be determined in the courtroom. Therefore, it would be remiss and unrealistic for physicians and ethicists to discount the importance of the impact of legal perspectives concerning end-of-life treatment by excluding judges and attorneys from their discussions. Instead, the focus of end-of-life treatment discussions should be expanded to include lay persons as well as judges and attorneys.

NOTES

1. *Cruzan v. Director, Missouri Department of Health*, 497 U.S. 261, (1990) at 277. As explained by Justice Sandra Day O'Connor in *Cruzan*, at 287, due to the inextricable interrelationship of the notions of liberty with those of physical freedom and self-determination, state invasions of the body often impermissibly burden those interests given to an individual under the Due Process Clause. According to Justice O'Connor, by imposing unwanted medical treatment on a competent adult, the state necessarily exercises some degree of restraint and intrusion. Therefore, forced treatment, like other forms of state coercion, can potentially burden the liberty interests of an individual.

2. *Brophy v. New England Sinai Hospital, Inc.*, 497 N.E.2d 626, (Mass. 1986) at 635; *Superintendent of Belchertown State Sch. v. Saikewicz*, 370 N.E.2d 417 (Mass. 1977) at 425; *John F. Kennedy Memorial Hospital v. Heston*, 279 A.2d 670, (N.J. 1971) at 673.

3. *Raleigh Fitkin-Paul Morgan Memorial Hospital v. Anderson*, 201 A.2d 537 (N.J. 1964) *cert. denied*, 377 U.S. 985 (1964); *In re Melideo*, 88 Misc.2d 974 (N.Y. Sup. Ct. 1976); *In re Jamaica Hospital*, 128 Misc. 2d 1006 (N.Y. 1985); *Fosmire v. Nicoleau*, 551 N.E.2d 77 (N.Y. 1989).

4. *Quinlan*, 355 A.2d 647 (N.J. 1976).

5. *Cruzan v. Missouri Department of Health*, 497 U.S. 261 (1990).

6. *In re Barry*, 445 So.2d 365 (Fla. Dist. Ct. App. 1984) at 370.

7. *In re Conroy*, 486 A.2d 1209 (N.J. 1985) at 1223; *In re Storar*, 420 N.E.2d 64, (N.Y. 1981) at 70, cert. denied, 454 U.S. 858 (1981); *Rosebush v. Oakland County Prosecutor*, 491 N.W.2d 633 (Mich. Ct. App. 1992) at 635.

8. *Rasmussen v. Fleming*, 741 P.2d 674 (Ariz. 1984) at 682-83.

9. *In re Barry*, 445 So.2d 365 (Fla. Dist. Ct. App. 1984); *In re L.H.R.*, 321 S.E.2d 716 (Ga. 1984); *In re Beth*, 587 N.E.2d 1377 (Mass. 1992); *In re Minor*, 434 N.E.2d 601 (Mass. 1982); *Rosebush v. Oakland County Prosecutor*, 491 N.W.2d 633 (Mich. Ct. App. 1992).

10. *In re Jane Doe*, 583 N.E.2d 1263 (Mass. 1992); *Superintendent of Belchertown State Sch. v. Saikewicz*, 370 N.E.2d 417 (Mass. 1977).

11. *Bartling v. Superior Court*, 163 Cal. App.3d 186 (1984) (malignant lung tumor); *Tune v. Walter Reed Army Medical Hosp.*, 602 F. Supp. 1452 (D.D.C. 1985) (malignant adenocarcinoma); *In re Saunders*, 129 Misc.2d 45 (N.Y. 1985) (progressive lung cancer without known medical cure).

12. *Foody v. Manchester*, 482 A.2d 713 (Conn. Super. Ct. 1984) at 721; *In re Torres*, 357 N.W.2d 332 (Minn. 1984) (en banc.) at 337-39; *In re Hamlin* 689 P.2d 1372 (Wash. 1984) at 1375.

13. *In re A.C.*, 573 A.2d 1235 (D.C. 1990); *In re Longeway*, 549 N.E.2d 292 (Ill. 1989); *In re Browning*, 568 So.2d 4 (Fla. 1990).

14. *In re Barry*, 445 So.2d 365 (Fla. Dist. Ct. App. 1984).
15. *In re Jane Doe*, 583 N.E.2d 1263 (Mass. 1992); *Superintendent of Belchertown State Sch. v. Saikewicz*, 370 N.E.2d 417 (Mass. 1977).
16. *In re O'Connor*, 531 N.E.2d 607 (N.Y. 1988); cf. *In re Browning*, 568 So.2d 4 (Fla. 1990); *In re Longeway*, 549 N.E.2d 292 (Ill. 1989).
17. At least one court has explicitly rejected the clear and convincing evidence standard in deciding whether to withdraw treatment from a minor precisely because "its adoption would always preclude the termination of life-support efforts for minors and other persons who have never been legally competent. . . ." *Rosebush v. Oakland County Prosecutor*, 491 N.W.2d 633 (Mich. Ct. App. 1992) at 688 n.7.
18. *Cruzan v. Missouri Department of Health*, 497 U.S. 261 (1990).
19. *Cruzan v. Harmon*, 760 S.W.2d 408 (Mo. 1988) (*en banc*) at 417-18.
20. *Cruzan* at 282.
21. Stuart J. Youngner, "Defining Death; A Superficial and Fragile Consensus," *Arch Neurol.* 49 (1992): 570-72.
22. Karen Grandstrand Gervais, *Redefining Death* (Stoughton, Mass.: Alpine Press, 1986), 4.
23. Charlotte K. Goldberg, "Choosing Life After Death: Respecting Religious Beliefs and Moral Convictions in Near Death Decisions," *Syracuse Law Review* 39 (1988): 1202.
24. Gervais, *Redefining Death*, 1.
25. James L. Bernat, "How Much of the Brain Must Die in Brain Death?" *The Journal of Clinical Ethics* 3 (Spring 1992): 22.
26. Ibid., 21.
27. President's Commission for the Study of Ethical Problems in Medicine and Biomedical and Behavioral Research, "Defining Death: Medical, Legal and Ethical Issues in the Determination of Death, The 'State of the Art' in *Medicine*," 9 July 1981, 21.
28. James L. Bernat, "Brain Death: Occurs Only with Destruction of the Cerebral Hemispheres and the Brain Stem," *Arch. Neurol.* 49 (1992): 569-70.
29. Ibid.
30. Goldberg, "Choosing Life After Death,"1207, n. 59-60. By contrast, brain-stem death is the commonly accepted alternative for determining death in the United Kingdom. U.S. physicians have rejected this criterion due to the remote possibility that a patient may maintain consciousness despite losing all other functions of the brain stem, according to Bernat, "How Much of the Brain Must Die in Brain Death?," 24.
31. James L. Bernat, "The Boundaries of the Persistent Vegetative State," *The Journal of Clinical Ethics* 3 (Fall 1992): 177.
32. Bernat, "How Much of the Brain Must Die in Brain Death?," 21.
33. Robert M. Veatch, *Death Dying and the Biological Revolution: Our Last Quest for Responsibility* (Binghamton, N.Y.: Vail-Ballou Press, 1989), 25-30.

34. Robert M. Veatch, "Brain Death and Slippery Slopes," *The Journal of Clinical Ethics* 3 (1992): 181-82. Veatch recognized the possibility that a state legislature may choose to allow the patient or next of kin to choose the definition of death to be applied; Veatch, *Death Dying and the Biological Revolution*, 54.

35. Gervais, *Redefining Death*, 18-44.

36. Damage to patients in persistent vegetative states occurs in the higher centers of the brain while the brain stem tends to be relatively normal. As a result, these patients have readily observable periods of normal wakefulness, yet remain unaware and unconscious. Ronald E. Cranford and David Randolph Smith, "Consciousness: The Most Critical Moral (Constitutional) Standard for Human Personhood," *American Journal of Law and Medicine* 13 (1987): 233, 238.

37. Anencephalic infants suffer from a severe congenital malformation and possess essentially no cerebral hemispheres. While these infants do have a type of functioning brain stem, it is abnormal. Consequently, these infants usually die from medical complications within a short period of days or weeks after birth; ibid., 238.

38. Veatch, "Brain Death and Slippery Slopes," 181-82.

39. *In re Wanglie*, No. PX-91-283 (Probate Ct. Div. Minn. 28 June 1991).

40. Steven H. Miles, "Informed Demand for Non-Beneficial Medical Treatment," *New England Journal of Medicine* 325 (1991): 513.

41. No. PX-91-283 (Probate Ct. Div. Minn. 28 June 1991).

42. Miles, "Informed Demand," 512, 514.

43. Ibid., 513.

44. No. PX-91-283 (Probate Ct. Div. Minn. 28 June 1991).

45. Miles, "Informed Demand," 514.

46. Marcia Angell, "The Case of Helga Wanglie: A New Kind of 'Right to Die' Case," *New England Journal of Medicine* 325 (August 1991): 511-12.

47. Ronald Cranford and Larry Gostin, "Futility: A Concept in Search of a Definition," *Law, Medicine and Health Care* 20 (1992): 309.

48. *In re Baby K*, 832 F.Supp. 1022, 1031 (E.D. Ca. 1993), affirmed, 1994 U.S. App. LEXIS 2215 (4th Cir. Feb. 10, 1994).

49. *Cruzan* at 281.

50. Ibid. at 288.

51. Miles, "Informed Demand," 514.

52. Ibid.

53. Hans Jonas, "Philosophical Reflections on Experimenting with Human Subjects," in *Contemporary Issues in Bioethics*, ed. Tom L. Beauchamp and LeRoy Walters (Belmont, Cal.: Wadsworth Publishing Co., 1978), 417.

54. Ann Alpers and Bernard Lo, "Futility: Not Just a Medical Issue," *Law, Medicine and Health Care* 20 (1992): 328; David Mechanic,

"Professional Judgment and the Rationing of Medical Care," *University of Pennsylvania Law Review* 140 (1992): 1748-52.

55.   A few cases have involved children who were wards of the state as a result of their parents' inability or unwillingness to assume responsibility for their children. *In re Beth*, 587 N.E.2d 1377 (Mass. 1992); *In re Minor*, 434 N.E.2d 601 (Mass. 1982).

56.   *In re Barry* , 445 So.2d 365 (Fla. Dist. Ct. App. 1984) at 371; *In re L.H.R.*, 321 S.E.2d 716 (Ga. 1984) at 722; *Rosebush v. Oakland City Prosecutor*, 491 N.W.2d 633 (Mich. Ct. App. 1992) at 683.

57.   *In re L.H.R.*, 321 S.E.2d 716 (Ga. 1984) at 722 (citing *Parham v. J.R.*, 442 U.S. 584 (1979). See also *In re Jane Doe*, 418 S.E.2d 3 (Ga. 1992) at 5.

58.   *Rosebush v. Oakland County Prosecutor*, 491 N.W.2d 633 (Mich. Ct. App. 1992).

59.   Ibid., 636-37.

60.   *Rasmussen v. Fleming*, 741 P.2d 674 (Ariz. 1987).

61.   *In re Barry*, 445 So.2d 365 (Fla. App. 1984) at 371; *In re Beth*, 587 N.E.2d 1377 (Mass. 1992) at 1381; *In re Minor*, 434 N.E.2d 601 (Mass. 1982) at 609.

62.   *Rosebush* at 637.

63.   *In re Minor*, 379 N.E.2d 1053 (Mass. 1978).

64.   *In re Jane Doe*, 418 S.E.2d 3 (Ga. 1992).

65.   1994 U.S. App. LEXIS 2215 (4th Cir. 10 February 1994).

66.   See supra note 37.

67.   *In re Baby K*, 832 F.Supp. 1022, 1025 (E.D. Va. 1993).

68.   Ibid., 1026.

69.   The child's parents are unmarried and the biological father has been involved with the child only minimally.

70.   The court determined that the guardian ad litem's role is limited statutorily to investigation of the facts and that consequently the guardian's recommendation regarding Baby K was irrelevant; ibid., 1031 n.2.

71.   This essay focuses on the constitutional issues implicated by this case. However, the court held that the hospital's refusal to provide the requested treatment would violate the Emergency Medical Treatment and Active Labor Act, the Rehabilitation Act of 1973, and the Americans with Disabilities Act; ibid., 1026-1029. The appellate court based its entire decision on the Emergency Medical Treatment and Active Labor Act.

72.   Ibid., 1030.

73.   Ibid., 1031.

74.   Alpers and Lo, "Futility: Not Just a Medical Issue," 327.

75.   George E. Taffet, "In-Hospital Cardiopulmonary Resuscitation," *Journal of the American Medical Association* 260 (1988): 2070.

76.   Tom Tomlinson and Howard Brody, "Futility and the Ethics of Resuscitation," *Journal of the American Medical Association* 264 (1990): 1277.

77. John D. Lantos, et al, "The Illusion of Futility in Clinical Practice," *American Journal of Medicine* 87 (1989): 81.
78. Leslie J. Blackhall, "Must We Always Use CPR?" *New England Journal of Medicine* 317 (1987): 1283.
79. Cranford and Gostin, "Futility : A Concept in Search of Definition," *Law, Medicine and Health Care* 20 (1992): 307-08.
80. Stuart J. Youngner, "Commentaries, Who Defines Futility?," *Journal of the American Medical Association* 260 (1988): 2094.
81. Steven H. Miles, "Medical Futility," *Law, Medicine and Health Care* 20 (1992): 310.
82. Youngner, "Commentaries, Who Defines Futility?" 2094-95.
83. Robert M. Veatch and Carol M. Spicer, "Medically Futile Care: The Role of the Physician in Setting Limits," *American Journal Law and Medicine* 18 (1992): 16.
84. Tracy E. Miller, "Do-Not Resuscitate Orders: Public Policy and Patient Autonomy," *Law, Medicine and Health Care* 17 (1989): 251.
85. Kathleen M. Boozang, "Death Wish: Resuscitating Self-Determination for the Critically Ill," *Arizona Law Review* 35 (1993): 23.
86. *In re Conroy*, 486 A.2d 1209 (N.J. 1985) at 1225.
87. *In re Peter*, 529 A.2d 419 (N.J. 1987) at 423.
88. For an example of such a case, see Lisa L. Kirkland, "Brain Death and the Termination of Life Support: Case and Analysis," *Journal of Clinical Ethics* 3 (Spring 1992): 78.
89. William G. Bartholome and Howard Morgan, "Discussion of Brain-Death Case,"*Journal of Clinical Ethics* 3 (1992): 82.
90. Goldberg, "Choosing Life After Death," 1197.
91. Unlike the right to die, one difficulty with this issue is whether we are dealing with the patient's or the next-of-kin's legal rights to dispose of the corpse.
92. Veatch, *Death, Dying and the Biological Revolution*, 56-57.
93. Ibid., 55.

8

Preserving the Moral Integrity of the Constitution: An Examination of Deconstruction and Other Hermeneutical Theories

DEREK DAVIS

The last fifteen years or so has witnessed a remarkable discovery by American academic lawyers: literary theory, especially in its hermeneutical aspects. Of course it is not that the legal community had never been interested in interpretive theory. To the contrary, the legal world, from the time of the Roman law system to the present, has always been one of texts—wills, contracts, deeds, court decrees, statutes, regulations, and constitutions—that carry the necessity of interpretation. Moreover, the word "hermeneutics" entered American legal discourse as far back as 1839 when Francis Lieber, a German immigrant, published *Legal and Political Hermeneutics or Principles of Interpretation and Construction in Law and Politics with Remarks on Precedents and Authorities*.[1] Yet the real work in hermeneutics has been done in the latter half of the twentieth century by literary theorists. Sanford Levinson, writing in 1988, observed that "increasingly within the last forty years, literary studies as a discipline has devoted more and more attention to the problematics of literary theory, and it is fair to say that the sophistication of the analyses has far surpassed anything that had previously occurred in the legal academy."[2] It is this body of work in hermeneutics described by Levinson that

academic lawyers have only recently discovered and have
sought to draw from in wrestling with interpretive problems in
legal texts.

In the discussion of the interpretation of legal texts, no text
takes on more importance than the United States Constitution.
William Gladstone, the great British statesman and prime
minister, once described the American Constitution as "the most
wonderful work ever struck off at a given time by the brain and
purpose of man."[3]   Americans cannot but be pleased by this
tribute, and it is accepted by most as an accurate assessment of
what has been regarded as, since the time of the American
founding, a sacred text. Certainly, the importance of the
Constitution in American life cannot be minimized. The
Constitution is the national charter of the United States. It is the
binding framework of law and public policy for the nation. It is
the starting place for a people committed to the rule of law in a
civilized society. Therefore, its meanings, to the extent they are
ascertainable, necessarily govern its interpreters.

The Constitution's meanings, however, are not always easily
determined. American legal scholars have debated the subject of
constitutional interpretation since the Constitution's adoption at
Philadelphia in 1787. The debate has become especially heated
in the last two decades, with the lines drawn between
"interpretivists" and "noninterpretivists," "originalists" and
"nonoriginalists," "strict" and "liberal" constructionists,
"textualists" and "nontextualists." While the labels are varied,
the controversy in the debate remains the same. Should the
Constitution be the sole source of law for purposes of judicial
review, or should judges supplement the text with an unwritten
constitution that is implicit in precedent, practice, and
conventional morality? That is, do we have a "static"
Constitution, or a "living" one? Or, stated another way, must the
United States Supreme Court confine itself to norms clearly
stated in the text of the Constitution, or may the Court protect
norms not mentioned in the Constitution? The debate is
important because at stake is the question of how much power a
set of nonelected judges should have in setting moral norms and
formulating major governmental policy for the nation.

Why has the legal academy suddenly begun to look to literary theory in the debate over how to interpret the Constitution? There are several possibilities. Stanley Fish has suggested that perhaps too many people with literary backgrounds have infiltrated the law schools.[4] Another theory is that academic lawyers now realize how little social science (fashionable in its applications to jurisprudence in the first half of the twentieth century) has to offer to interpretational problems and are impressed by literary theory as a new and heady slant on the hermeneutical debate.[5] The best explanation, however, is that constitutional hermeneutics, in the 1980s when its own debate seemed hopelessly unsolvable, found room for literary theories, themselves scarcely a few decades old, in the hope that it had discovered a new wellspring of data to resolve the debate. The outcome, though, has not so far been what those involved in the field of constitutional hermeneutics had hoped for. The claim to textual autonomy— the claim that a text can somehow escape subjective readings— has been challenged. Deconstructionist and reader-response terminology has infiltrated the legal literature. And as Richard Weisberg has noted, interjected now is the unsettling view that interpreters stand outside of the text, that the Constitution itself exists independently of the readers who talk and write about it, and, indeed, the enormously disquieting view that there are *no* meanings in the Constitution to be discovered.[6]

Thoughtful traditionalists such as Owen Fiss have described the new merger of constitutional hermeneutics and literary theory as "nihilistic,"[7] and other more "objectivist" theorists, such as Raoul Berger, as downright "distorted."[8] Even commentators sympathetic to the deconstructionist view that language is infinitely variable, and legal interpretation virtually unconstrained, have recognized the potentially radical effect of the new synthesis for the American political structure. As one writer put it: "If the trend toward literary lawyers and lawyerly critics gains further momentum, I can imagine a senate confirmation hearing in the near future where a Supreme Court nominee is asked: Are you a strict constructionist or a deconstructionist?"[9] In short, many scholars are concerned with the potentially destructive effects of the new thinking upon the integrity of the Constitution.

The most popular and influential contemporary approach to literary analysis is deconstruction. The popularity of deconstruction has spilled over into legal writings, although it is still strange territory for most legal academics who are accustomed to reading only what other lawyers have said about textual interpretation. The Frenchman, Jacques Derrida, is the leading deconstructionist and has won a large following in America. Derrida's dominant idea concerning the literary text is that, since language is a chain of signifiers that does not point to independently existing signifieds, texts do not portray a real world that exists independent of language.[10] Thus we have Derrida's best known aphorism, "there is nothing outside of the text."[11] Consequently, the world as we know it is only a world of representation, and representations and representations, ad infinitum. Every signified is actually a signifier in disguise.

It is easy to see how Derrida's critique can be viewed as nihilistic because it appears to deny the existence of objective truth. In fact, deconstructionists often argue that texts have *no* determinative meanings. Many critics have been bitter in their criticisms of a form of analysis that leaves them with no "truth" and no determinative meanings. As one writer has said, "Derrida's deconstructive readings are, at one level, a remarkably far-reaching attempt to loosen the moorings of virtually every intellectual tradition in Western thought."[12] On this interpretation, deconstruction is, at bottom, the fashionable, modern version of nihilism.

Yet Derrida himself has said that deconstruction only means "undoing," not "destroying."[13] And some commentators like J.M. Balkin have been more sympathetic to Derrida's project, arguing that deconstruction is a useful "tool of analysis" and that it does not deny the existence of objective truth as much as it affirms the interpretive character of our attempts to comprehend truth.[14]

Several questions, then, can be asked about deconstruction. Is it destructive or constructive? Does deconstruction make any difference? Can it aid those who are investigating the field of constitutional hermeneutics? Will it help resolve the current debate over how the Constitution should be interpreted? Are there moral consequences to a deconstructed Constitution? These and related questions are addressed in this essay by focusing on two areas of discussion. First, a brief description of the current debate on constitutional interpretation is presented. The debate is discussed in language typically employed by legal academics, that is, language free from the influence (or awareness) of literary theory. Seeing the debate in this context will make it easier to see how legal academics have rushed, rightly or wrongly, to literary theory with its greater sophististication and its own erudite verbiage, in search of help for resolution of the debate. Second, deconstruction is discussed, with particular attention being given to the implications of a deconstructive approach to constitutional hermeneutics. The goal is to determine whether deconstruction can help to solve the contemporary debate on constitutional interpretation and to identify the moral implications of a deconstructed Constitution.

THE CONTEMPORARY DEBATE ON CONSTITUTIONAL HERMENEUTICS

There are two basic responses to the question of the beliefs on which a judge should rely in making constitutional decisions. As already noted, the nomenclature for these two responses vary, but the terms used here will be "originalism" and "nonoriginalism,"[15] only because they seem best to capture the central focus of the debate: the degree that modern interpretation should be guided by the "original" intentions of the Constitution's framers and ratifiers.

Originalism holds that a judge, in deciding whether public policy regarding some matter is constitutionally valid, should rely upon "original" beliefs, motives, and intentions of those who were responsible for drafting and ratifying the Constitution. This view at first seems overly rigid; after all, how can the beliefs of the framers and the ratifiers ever be completely determined, especially when one considers the scarcity of written records of the Constitutional Convention and the state ratifying conventions. It also tends to minimize the significant disagreements that prevailed over the final wording of the Constitution. Originalists hold, however, that the wording of the Constitution itself is clear evidence of the intentions of the framers and ratifiers, and because the Constitution in its final wording was passed in democratic course, original disagreements on its content are to be disregarded, except to the extent that those disagreements can illumine the reasons for the approval of the final language. Moreover, they argue, the constitutional text anticipates the need to depart from its original provisions by providing a process for amendment. The original intentions, then, are the rudder of the nation; remove the rudder and the nation will drift aimlessly, ultimately to be ruled (and ruined) by nine nonelected judges who can make whatever laws they want.

A common misconception of originalism is that it requires judges to answer a question the way the framers/ratifiers would have answered it in our day, if they were living. However, there is no way a judge can know how the framers would have answered a constitutional question— the abortion question, say — in our day, were they still living. The originalist project is not to speculate about what the framers' beliefs would have been in our day, were they still living, and then to decide the case on the basis of those beliefs. Rather, the originalist project is to discover what beliefs the framers "constitutionalized," and then to decide the case on the basis of those beliefs.[16] As Robert Bork, a prominent originalist, has written: "The objection that we can never know what the Framers would have done about specific modern situations is entirely beside the point. The originalist attempts to discern the principles the Framers enacted, the values they sought to protect."[17]

Yet, "discern[ing] the principles the Framers enacted, the values they sought to protect," is not an easy assignment. It requires, according to Michael Perry, entering into a hypothetical conversation with the framers in an effort to discern which principle *they* likely would have chosen, that is, selecting from among the various candidate principles, the one that best captures the purpose or point or meaning of what they said in the Constitution.[18]   Even Bork understands that this leaves room for self-serving conclusions: "Enforcing the Framers' intentions is not a mechanical process and . . . even a judge purporting to be an . . . [originalist] can manipulate the levels of generality at which he states the Framers' principles."[19]

Originalism, then, even in its most sophisticated form, readily acknowledges that the judge can never retrieve the actual "original understanding" any more than one can come to see the world through another person's eye. The sophisticated originalist is fully aware that the best the judge can do is construct an imagined "original understanding" by means of a hypothetical conversation that is sensitive to the available historical materials. But, for the originalist, the best the judge can do is quite good enough— far better, at least, than a nonoriginalist approach, uncommitted, fundamentally, to original intent.[20]

To the nonoriginalist, unlike the originalist, what the Constitution means is not merely what it originally meant. As Michael Perry has said, the Constitution may mean original beliefs, but it may also mean the aspirations or ideals or principles signified by the Constitution. The best examples of provisions bearing constitutional aspirations are the First Amendment, signifying the aspiration of freedom of speech, press, and religion; the Fifth Amendment, signifying the aspiration to due process of law; and the Fourteenth Amendment, signifying the aspiration to due process of law and to equal protection of the laws.[21]

Constitutional provisions signifying constitutional aspirations are usually vague, the nonoriginalist claims. When the framers were vague or ambiguous, the likely reason is that they meant to be. The nonoriginalist assumes that the framers intended their vagueness and ambiguity to be pregnant with meaning for unborn generations, rather than be restricted to whatever meaning then existed. Thus, a wide open term like "freedom of speech" was chosen by the framers deliberately, leaving room for the widest possible interpretation.[22] The framers could have given a comprehensive definition of freedom of speech, but they chose not to. They meant, then, that the aspirational meaning of freedom of speech would emerge over time— in the course of constitutional adjudication and political discourse. As a progressive generalization of the original meaning, the aspirational meaning of freedom of speech is not inconsistent with, but indeed includes, the narrow original meaning.[23]

The "fundamental aspiration" approach to constitutional interpretation has traditionally been practiced by the Supreme Count's more liberal members. Former Associate Justice William Brennan often expounded the fundamental aspirations theme. For example, he once wrote that "the Constitution embodies the aspiration to social justice, brotherhood, and human dignity that brought this nation into being. . . . [W]e are an aspiring people, a people with faith in progress. Our amended Constitution is the lodestar for our aspirations."[24] Moreover, Brennan frequently found justification for the fundamental aspirations approach in the ambiguity of certain provisions of the Constitution. According to Brennan, the "majestic generalities and ennobling pronouncements [of the Constitution] are both luminous and obscure. The ambiguity of course calls forth interpretation, the interaction of reader and text."[25] It should be made clear that not every provision of the Constitution signifies a fundamental aspiration. Some provisions of the Constitution, after all, pertain only to mundane yet essential matters. In Article I, Section 3, for example, it is provided that "The Vice President of the United States shall be President of the Senate, but shall have no vote, unless they be equally divided." Unambiguous provisions like this one do not preclude an originalist approach, even for the nonoriginalist.

The nonoriginalist, then, is free to consult original beliefs, but is also free to search for the ideals and aspirations behind certain provisions of the Constitution. It is a process of being true to the original text, but acknowledging that there is room for play in the joints to keep the Constitution "up to date" and reflective of modern values. Alexander Bickel has summarized the key factor that constrains the nonoriginalist to look beyond original intent:

[A]s time passes, fewer and fewer relevantly decisive choices are to be divined out of the tradition of our founding. Our problems have grown radically different from those known to the Framers, and we have had to make value choices that are effectively new, while maintaining continuity with tradition.[26]

Thus there are two competing paradigms of constitutional decision making: originalism and nonoriginalism. The contemporary debate has been spurred, no doubt, by political and judicial conservatives who, arguing for originalism, are vitally concerned about the wave of liberal decisions that the Supreme Court has handed down in the last fifty years, especially since the Warren Court began in 1954. And of course, virtually every decision of the Court since that time, until the Rehnquist Court began in 1987, reflects a nonoriginalist methodology. Many examples can be cited. The ambiguous language of the Equal Protection Clause did not compel the Court to end school desegregation in *Brown v. Board of Education*.[27] The Constitution does not require the exclusion of evidence obtained in violation of the Fourth, Fifth, and Sixth Amendments.[28] The right to a fair trial embodied in the Sixth Amendment does not necessarily mean that the government has the duty to provide free legal counsel to indigents; in fact, the Court had previously held that no such requirement exists.[29] State sanctioned prayers in public schools and financial aid to sectarian schools are not explicitly forbidden by the First Amendment.[30] Nothing in the Constitution's text prevents a state from prohibiting the use of contraceptives or forbidding abortion.[31] In fact, the Constitution does not even state that the Bill of Rights must apply to the states.[32]

Strong disagreement with decisions like these that protect rights not stated or implied in the Constitution has compelled conservative critics to mount an attack on the nonoriginalist methodology of constitutional interpretation. The foundational argument of conservatives is that the principle of majority rule is violated if judicial decisions are based upon values not clearly stated or implied in the Constitution. They contend that democracy requires unelected judges to defer to the decisions of

elected officials unless there is a clear violation of the rights
protected by the text of the Constitution.[33]

The most common nonoriginalist counterargument to this
claim is that it is wrong to define democracy solely as majority
rule. Erwin Chemerinsky, for example, argues not only that a
description of democracy as majority rule is not what the
framers of the Constitution intended, but also that it is
impractical to reject nonmajoritian elements in a scheme of
democratic government. James Madison, he points out, who
was particularly influential in the drafting and ratification of the
Constitution, was especially distrustful of majorities and wanted
to create a "republic," not a purely majoritarian democracy. A
"republic," in Madison's view, would have features that would
guarantee the liberties of certain minorities from the tyranny of
majorities. Few would dispute, moreover, that the republican
form of government under which the United States has operated
for more than two hundred years has functioned quite well. The
clearest example of the nonmajoritarian dimension of the
American "republic," Chemerinsky argues, is the power of the
judiciary. Since *Marbury v. Madison* in 1803, the Supreme Court
has had the power to invalidate legislative acts. This power is
not explicitly in the Constitution, yet it has been accepted as a
wise and necessary check on legislative acts. Moreover, the
Marbury decision itself established the nonoriginalist mode of
review in protecting rights not stated or implied in the
Constitution. These are important points, says Chemerinsky,
because they reveal that from the earliest days of the Republic,
our society has not required that all decisions be made by
electorally accountable officials.[34]

The originalist could argue, of course, that the kind of
evidence cited by Chemerinsky—that an independent judiciary
has functioned since the early days of the Republic—is the
source of the problem. Yet even when the opposition to the
Supreme Court was at its height in the 1930s, the institution
retained its credibility. In the midst of a depression, the Court
was striking down statutes thought to be necessary to economic
recovery. President Franklin D. Roosevelt, irate over the Court's
rejection of recovery measures that he had initiated, sought to

alter the Court's power by increasing its membership. Roosevelt's "court packing" proposal received little support. The Senate Judiciary Committee rejected the proposal and strongly reaffirmed the need for an independent judiciary:

Let us now set a salutary precedent that will never be violated. Let us, the Seventy-fifth Congress, declare that we would rather have an independent judiciary, a fearless Court, that will dare to announce its honest opinions in what it believes to be a defense of liberties of the people, than a Court that, out of fear or sense of obligation to the appointing power of factional passion, approves any measure we may enact.[35]

The Committee's statement is a powerful affirmation of the legitimacy of the Court's independent status.

The Supreme Court decision that has most incensed originalists, and that perhaps best illustrates the competing paradigms of originalism and nonoriginalism, is the 1973 case of *Roe v. Wade*.[36] In that case the Supreme Court ruled that no state may prohibit abortions that take place prior to viability of the fetus. The originalist critique is not merely that the Court wrongly decided *Roe;* it is that the Court was wrong to wrest from the states the question of what public policy should be for abortions.

The *Roe* decision was grounded in a "right to privacy" that the Court said was an aspect of the "liberty" guarantee of the Fourteenth Amendment. Section 1 of the Fourteenth Amendment says, in part: "nor shall any State deprive any person of . . . liberty . . . without due process of law. . . ." The crucial words, of course, are "liberty" and "due process of law." The basic meaning of the provision is that a state may deprive a person of some part of his or her "liberty," but not without "due process of law." It is agreed by virtually all that the "liberty" guarantee of the Fourteenth Amendment, as one of the post-Civil War amendments of 1868, was enacted primarily to ensure that black citizens would no longer be subjected to slavery. But does it mean more? By a process of interpretation at the hands of the Supreme Court, "liberty" has taken on increased judicial

meaning. Many provisions of the Bill of Rights—the guarantees
of freedom of religion, speech, and press, for example—have
been construed to be "liberties" against which no state, not just
the federal government, may deprive a citizen without due
process of law.

But did the framers of the Bill of Rights or the Fourteenth
Amendment intend to protect a right of privacy? No such right
receives explicit mention in the Constitution. In the 1965 case of
Griswold v. Connecticut,[37] however, the Court ruled that a
married couple's right of privacy prevented the State of
Connecticut from banning the use of contraceptives. The Court
understood a right of privacy to exist as a result of various
"penumbras" and "emenations" from several provisions of the
Bill of Rights. The First Amendment's peripheral right to
association entails a penumbra of privacy to be protected from
government intrustion, the Court said. The Third Amendment
ban on the quartering of soldiers in homes during peacetime
without the owner's consent, the Court noted, is another facet of
privacy. The Fourth Amendment's protection against
unreasonable searches and seizures protects a right to privacy, as
does the self-incrimination clause of the Fifth Amendment.
Finally, the Court said the Fourteenth Amendment's protection
of "liberty" includes a right to privacy. On the basis of these
"penumbras" of privacy, especially that arising out of the concept
of "liberty" embodied in the Fourteenth Amendment, the Court
in *Roe* held that a woman's right to have an abortion was
protected by a constitutional right to privacy.

Robert Bork has ridiculed such reasoning about the right to
privacy, which he denies that the Constitution protects. The
Court, he says, "performed a miracle of transubstantiation" by
reasoning that was "utterly specious: and constituted an
"unprincipled decision."[38] Bork believes that nonenumerated
rights do not exist and cannot be derived from the Constitution,
because the judges who discover such rights are "enforcing their
own morality upon us and calling it the Constitution."[39] For
Bork and other originalists, democratic government requires that
only the people, acting through their elected representatives,
have the right to discover and protect such rights. If perma-

nence is sought, the Constitution can be amended to enumerate the right.

Much more could be said about the debate, but it is not necessary here. The purpose of the foregoing discussion has been only to give an abbreviated summary of the basic issues. Before proceeding to a consideration of what deconstructive theory might contribute to this ongoing controversy, however, it should be said, somewhat parenthetically, that wholly apart from redirectives that deconstruction or any other literary theory might supply, this writer is personally compelled to side with the nonoriginalist view of constitutional interpretation for the simple reason that the Constitution is an antimajoritarian document reflecting a distrust of government conducted entirely by majority rule. The Constitution protects substantive values from majoritarian pressures, and judicial review enhances democracy by safeguarding these values. To deny the Supreme Court the right to permit the Constitution to evolve over time to protect values not contemplated or specifically enumerated in the Constitution is to deny the Court the right to *interpret* the Constitution. If the Constitution is to serve its function of protecting fundamental values and unifying society, the Supreme Court should have substantial discretion in determining the meaning of specific constitutional provisions. This discretion should not be unlimited, however. The fundamental aspirations that a judge perceives in a particular provision of the Constitution should not merely be his or her own, but those of the framers. If judges can give a provision almost any meaning, why have a constitution at all? Accordingly, any judicial interpretation must retain this linkage to the constitutional text. And it is recognized, of course, that the exercise of discretion does not guarantee good results, and thus there always exists a risk of judicial discretion being used to frustrate political and social progress. Nonetheless, it is suggested here that, on balance, judicial discretion in constitutional interpretation is a good thing that is essential to the advancement of society.

In the foregoing discussion of the contemporary debate on constitutional hermeneutics, nothing has been said about the

contribution that a deconstructive analysis of the Constitution
might make to the debate. In proceeding, then, to a discussion of
deconstruction, the central questions we ask are: How should
meaning be given to the provisions of the Constitution? Can
deconstruction help in this process? And, what are the moral
implications of a deconstructed Constitution?

DECONSTRUCTION AND THE CONSTITUTION

Until 1950 or so, literary theory was fairly uncontroversial
and of limited interest to anyone other than academics who
studied literature as a life's work. Discussions about literature,
whether in book reviews or on radio and television, were
addressed to the ordinary reader. Most literary critics assumed
that great literature was universal and expressed general truths
about human life, and that readers therefore required no special
knowledge or language. Critics believed they talked sensibly
about the writer's personal experience, the social and historical
background of the work, the human interest, and the beauty of
literature. That is, criticism spoke about literature without
disturbing our picture of the world or of ourselves as readers.
Then, suddenly, things began to change.[40]

In the last forty years or so, students of literature have been
troubled by a seemingly endless series of challenges to the
consensus of common sense. A number of schools of literary
theory have taken shape, all challenging the conventional
thinking about literature. In reader-response criticism, for
example, a work of literature is deemed to be the creation (not
necessarily the same creation) of each reader. Intentionalism has
combatted this approach, claiming that the purposes of the
author are paramount: the author is assumed to have had a
reason for everything in the work; to understand the work
means to discover and understand those reasons. New Criticism
has also developed, occupying a middle ground: literature
inhabits its own space without reference to the reader or the
author. Other schools have arisen— Feminist, Freudian,
Nietzschean, Nuclear, Marxist, and others. But all of the new
schools of criticism seem to have a common characteristic: they

challenge what previously had been considered common sense understanding of the meaning of texts. Interpreting texts is no longer a simple enterprise; in some very serious ways, the ground of meaning for all texts has disappeared.

In 1966 deconstruction was introduced in America by the French philosopher and literary critic, Jacques Derrida.[41] Deconstruction has since become the critical rage, and according to Richard Posner, is the critical method least understood by lawyers.[42] What is deconstruction? Greatly simplified, deconstructive theory holds that we create from our perceptions concepts (for example, the concept that the ceiling in the room is high) that are outside of time and space and are also distinct from the perceptions out of which they are made. If I want to share this concept, I have to encode it in some physical form ("signifier," in Derrida"s language)— a writing, a sound, a gesture, or some other communication. Upon hearing or seeing the signifier, someother person will mentally recreate the same concept (the "signified").[43]

Of course, the process of conveying the concept in my mind to another person's mind may break down; the communication, Posner notes, is not free of "noise." For one thing, the link between signifier and signified is a matter of convention, and conventions are not universal. A ceiling is *ceiling* in English, *techo* in Spanish, *decke* in German. Another source of failure in conveying concepts relates to vagueness. There are different kinds of ceilings, different kinds of rooms, and different notions of high. Even though I may have had a very clear picture of these terms when I communicated them, the mind of the other person may obtain a vastly different picture. I may have been thinking of a frescoed ceiling in a rotunda; the person hearing or reading my statement may have pictured the bedroom ceiling at home. So translation is often problematic. Since conversation is a two-way exchange, the person to whom I am speaking can seek clarification of my utterance, but this course is unavailable if the signifiers are written instead of spoken or if the writer is dead or is otherwise unavailable for consultation.[44]

One might normally assume that these kinds of impediments to conceptual transfer can be overcome because they are natural or are insignificant enough not to be essential to communication. But this is the point against which deconstruction mounts its assault: it insists that to regard those properties of signifiers that impede communication as secondary is not at all natural or insignificant. It is just as natural, deconstructionists insist, to subordinate the communicative functions of discourse to the communication-impeding effects of the signifiers that the speaker or writer uses, and thus to attend to the "play of the signifiers" (Derrida's term), which is to say to the relations between the signifiers and the signified that there may be other concepts besides the one intended to be signified.[45]

Thus, the deconstructionist project involves the reversal of hierarchical opposition. This establishes new priorities in the investigation of concepts and ideas, since the usual, typical, traditional, or "common sense" arrangement is reversed. For Derrida and other deconstructionists, hierarchies of thought are everywhere, and all are open to deconstructive reversal. For example, if A is the rule and B is the exception, then B might also be the rule and A the exception. If A is simple and B complex, then B might also be simple and A complex. If A is normal and B is abnormal, then B might also be normal and A abnormal. Deconstruction shows that the property we ascribe to A is true of B and the property we ascribe to B is true of A; the deconstruction shows that A's privileged status is an illusion, for A depends upon B as much as B depends upon A. We will discover, then, that B stands in relation to A much like we thought A stood in relation to B. Indeed, it is possible to find in the very reasons that A is privileged over B the reasons that B is privileged over A. Having reversed the hierarchy, we are able to see things about both A and B that we had never noticed before.[46]

Any hierarchical opposition of ideas, no matter how trivial, can be deconstructed in this way. It is a means of intellectual discovery that operates by wrenching us from our accustomed modes of thought. In fact, Derrida was led to this practice of deconstruction by his dissatisfaction with Western philosophy and political practice from Plato's time to our own.[47]

Nothing retains its privileged status when subjected to deconstructive analysis. The world in which we live is full of texts that can be deconstructed— objects, ideas, persons, or whatever. Nothing is sacred; any "text" can always be only a representation of something else, which in turn is only a representation of something else, ad infinitum. Every signified is actually a signifier in disguise. One never reaches a foundational basis upon which a "truth" can be affirmed. Indeed, it is Western foundational epistemology that deconstruction attacks. It is this endless chain of signifiers to which Derrida is referring when he says "there is nothing outside the text." It is a metaphor which proclaims that all understanding is merely metaphorical.[48] As Balkin says, "Deconstruction awakes us from our dogmatic slumber, and seeks to remind us that our 'truth' is only an interpretation."[49]

Richard Weisberg provides an excellent example of how a very basic provision of the Constitution might be deconstructed. Article I, Section 7, provides that if a "Bill shall not be returned by the President within ten days (Sundays excepted)" then the bill shall become law.[50] Upon close examination, the parenthetical words "Sundays excepted," become problematic. Now this provision is not as provocative as, say, the Fourteenth which contains loaded terms like "liberty," "due process," and "equal protection," but nevertheless, it presents interpretive difficulties.[51]

The "plain meaning" of this provision eludes us because it could mean at least either of the following:

1) The president has only ten days to veto a bill, unless the bill was presented to him on Thursday, in which case he may take an extra day the very end of the period (which is a Sunday).
2) The president has eleven days in any event, and sometimes twelve.

The originalist who believes that intentions control meaning is relegated to saying that this provision carries the *meaning* intended by its authors, and even though the constitutional debates are silent on the point, the meaning is discoverable although possibly not without some subjective bias.[52] The nonoriginalist might look for values or aspirations "constitutionalized" in this provision. He might, for example, "discover" that the framers assigned a religious significance to Sundays which would make the second option preferable.

It is important to note that the originalist and nonoriginalist methodologies both involve a privileging. There are several possible readings of the text, and these readings can take place in a multitude of different factual and legal contexts. However, the effect of the privileging that takes place is that some of those readings are correct or best, and others are incorrect or less than best. Therefore, the goal of interpretation under the traditional originalist and nonoriginalist methods is to separate the correct or best readings from the incorrect or less than best readings.

A deconstructive approach would look at the possible readings of the text, but refuse to assign any privileging. Deconstructing the provision will show that all readings are actually misreadings. Each reading is only partial, and therefore not "correct" because it depends on other possible readings. The first reading is deemed privileged because it is accepted in rejection of the second reading. The second reading is deemed privileged because it is accepted in rejection of the first reading. Therefore, neither is definitive. Moreover, because consideration may have been given by the framers to the heightened religious significance of Sundays if they intended the second reading, this automatically implies that its opposite— that the "Sundays excepted" carries a totally secular meaning— might have been in the minds of some of the framers. This reading would reflect the thinking of the framers that the constitutive group in particular needed a day of rest, not so much for religious as for "cooling off" or even private political purposes.[53] Each reading (the "signified") is only reflective of some other reading (the "signifier"); each value reflected in a reading is only reflective of some similar or contrary value.

The problem with this approach is that one is never able to get to the "true" meaning. In addition, as Jonathan Culler has demonstrated, my own deconstructive reading of the provision is done in a necessarily selective and ordered fashion. Therefore, my reading may be classified as a "misreading."[54] One is never able to arrive at a preferred reading; by definition, that is not the goal of deconstruction. The goal is merely to open up new possibilities of meaning.

It is not difficult then to see how deconstruction expands the possibilities of meaning for a particular text. In the Constitution, the more vague and obscure the text, the more expanded the possibilities of interpretive meaning become. So, is deconstruction of any help in interpreting the Constitution, or is it simply a nuisance device that confuses meaning? Many persons who use the word "deconstruction" regard it as no more than another expression for "trashing," that is, showing how legal texts, including the Constitution, are self-contradictory, ideologically biased, or indeterminate.[55] Some legal writers, however, have found deconstructive techniques to offer both a new kind of interpretative strategy and a critique of conventional interpretations of legal texts. J.M. Balkin, for example, explains the usefulness of deconstruction in the following way:

The purpose of the deconstruction is not to establish that any interpretation of a text is acceptable, but that the yearning for originary meaning . . . is incomplete and cannot serve as a foundation for interpretation. . . .

Deconstruction by its very nature is an analytic tool and not a synthetic one. It can displace a hierarchy momentarily, it can shed light on otherwise hidden dependence of concepts, but it cannot propose new hierarchies of thought or substitute new foundations. These are by definition logocentric projects, which deconstruction defines itself against.[56]

The Critical Legal Studies (CLS) movement has also flaunted the banner of deconstruction. CLS began in 1977 as an organized effort among many American lawyers to oppose the intellectual and political dominance of the liberal establishment. They seek to clear the ground for different and transformative ways of thinking about law and society. In its uncompromising assault on traditional legal theory, it holds that "legal reasoning consists of an endless and contradictory process of making, refining, reworking, collapsing, and rejecting doctrinal categories and distinctions."[57] Believing that contemporary law functions in a framework of bounded objectivity, CLS seeks to reveal the true state of indeterminancy that exists in political and judicial decisionmaking. Therefore, it explores new avenues of thought that will bring about a break from the trappings of modern liberalism. It is not surprising, then, that included in the eight hundred or so articles and books in print that can be grouped loosely under the rubric of CLS, many deal with modern literary theory, including deconstruction.[58]

In assessing the usefulness of deconstruction in interpreting the Constitution, it is difficult not to be skeptical of its potential for positive contributions for two basic reasons. First, the Constitution is a hallowed and sacrosanct document in American society possessing a number of deeply imbedded meanings which defy the deconstructive notion that a text has no determinative meanings. If the interpretation of the Constitution depends upon a deconstruction of each of its provisions, authoritative meanings would vanish. Turning a text upside down can be done rather harmlessly, and even fruitfully, when we are dealing with a nonsacrosanct text. Literary theorists and legal academics drawing from the well of literary theory often forget to make the important distinction between sacrosanct texts which carry authority and nonsacrosanct texts which do not. The sacrosanctity of religious texts, for instance, would not survive deconstructive readings. Such texts are deemed by many to carry *determinate* meanings.[59] In the same way, the Constitution, virtually from the moment of its ratification, has been considered a sacred text, the most potent emblem (along with the flag) of the nation itself. As Thomas Grey has demonstrated, in many ways the Bible and the Constitution are much alike. Just as Christians and Jews take the word of God as sovereign and the Bible as the word of God, so Americans take the will of the people as sovereign, at least in secular matters, and the Constitution as the most authoritative expression of that popular will.[60]

In considering the special character of the Constitution, it is important to view it not only as an object of interpretation, but to realize that it is also an interpretation of what its authors considered fundamentally important. Constitutional concepts such as the separation of powers among three branches of government, a system of checks and balances to prevent tyranny, and the protection of individual freedoms from majoritarian reach were considered fundamentally important by the framers and are now virtually sacred concepts in American life. Although interpretation of concepts such as these is complex, it is their institutionalized sacredness that blocks their deconstruction. For the deconstructionist, it makes little difference whether a text is viewed as holding all meanings, some meanings, or no meanings. But the Constitution has never been regarded as merely a hierarchically superior statute whose privileged status can be reversed and made inferior to inferior statutes or ideas so that all possibilities of meaning may be explored. Rather, the Constitution is widely regarded as having definite meaning — specifically, that it embodies the fundamental public values of our society.[61]

Owen Fiss has given a second reason why a deconstruction of the Constitution will not succeed. It is that the rule of law in American society depends upon the foundational "truths" embodied in the Constitution.[62] Interpretation of the Constitution, says Fiss, is constrained by rules that derive their authority from an interpretive community that is itself held together by the rule of law. Fiss is right. To hold otherwise, says Fiss, would mean that:

The great public text of modern America, the Constitution, would be drained of meaning. It would be debased. It would no longer be seen as embodying a public morality to be understood and expressed through rational processes like adjudication; it would be reduced to a mere instrument of political organization distributing political power and establishing the modes by which that power will be exercised. Public values would be defined only as those held by the current winners in the processes prescribed by the Constitution; beyond that, there would be only individual morality, or even worse, only individual interests.[63]

In short, Fiss is saying that if deconstructive techniques reigned over the process of constitutional interpretation, America would be courting anarchy. One can only wonder, though, if this is not what some deconstructionists want— a new social order in which there are only individual interests and no public ones, only voluntary choices and no binding rules.

It should also be remembered that judges who are called upon to interpret the Constitution are exercising social power. Literary theorists can espouse and practice interpretive techniques without doing real harm to anyone. The interpretive function of judges, however, affects lives very directly. Literary theorists need only interpret; judges must interpret and rule. Judges must make choices; but as Sam Setterlund has said, "one of the things deconstruction cannot do is to help with choices. Deconstruction can push right up against evaluation but never cross over."[64] Richard Posner, who has been described by one of his colleagues as the single most influential academic in the last thirty years,[65] and presently a judge serving on the U.S. Court of Appeals for the Seventh Circuit, also sees literary theory as impotent to aid judicial decision-making. "Law is a branch of government concerned with regulating behavior, and legal texts are tools in the government process," he said in a recent interview. "Literature, at least in present society, is primarily a form of superior entertainment, and texts are complex artifacts. Judges can command compliance; literary critics have no such power."[66]

No one claims perfection for originalism or nonoriginalism as theories of constitutional interpretation. But they both at least represent attempts to provide real answers to real problems in a real world. As interpretive theories, they lack the urbane and recondite vocabularies of modern literary theories, but as theories built on common sense approaches to interpretation, they both seek to give definitive meaning to the Constitution. Constitutional interpretation requires deciding upon a reading. Deconstruction does not, and maybe this is why deconstruction is inappropriate for constitutional analysis. David Couzens Hoy has said that "Deconstruction is a reasonable procedure as the practical attempt first to find the rhetorical devices that function to give the text the appearance of coherence, and then to show that since they are *rhetorical* devices there are other elements that disrupt this coherence."[67] Deconstruction may be well-intended in its desire to insure that the potential complexity of a text is not underestimated, but projecting it as a fundamental principle of understanding and interpretation is philosophical overkill — especially for a text like the Constitution whose interpreters must discover meanings, not disruptions.

If indeed Richard Posner is the single most influential legal academic in the last thirty years, we must hope that those who are now fleeing to literary theory in the hopes of finding assistance to interpret the Constitution will heed his advice:

The proposition that literary critics can point the way to solving the puzzles of statutory and constitutional interpretation is the falsest of the false hopes of the law and literature movement, while the antipodal proposition that deconstruction and other skeptical strains in contemporary literary criticism can demonstrate the futility, or the inescapable subjectivity, of statutory and constitutional interpretation is one of the hollower cries of the critical legal studies movement. The social function and the conditions of composition of literary texts are so different from those of legislative texts that the best interpretive methods to use on the one type are radically different from the best methods to use on the other.[68]

In the end, deconstruction scoffs at the idea that the Constitution has any meaning. This form of thinking is thoroughly at odds with the most elemental reading of the Constitution and with more than two hundred years of constitutional history. Such thinking threatens the social existence of American citizens and the nature of public life as it is known in America.[69] Deconstruction, then, has its functional limits; it provides no interpretive answers. Literary theory generally, and deconstruction specifically, fail to add much that is useful in the debate over how best to interpret the Constitution.

The traditional categories of originalism and nonoriginalism offer as much as can be reasonably expected of interpretive theories to determine constitutional meaning. Like deconstruction, they both have their functional limitations, but nonoriginalism must be regarded as far more accommodating to the changing needs of American society. Originalism provides interpretive answers that are too simple and too rigid; nonoriginalism is more flexible, viewing the Constitution as a document serving a society forever changing and progressing. Both theories look backward to the constitutional founding but nonoriginalism possesses the added dimension of looking forward to the evolving needs and demands of society. Nonoriginalism has stood the test of time as a common sense means of constitutional interpretation and will continue to do so—without the aid of deconstructive techniques—for as long as America has a written constitution that demands interpretation.

NOTES

1. Francis Lieber, *Legal and Political Hermeneutics*, 3rd ed. (St. Louis, Mo.: F.H. Thomas, 1880).
2. Sanford Levinson and Steven Mailloux, eds., *Interpreting Law and Literature: A Hermeneutic Reader* (Evanston, Ill.: Northwestern University Press, 1988), xx.
3. Quoted in Alfred H. Kelly and Winfred E. Harbison, *The American Constitution: Its Origins and Development*, 3rd ed. (New York: W.W. Norton, 1963), 205.
4. Stanley Fish, "Pragmatism and Literary Theory," *Critical Inquiry* 11 (1985): 454.
5. Robin West, "Authority, Autonomy, and Choice: The Role of Consent in the Moral and Political Visions of Franz Kafka and Richard Posner," *Harvard Law Review* 99 (December 1985): 384.
6. Richard H. Weisberg, "Text Into Theory: A Literary Approach to the Constitution," *Georgia Law Review* 20 (Summer 1986): 940. Weisberg is professor of law at the Benjamin N. Cardozo School of Law, Yeshiva University, and president of the Law and Humanities Institute.
7. Owen Fiss, "Objectivity and Interpretation," in Levinson and Mailloux, eds., *Interpreting Law and Literature*, 230.

8. Raoul Berger, "Paul Best's Brief for an Imperial Judiciary," *Maryland Law Review* 40 (1981): 36.
9. Arnold Wishingrad, "Literary Lawyers and Lawyerly Critics," *New York Law Journal* 194 (1985), 1-2.
10. Art Berman, *From the New Criticism to Deconstruction: The Reception of Structuralism and Post-Structuralism* (Chicago: University of Illinois Press, 1988), 208.
11. Jacques Derrida, *Of Grammatology*, trans. Gayatri Chakravorty Spivak (Baltimore, Md.: Johns Hopkins University Press, 1976), 158.
12. Raman Selden, *Practicing Theory and Reading Literature: An Introduction* (Lexington, Ky.: University Press of Kentucky, 1989), 88.
13. Jacques Derrida, "Deconstruction: A Trialogue in Jerusalem," Mishkenot Sha'ananim Newsletter, no. 7 (December 1986), 2; cited in Levinson and Mailloux, *Interpreting Law and Literature*, xx.
14. J.M. Balkin, "Deconstructive Practice and Legal Theory," *Yale Law Journal* 96 (1987): 761, 786.
15. Paul Brest apparently introduced the terminology. See Paul Brest, "The Misconceived Quest for the Original Understanding," *Boston University Law Review* 60 (1980): 204.
16. Michael J. Perry, *Morality, Politics, and Law: A Bicentennial Essay* (New York: Oxford University Press, 1988), 126.
17. Robert H. Bork, "Original Intent and the Constitution," *Humanities* (February 1986), 26.
18. Perry, *Morality, Politics, and Law*, 127.
19. Robert H. Bork, Foreword to Gary McDowell, *The Constitution and Contemporary Constitutional Theory* (Cumberland, Va.: Center for Judicial Studies, 1985), xx.
20. Perry, *Morality, Politics, and Law*, 127-28.
21. Ibid., 133.
22. Leonard Levy, *Original Intent and the Framers' Constitution* (New York: MacMillan, 1988), 349.
23. Perry, *Morality, Politics, and Law*, 133-34.
24. William J. Brennan, "The Constitution of the United States: Contemporary Ratification," *South Texas Law Review* 27 (1986): 434.
25. Ibid.
26. Alexander Bickel, *The Least Dangerous Branch* (Indianapolis, Ind.: Bobbs-Merrill, 1982), 39.
27. *Brown v. Board of Education*, 347 U.S. 483 (1954).
28. See *Wolfe v. Colorado*, 338 U.S. 25 (1949), holding that the Constitution does not require the exclusion of illegally obtained evidence in state proceedings, but which was overruled by *Mapp v. Ohio*, 367 U.S. 643 (1961), where the Court held that the exclusionary rule applies to states.

29. See *Betts v. Brady*, 316 U.S. 455 (1942), where it was held that the Constitution does not require the provision of counsel to defendants in state proceedings, but which was overruled by *Gideon v. Wainright*, 372 U.S. 335 (1963).

30. See *Engle v. Vitale*, 370 U.S. 421 (1962), where the Court invalidated public school prayers. But see *Lemon v. Kurtzman*, 403 U.S. 602 (1971), articulating guidelines for when aid to sectarian schools violates the Establishment Clause.

31. See *Griswold v. Connecticut*, 38 U.S. 479 (1965), holding that the right to privacy includes a married couple's use of contraceptives; *Roe v. Wade*, 410 U.S. 413 (1973) (right to privacy includes a woman's right to terminate an abortion).

32. See Charles Fairman, "Does the Fourteenth Amendment Incorporate the Bill of Rights?: The Original Understanding," *Stanford Law Review* 2 (1949): 5 (arguing that the framers of the Fourteenth Amendment did not intend to apply the Bill of Rights to the States).

33. Erwin Chemerinsky, *Interpreting the Constitution* (New York: Praeger, 1987), 1.

34. Ibid., 6-11.

35. Senate Judiciary Committee, S. 711, 75th Cong., lst Session. 13-14 (1937); quoted in ibid., 135.

36. *Roe v. Wade*, 410 U.S. 113 (1973).

37. *Griswold v. Connecticut*, 381 U.S. 479 (1965).

38. Robert H. Bork, "Neutral Principles and Some First Amendment Problems," *Indiana Law Journal* 47 (1971): 6, 8-9.

39. Robert H. Bork, "Original Intent and the Constitution," 26.

40. Raman Selden, *Reader's Guide to Contemporary Literary Theory* (Lexington, Ky.: University Press of Kentucky), 1.

41. G. Douglas Atkins, *Reading Deconstruction: Deconstructive Reading* (Lexington, Ky.: University Press of Kentucky, 1983), 1.

42. Richard A. Posner, *Law and Literature: A Misunderstood Relation* (Cambridge, Mass.: Harvard University Press, 1988), 211.

43. Ibid., 212.

44. Ibid.

45. Ibid.

46. Balkin, "Deconstructive Practice," 747.

47. Derrida, *Of Grammatology*, 3, 10-18.

48. Ibid., 158.

49. Balkin, "Deconstructive Practice," 761.

50. U.S. Constitution, Art. 1, Sec. 7, clause 2.

51. Richard Weisberg, "On the Use and Abuse of Nietzsche for Modern Constitutional Theory," in Levinson and Mailloux, eds., *Interpreting Law and Literature*, 189.

52. Walter Benn Michaels, "Response to Perry and Simon," *Southern California Law Review* 58 (1985): 673-675.

53. One recent history of the Constitutional Convention makes clear that Sundays were often used to negotiate crucial compromises: See Christopher Collier and James Lincoln Collier, *Decision in Philadelphia* (New York: Random House, 1986): 94-95.

54. Jonathan Culler, *On Deconstruction: Theory and Criticism after Structuralism* (London: Routledge and Kegan Paul, 1983), 176.

55. For example, Girardeau A. Spann, "Deconstructing the Legislative Veto," *Minnesota Law Review* 68 (1984) 473, where the author associates deconstruction with the general project of demonstrating that legal reasoning is indeterminate.

56. Balkin, "Deconstructive Practice and Legal Theory," 785-86.

57. Alan C. Hutchinson, ed., *Critical Legal Studies* (Totowa, N.J.: Rowman and Littlefield), 4.

58. See, for example: Clare Dalton, "An Essay in the Deconstruction of Contrast Doctrine"; Mark Tushnet, "Following the Rules Laid Down: A Critique of Interpretivism and Neutral Principles"; and Catherine MacKinnon, "Feminism, Marxism, Method, and the State: Toward Feminist Jurisprudence"; all reprinted in Hutchinson, *Critical Legal Studies.*

59. David Couzens Hoy, "Interpreting the Law: Hermeneutical and Poststructuralist Perspectives," in Levinson and Mailloux, *Interpreting Law and Literature,* 331.

60. Thomas Grey, "The Constitution as Scripture," *Stanford Law Review* 37 (November 1984): 3.

61. Owen Fiss, "Objectivity and Interpretation," in Levinson and Mailloux, eds., *Interpreting Law and Literature,* 248.

62. Ibid.

63. Ibid.

64. Sam Setterlund, "Deconstruction: Persistent, Pervasive, and Troubling," *Cimmarron Review* 92 (July 1990), 145.

65. Karen J. Winkler, "Controversial Judge and Legal Theorist Jumps Into the Debate on Law and Literature," *The Chronicle of Higher Education,* 7 December 1988, A6.

66. Ibid.

67. Hoy, "Interpreting the Law: Hermeneutical and Poststructuralist Perspectives," 332-33.

68. Posner, *Law and Literature,* 17.

69. Fiss, "Objectivity and Interpretation," 248-49. On the nihilistic tendencies of deconstruction generally, see Peter Shaw, "The Rise and Fall of Deconstruction," *Commentary* 92 (December 1991): 50.

9

Killing Compassion

STANLEY HAUERWAS

COMPASSION: THE LIBERAL VIRTUE

This author first became aware that compassion can kill while viewing a commercial film sponsored by The National Association for Retarded Citizens. The commercial depicted a couple looking into a crib. The room is dark and the viewer does not see who is in the crib. The young mother looks up and says, "Don't let this happen to you. Our baby was born retarded. Our lives are crushed and we do not know where to turn. Do not let this happen to you. Get prenatal counseling. Help us eliminate retardation."

The commercial was stunning. It had been developed with the best intentions. The National Association for Retarded Citizens thought the commercial was a way to mobilize support for research monies from the government to help find cures for retardation. Just as people think that cancer should be eliminated, so they believe that retardation should be eliminated as well. Of course, there is one difficulty. Cancer treatment can be effected without destroying the patient, but retardation cannot be eliminated without destroying the person who is retarded.

It is important to reflect on what could possibly fuel this extraordinary desire to eliminate the retarded in the name of caring for them. There is no question that the most compassionate motivation often lies behind the call to eliminate retardation, to help the old to die without pain, to insure that no unwanted children be born, and so on. Such policies seem good because we assume that compassion requires us to try to rid the world as much as possible of unnecessary suffering. Those born retarded seem to be suffering from outrageous fortune, cruel fate that, if possible, should be eliminated. Ironically, in the name of responding to suffering, compassion quite literally becomes a killer.

Nowhere is this seen more powerfully than in issues raised through the practice of medicine. For modern medicine has had its task changed from care to cure in the name of compassion—a "killing" compassion. For example, the recent discussion of doctor-assisted death, or what perhaps should be called doctor-assisted suicide, might be seen in this context.[1] Unable to cure those who are dying, one might think that the compassionate alternative is to help them to their death. Euthanasia thus becomes the other side of the medical and technological imperative to keep the dying patient alive at all cost.[2]

There is a kind of madness in our modern souls when we contemplate the overwhelming degree of suffering that exists in the world. How do we work to care for some when not all can be cared for? We thus work to save starving children knowing all the time that their survival only makes it more difficult to feed the thousands more being born daily in poverty. Thus, compassion perpetrates cruelty and we are driven mad by this awareness. Some in their madness turn to strategies that require them to sacrifice present generations in the hope of securing a better future for those that are left—all in the name of compassion. The philosophical name we give to this compassion as an ethical alternative is sometimes called utilitarianism.[3] Even though utilitarianism is often thought to be a radical secular philosophical alternative, it can be seen as a form of Christianity gone mad. For the utilitarian is radically self-denying exactly to the extent that the consistent utilitarian gives himself or those near him no more value than anyone else. So each person is equal to every other person— that is, each one is but another unit seeking to maximize his self-interest. Utilitarians, with the greatest compassion, are thus willing to sacrifice some, which may include themselves, so that the greater number may flourish. Of course it is difficult to know who counts as the greater number and over what time sequence.

Confronted with this kind of killing compassion, one is tempted to quite literally kill compassion. Years ago this author published an article called "Love's Not All You Need"[4] which in part was an attack on those who construe the nature of the Christian moral life primarily in terms of love. When compassion becomes the overriding virtue, linked with liberal political practice, it cannot help but be destructive. As Oliver O'Donovan observes in his book, *Begotten or Made?*, "Compassion is the virtue of being moved to action by the sight of suffering— that is to say, by the infringement of passive freedoms. It is a virtue that circumvents thought, since it prompts us immediately to action. It is a virtue that presupposes that an answer has already been found to the question 'what needs to be done?,' a virtue of motivation rather than of reasoning. As such it is the appropriate virtue for a liberal revolution, which requires no independent thinking about the object of morality, only a very strong motivation to its practice."[5]

It is not this author's intention to try to defeat the over-determined emphasis on compassion by pointing to the negative results in societies like our own. There is no question that charity is, in Aquinas phrase, the form of all virtues.[6] But that charity is first and foremost disciplined by the witness of our God who would have us die, yea even have our children die, rather than to live unworthily.[7] Therefore, Christians are formed by a harsh and dreadful love, but one we think truthful, rather than the generalized forms of sentimentality that we call compassion.

To call attention to compassion as the central norm and virtue that characterizes our lives is a way to help us locate those stories that hold us captive.[8] For there can be no question that the generalized commitment to compassion characteristic of enlightenment societies forms the Christian as well as the non-Christian soul. One way of putting this is to say that today we are all liberals. We are all liberals because we have no choice but to be liberals.

It was the project of modernity to create social orders that would produce something called the free individual. The powerful institution of the division of labor makes it almost impossible to escape the fate of being an individual whose sole moral focus is that of compassion. Put quite simply, the story of modernity is that one's only story is the story chosen when one has no story. Thus the modern presumption that a person never be held responsible for commitments which were not freely chosen even if, at the time, that person thought that he was freely choosing. Compassion and the creation of compassionate societies try to make it possible for each person in a society of individuals to have the social, economic, and political status to choose who he wants to be. The project of liberal societies is to make freedom of choice a necessity. Thus a successful liberal order achieves the goal of making freedom the fate of each individual.

That, of course, creates the peculiar form of self-deception at the heart of the modern project. For ironically, what liberal societies cannot acknowledge is that we did not choose the story that we should have no story except the story we have chosen from the position where we had no story. Therefore, modern liberal societies cannot acknowledge that they are coercive since they derive their legitimation from the presumption that no one, if he has appropriate social and economic power, is coerced to be a member of such social orders. Our task, our social idealism, is now to work for societies where everyone has the economic power to be whatever he or she wants.[9]

This compassionate ideal renders problematic some of our most basic practices as they cannot help but appear unintelligible as liberal and compassionate grounds for ordering our behavior as human beings. For example, at the University of Notre Dame, where this author once taught, part of the regular offerings in the theology department was a course on marriage. I did not want to miss the opportunity to teach such a course, but I knew that my approach would be a disappointment for both the parents who wanted their children to take the course as well as the students that took it. For I knew that they would want the course taught from the perspective of how to do marriage and I could only teach the course from the perspective of why anyone would want to. Marriage for Christians, after all, is not a necessity since we believe our lives as Christians do not require marriage since the true family is now the Church.[10]

However, trying to satisfy as many people as possible, I knew that students had been sent to Notre Dame because it had the reputation of being a relatively conservative school. By conservative most meant that students at Notre Dame would be taught some absolutes. Not wanting to disappoint those expectations I always taught what I called Hauerwas's law: you always marry the wrong person. Though such a law sounds cynical, it is not in fact meant to be since it is also reversible: you also always marry the right person.

I did not teach Hauerwas's law simply to challenge the romantic conceptions of marriage shared by both my students and their parents. Rather, I taught Hauerwas's law to challenge some of the basic liberal presuppositions I thought were destroying the very notion of marriage as a Christian institution and practice. For it is the peculiar sensibility of modernity to think that if our marriages have gone bad it is because we did not know what we were doing when we "chose" the person we married. If we just become more intelligent and more thoughtful we will surely get it right the second time.

The anomaly behind this set of presumptions is that one could ever realize what one was doing when one got married. It is this author's opinion that the wisdom of the Christian tradition has been that the church witnesses a couple's marriage, not because it thinks it knows what the couple is doing, but because it does not. That is why Christians should insist that marriage should be witnessed in the church by people who will hold the couple to their marriage vows. Marriage provides the set of practices and expectations that allow husband and wife over a lifetime to name their lives together as love. Without the time that fidelity in marriage creates there is no possibility of love.

Of course, the other anomaly behind the liberal presuppositions about marriage has to do with the way that family members feel about one another. Family life creates certain duties that are sometimes undesirable. Why, for example, should people be responsible for other people who they did not choose to become part of their lives? Children, for example, eventually discover that their parents are simply given to them and they are stuck with them and in being so stuck, they learn that their lives are not their own. The same can often be said for parents and the feelings they have for their children. Yet it is exactly such limits that the compassionate imperative of liberalism to create a society where we are freed from such "fate" renders problematic.

That is why liberal compassion has so much difficulty understanding why we may have obligations to near neighbors who come in the form of our children in a manner that those obligations cannot be overridden for the good of future generations.[11] Of course, the kind of obligation we have to our own children does not mean that they can have computers while children in Somalia are starving. The difficulty we face, however, is that we do not know how to say or express our care for children in Somalia without underwriting the liberal project of compassion. We thus throw up our hands acknowledging that if we cannot do everything necessary to make the world free of starving children then we might as well do nothing.

Failing to meet the demands of compassion leads many to adopt the other virtue of modernity—cynicism. It is odd to think of cynicism as a virtue, but it is at the heart of the liberal moral project. For in the absence of any agreed upon goods people are forced to create their own values. The difficulty is that most people do not trust the values they have chosen exactly because they have chosen them. So they adopt a cynical stance toward their own and others' project; that is, they believe that they must always preserve their autonomy by being able to step back from their engagements by describing them as self-interested pursuits. That is why people are so hesitant to ask others, and in particular their own children, to make sacrifices for their convictions.[12]

Perhaps no place is this particular set of virtues better exhibited than in the area of education. The task of education in most liberal societies becomes that of providing information for students to "make up their own minds." The most feared perversion of such education is called indoctrination. It never seems to occur to us that in the name of respecting students' individual desires, our educators indoctrinate them to believe that their own individual desires should matter. Any education that is worthy is obviously indoctrination. An inability to acknowledge education as such in the name of respect and love for the student is but a sign of one's corruption.

THE DISCOVERY OF EVERYDAY LIFE:
CHARLES TAYLOR'S *SOURCES OF THE SELF*

Rather than continue to describe the anomalies created by the domination of compassion in our lives, it is important that we attempt to understand how this has happened by drawing on Charles Taylor's *Sources of the Self: The Making of Modern Identity*.[13] Taylor makes some extremely acute observations about the discovery of the significance of ordinary life that are the necessary background for the ethics of compassion. By ordinary life, Taylor means "those aspects of human life concerned with production and reproduction, that is, labor, the making of the things needed for life, and our life as sexual beings, including marriage and the family."[14]

Taylor is not making the absurd claim that prior to modernity people did not love their children or marry for love. Nor prior to modernity did they value less their everyday work. People of all ages in societies have cared for their children, although what "care" meant obviously varied. It is not the actual place of affection that Taylor is calling to the reader's attention, but rather the sense of its importance. As he says, "What changes is not that people begin loving their children or feeling affection for their spouses, but that these dispositions come to be seen as a crucial part of what makes life worthy and significant. For whereas previously these dispositions were taken as banal, except perhaps that their absence in a marked degree might cause concern or condemnation, now they are seen as endowed with crucial significance. It is of course true that beginning to make something of them also alters these dispositions."[15]

Taylor notes that Aristotle managed to combine in his account of the eudaemonistic life two activities— theoretical contemplation and participation as a citizen in the polity. Yet Plato looked unfavorably on the second and the Stoics challenged both. At least for some of the Stoics the sage should be detached from the fulfillment of his vital and sexual needs. Taylor calls our attention to Aristotle, Plato, and the Stoics to note that in contrast to the valuing of ordinary life stand those forms of social existence that are intrinsically hierarchical. It is the life of contemplation and political participation, the latter often exemplifying the Aristocratic ethic of honor, that render the minor householder as inferior.

Taylor suggests that the transition he thinks so significant is when these hierarchies are displaced in favor of labor and production on the one hand, and marriage and family life on the other. All previous "higher" activities are now rendered problematic. For example, under the impact of the scientific revolution the intellectual project of grasping the order of the cosmos through contemplation is now seen as vain. Rather now the object is to engage in the detailed work of discovery. Accordingly, Francis Bacon reorientates science to be about relieving the condition of man, not understanding the beauty of planetary motion. As Bacon himself said, "Science is not a higher activity which ordinary life should subserve; on the contrary, science should benefit ordinary life."

According to Taylor, inherent in this new evaluation of ordinary life is a commitment toward social leveling. The good life is about what everyone can and/or should achieve. The elitism of the ethic of the gentleman, the ethic of honor, is slowly eroded in favor of the virtues necessary to sustain the life of commerce, the science that serves that commerce, and for the goods of work and family. Even, or especially, revolutionary thought such as Marxism has as its goal to find our highest dignity in labor and the transformation of nature in the service of life.[16]

Taylor argues that to rightly understand this transformation of the significance of ordinary life one cannot attribute it to the process of secularization. Indeed Taylor suggests that the origin of this discovery of the everyday came first of all from the Reformation. For it was one of the central points of the

Reformation to reject hierarchy and meditation. In particular the Reformation criticized the Catholic presumption that some in the corporate body of Christ could be more dedicated making them more capable of winning merit and salvation than others who were less so.

The rejection of mediation was interconnected with the reformers' denial that the sacred could be found in some places and times more than others— no holy objects, land, or people.[17] Salvation as now the exclusive work of God required the rejection of the Catholic understanding that the Church is the necessary mediator of God's salvation. The very idea that there were special places or times for actions where the power of God is more intensely present became the hallmark of those people called Protestant.

When salvation is no longer thought mediated then the personal commitment by the believer becomes all important. No one can belong to the people of God by a connection to a wider order that sustans a sacramental life, rather, one's wholehearted personal commitment is now required. Monasticism accordingly is rendered problematic. Monasticism flourished, says Taylor, when members of the church drew "on the merits of those who are more fully dedicated to the Christian life, through the mediation of the church, and because I am accepting this lower level of dedication, I am settling for less than a full commitment to the faith. I am a passenger in the ecclesial ship on its journey to God. But for Protestantism, there can be no passengers. This is because there is no ship in the catholic sense, no common movement carrying humans to salvation. Each believer rode his or her own boat."[18]

Accordingly the very notion of vocation changes. In Catholic cultures the term vocation is usually used in connection with the priesthood or the monastic life, but for the Puritans vocation becomes any employment understood as useful to mankind and imputed to use by God. "The highest life," notes Taylor, "can no longer be defined by an exalted *kind* of activity; it all turns on even the most mundane existence."[19] For Taylor, such a view of vocation assumes that the creator intends the preservation of all creatures: "Humans serve God's purposes in taking the appointed means to preserve themselves in being. This doesn't mean that we are called upon to preserve others at our own expense; it is no question of renunciation. Rather we are called upon to serve both ourselves and others as being equally humans and God's creatures."[20] Vocation thus is alleged to have intrinsic rules, determined by the order of creation or sovereign spheres, to which believers must submit as part of their service to their neighbor.[21]

Taylor argues that it was not accidental that the Puritan discovery of ordinary life articulated through a theology of work provided a hospitable environment for the scientific revolution. Bacon's outlook on science was, in fact, made possible by those Puritan presuppositions. Baconian science and Puritan theology equally "rebelling against a traditional authority which was merely feeding on its own errors and as returning to neglected sources: the Scriptures on one hand, experimental reality on the other. Both appealed to what they saw as living experience against dead received doctrines— the experience of personal conversion and commitment, and that of direct observation of nature's workings."[22]

Baconian science thus institutionalized the shift from contemplation as the goal of science to science becoming the means for humans to be stewards of God's creation. Accordingly, Baconian science served to legitimate an instrumental stance toward the world which, ironically, made science all the more powerful as it is now filled with spiritual meaning. Now our task through science is to gain rational control over ourselves and the world for the good of the world. Instrumentalizing is crucial to this approach to the world since we are constantly reminded to treat the things of creation merely as instruments and not as ends valuable in themselves. Taylor argues as a result that "the tremendous importance of the instrumental stance in modern culture is over determined. It represents the convergence of more than one string. It is supported not just by the new science and not just by the dignity attaching the disengaged rational control; it has also been central to the ethic of ordinary life from its theological origins on. Affirming ordinary life has meant valuing the efficacious control of things by which it is preserved and enhanced as well as valuing the detachment from purely personal enjoyments which would blunt our dedication to its general flourishing."[23]

It was that form of rationalized Christianity called deism that resulted from those developments. The Puritans stress to work for the common good becomes the Enlightenment presumption that there is a way of life which can conciliate self service and beneficence. Just to the extent that our service to the self can take a productive form, such service can be furthered without invading other people's rights and property. The Puritan presumption that one's purpose is to worship God is now translated into living rationally, that is, productively.[24] Instrumental rationality now becomes the avenue of participation in God's will. This is not an abasement of God's will to the status of a factor in our game, but rather it exalts our reasoning to a level of collaboration in God's very purpose.[25]

Thus, the affirmation of ordinary life went hand in hand with the notion that the very purpose of God's creation was for the human good. This took the form of a belief in the good order of nature. Miracles in fact had to be excluded not simply because the presumptions of an ordered universe required that they be eliminated, but because if miracles were a possibility then we were less sure of developing predictable sciences necessary for serving the human good.[26] Of course, as Taylor observes, to make the order of nature so paramount that miraculous interventions are excluded, means also history that is marginalized. The great historical events of Exodus and the Cross require that Christians maintain unbroken continuity with these moments through tradition. Taylor makes the point that "once the notion of order becomes paramount, it makes no more sense to give them a crucial status in religious life. It becomes an embarrassment to religion that should be bound to belief in particular events which divide one group from another and/or in any case open to cavil. The great truths of religion are all universal. Reason extracts these from the general course of things. A gap separates these realities of universal import on the particulate facts of history. These latter cannot support the former."[27]

What is extraordinary about Taylor's analysis is how it helps us see that the loss of a christological center for any Christian account of love is necessary, not because of science, but because of the moral presuppositions commensurate to the valuation of everyday life. If compassionate societies are to be created in which the value of each individual is thought to be equal to another individual, then the extraordinary must be devalued. The extraordinary, of course, comes in the form of extraordinary people as well as extraordinary events. But in the interest of creating compassionate societies, that is, societies that are driven by the imperative of technology to render existence as much as possible free of suffering, it is found that one must live in a world in which the ordinary reigns. Ironically, the story of modernity is that modernity was created by Christianity which then rendered its creator irrelevant and trivial at best and perverse at worst.

PATIENCE: THE CHRISTIAN VIRTUE

This brings us back to O'Donovan's worries in *Begotten or Made?* O'Donovan has seen clearly how the technological imperatives driven by the ethics of compassion can only end ironically in murder. What do Christians have to offer as an alternative to this set of events? According to Donovan, there are four things Christians can do. First, he says, Christians should confess their faith in the natural order as the good creation of God. "To do this," he says, "is to acknowledge that there are limits to the employment of technique and limits to the appropriateness of 'making.' These limits will not be taught thus by compassion, that only by the understanding of what God has made, and by discovery that it is complete, whole and satisfying. We must learn again the original meaning of the great symbolic observance of Old Testament faith, the Sabbath, on which we lay aside our making and acting and doing in order to celebrate the completeness and integrity of God's making and acting and doing, in the light of which we can dare to undertake another week of work. Technique, too, must have its Sabbath rest."[28]

Second, according to O'Donovan, Christians must confess at this juncture their faith in the providence of God as the ruling power of history. To do this Christians make clear their limits to their responsibility with regard to the future. The future is not an artifact which one can mold to his or her will. Rather, Christians must see that there are ways of acting that contribute to the course of events a deed, which, whatever its outcome, is fashioned rightly in response to the reality which confronts the agent as they act.

Third, Christians should confess that their faith is in a transcendent ground if they are to affirm human community at all. Here, O'Donovan tells us that "in our time the notion of brotherhood has broken up into two inadequate substitutes: on the one hand, the notion of bearing responsibility for someone, which implies care for the others freedom without mutuality of action, and, on the other hand, the notion of association in a common project, which implies mutuality of action without care for the others freedom. If we are to recover the mutual responsibility between doctor and patient, we need to think of their quality as co-operating human agents, in ways that only the Christian confession can open up to us."[29] Fourth, Christians should confess their faith that creation from beginning to end is made through the word which they call Jesus. Only on that understanding is one capable of acknowledging the kind of order that is rightly to be found in the world.

O'Donovan's suggestions for how we as Christians are to respond to the ethos of compassion are wise and profound. This author, however, does not think that they are adequate. It seems that O'Donovan's appeals to order and the correlative confessions in God's creation that sustain them are worrisome because it is doubtful that such order is knowable apart from the Cross and Resurrection. O'Donovan seeks an account of natural law that is not governed by the eschatological witness of Christ's Resurrection. It is not possible to write about *Resurrection and Moral Order* because any order that we know as Christians is resurrection. It is not denied that people are creatures of a good creator. This author simply suggests that Christians know nothing about what is meant by creation separate from the new order we find through the concrete practices of baptism and eucharist correlative as they are to Christ's resurrection.[30]

There is no way to protect ourselves from the ethos of compassion by appealing to the order guaranteed by God's good creation. It makes no difference whether it is called orders of creation, or sphere sovereignty, or common grace. What must be recognized is the ethos of compassion that currently threatens to destroy mankind will not be checked by appeals to the integrity of creation but rather by people who know that their lives have meaning only as they are called to serve one another through the body and blood of Jesus of Nazareth. Only such a people can know how to love some when not all can equally be cared for.

Albert Borgmann notes that our lives are characterized by a kind of addiction to hyperactivity. Since we believe we live in a world of endless possibilities secured through technology, we find ourselves constantly striving restless, for what we are not sure. Such hyperactivity creates, according to Borgmann, a kind of sullen leisure resentful of our inability to be satisfied.[31]

Borgmann does not think it possible or wise to deny that technology is now our "postmodern destiny." Rather, he suggests that our task is to shape that destiny through a recovery of the virtue of patience as an alternative to power: "When power prevails in its paradigmatic modern form, it establishes order on the ruins of inconvenient circumstances and on the suppression of uncooperative people. Regardless, power rests on destruction and remains haunted by it. Patience has the time and strength to recognize complicated conditions and difficult people, to engage them in cooperation and conversation. The powerful provoke envy and fear; the patient earn admiration and affection. By patience I do not mean passivity but endurance, the kind of strength we admire in an athlete who is equal to the length of a run or the trials of a game."[32]

Borgmann notes that such patience is required not only by our need to learn the limits of the land but by the frailty of our bodies which call for social and individual patience. Noting that this country is terribly confused about health care, he suggests that there is little hope of clarification about such matters "until we learn a common and, indeed, communal patience with the pains of fatal diseases, the debilities of old age, and the aches and pains of daily life. Only a shared understanding will encourage the individual to endure and society to agree on explicit and reasoned limits to medical intervention. More properly put, it is only when society becomes something like a community and the individual more of a member in that community that health and patience will be reconciled."[33]

Borgmann ends his powerful book noting that such patience is possible only through communal celebration. Christians call such celebration worship, believing that in a world of deep agony, there is nothing more important than to take the time to worship a God whose patience took the form of a cross.[34] Hopefully, if caring Christians learn to live out such patience, they might help themselves and others learn more wisely how medicine might be patiently ordered to care for the ill and the dying.

NOTES

1. That most of the victims of Dr. Jack Kevorkin have been women, this author does not think accidental. Doctors, even doctors such as Dr. Kevorkin, become priests of the new ethic of death, in which people are given the permission to die.
2. Daniel Callahan has acutely depicted the relationship between the movement toward euthanasia and the imperative for medicine to cure in his *What Kind of Life* New York: (Simon and Schuster, 1990), 242-43. For a similar assessment, see my *Naming the Silences: God, Medicine, and the Problem of Suffering* (Grand Rapids: William B. Eerdmans, 1990), 97-112.
3. I am aware that utilitarianism comes in many different varieties but I think the distinction between different kinds of utilitarianism is not important for the general point made here.
4. This article can be found in my book, *Vision and Virtue* (Notre Dame, Ind.: University of Notre Dame Press), 111-26. My concern with the overconcentration on love as the central moral concept in Christian ethics involves not only moral issues but also Christological questions. Often hand in hand with the concentration on love is a

correlative low Christology. For example, it is difficult to account for Jesus' death if all he was about was recommending that we ought to love one another. The concentration on love as the heart of Jesus' teaching is often associated with the ignoring of Jesus' eschatological proclamation of the Kingdom of God.

5. Oliver O'Donovan, *Begotten or Made?* (Oxford: Clarendon Press, 1984), 11.

6. See, for example, Paul Wadell, *The Primacy of Love: An Introduction to the Ethics of Thomas Aquinas* (New York: Pauline Press, 1992).

7. One, among many passages in William Willimon and Stanley Hauerwas, *Resident Aliens* (Nashville, Tenn.: Abingdon Press, 1989) that most angered readers was the suggestion that Christians might contemplate the death of their children as a consequence of their children's baptism (pp. 148-49). This seemed obvious to us given the language of baptism in Romans 5, but it seems today that most Christians assume that Christianity is about the project of making existence safe for ourselves and our children.

8. For some extremely illuminating remarks on the interrelation of theory and story-telling, see Ronald Beiner, *What's the Matter with Liberalism?* (Berkeley, Calif.: University of California Press, 1992), 10-14.

9. Beiner, *What's the Matter with Liberalism?*, 22-23, reminds us that liberal theory as well as social practice is various as well as interrelated in a complex fashion. He provides an adequate characterization by noting "liberalism is the notion that there is a distinctive liberal way of life characterized by the aspiration to increase and enhance the prerogatives of the individual; by maximal mobility in all directions, throughout every dimension of social life in and out of particular communities, in and out of socioeconomic classes, and so on; and by a tendency to turn all areas of human activity into matters of consumer preference; a way of life based on progress, growth, and technological dynamism. This liberal mode of existence is marked by tendencies toward pluralistic fragmentation, but paradoxically it is also marked by tendencies toward universalism and even homogenization."

10. For a more extensive, but still inadequate account of the Christian practice of singleness and marriage, see my *After Christendom?* (Nashville, Tenn.: Abingdon Press, 1991), 113-32.

11. In a series of publications, Steven Post has illumined this issue in an extraordinarily fruitful fashion. See, for example, his "Love and the Order of Beneficence," *Soundings* 4 (Winter 1992): 499-516.

12. This particular set of trade-offs creates what this author calls the Groucho Marx problems of ethics. Groucho Marx noted that he would not want to be a member of a country club that would have him as a member. Most people do not want a life that they have chosen.

13. Charles Taylor, *Sources of the Self: The Making of Modern Identity* (Cambridge, Mass.: Harvard University Press, 1989). For a more critical analysis of Taylor's book, see mine and David Matzko's, "The Sources of Charles Taylor," Religious Studies Review 18 (October 1992): 286-89.

14. Taylor, *Sources of the Self*, 211.

15. Ibid., 292.

16. Ibid., 215.

17. For a wonderful account of how the land of Palestine became holy for Christians, see Robert Wilken, *A Land Called Holy* (New Haven, Conn.: Yale University Press, 1992), 113. Wilken notes, "The narrative character of the gospels recording Jesus' life from birth through death indelibly imprinted on the minds of Christians the sanctity of time. For Christians in Jerusalem, however, the proximity of the holy places made possible a sanctifiction of space."

18. Taylor,*Sources of the Self*, 217.

19. Ibid., 224.

20. Ibid., 225.

21. In effect, vocation becomes the Protestant substitute for natural law reflection. Indeed, the natural law tradition in principle held out greater possibility for Christians to take a critical stance toward their behavior in "the world" than the language of vocation. Honor and duty became self-justifying norms that could not be challenged since there was no place from where they might be called into question.

22. Taylor, *Sources of the Self*, 230.

23. Ibid., 232.

24. It is not accidental, as George Marsden has documented, that fundamentalism drew on Baconian presupposition for their reading of the Bible. See George Marsden, *Fundamentalism and American Culture: The Shaping of Twentieth-Century Evangelicalism, 1870-1925* (New York: Oxford University Press, 1980), 112.

25. Ibid., 244.

26. No doubt part of the story also involves the increasing belief in progress as an end in itself. See, for example, Christopher Lasch, *The True and Only Heaven* (New York: Morton and Company, 1991).

27. Alasdair MacIntyre rightly argues in *After Virtue* (Notre Dame, Ind.: University of Notre Dame Press, 1984), 88-101, that the distinction between fact and values derived not from any obvious epistemological theory, but rather was a necessity to legitimate the authority of the bureaucrat. The latter depends on "expert advice" which correlatively depends on predictability which depends on the control of "facts." Without denying that human activity is capable of some generalization, MacIntyre argues that human

affairs are characterized by a "systematic unpredictability" that cannot be suppressed even by the supervising strategies of bureaucratic liberalism.

28. O'Donovan, *Begotten or Made?*, 12.
29. Ibid., 13.
30. There are obviously complex issues that cannot be adequately discussed in this context— or perhaps anywhere. Indeed, this author is confident that he rightly understands O'Donovan's position. At the beginning of *Resurrection and Moral Order* (Grand Rapids, Mich.: William B. Eerdmans, 1986), 31-52, O'Donovan rightly castigates those who would have us choose between resurrection and creation as moral sources. Yet his fear of "historicism" leads him throughout the remainder of the book to appeal to the created order for moral reflection. He rightly senses that the eschatological character of the resurrection in fact makes a kind of historicism unavoidable for Christian moral reflection. This is not as problematic for this author as O'Donovan since this author makes no pretense to think about the moral life for those who do not share in the baptism made possible by Christ's death and resurrection.
31. Albert Borgmann, *Crossing the Postmodern Divide* (Chicago: The University of Chicago Press, 1992), 97-102.
32. Ibid., 124.
33. Ibid., 125.
34. In *The Peaceable Kingdom* (Notre Dame, Ind.: University of Notre Dame Press), this author argued that patience, with hope, are the central Christian virtues given by the eschatological character of Christian faith.

A SELECTED BIBLIOGRAPHY

Anderson, Gordon L. and Morton A. Kaplan, eds. *Morality and Religion in Liberal Democratic Societies: Their Present and Future.* New York: Paragon House, 1992.

Baird, Robert M. and Stuart E. Rosenbaum, eds. *Morality and the Law.* Buffalo, N.Y.: Prometheus Books, 1988.

_____: *Pornography: Private Right or Public Menace.* Buffalo, N.Y.: Prometheus Books, 1991.

Bartley, W. W. *Morality and Religion.* London: Macmillan, 1971.

Bayne, David Cowan, S.J. *Conscience, Obligation, and the Law: The Moral Binding Power of the Civil Law.* Chicago: Loyola University Press, 1966.

Berman, Harold J. *Faith and Order: The Reconciliation of Law and Religion.* Atlanta: Scholars Press, 1993.

Bickel, Alexander M. *The Morality of Consent.* New Haven, Conn.: Yale University Press, 1975.

Cahn, Edmond. *The Moral Decision: Right and Wrong in the Light of American Law.* Bloomington, Ind.: Indiana University Press, 1955.

Devlin, Patrick. *The Enforcement of Morals.* New York: Oxford University Press, 1965, rpt. 1977.

Donnerstein, Edward, Daniel Linz, and Stephen Penrod. *The Question of Pornography: Research Findings and Policy Implications*. New York: Free Press, 1987.

Drinan, Robert F., S.J., *Cry of the Oppressed: The History and Hope of the Human Rights Revolution*. San Francisco: Harper and Row, 1987.

Elazar, Daniel J., ed. *Morality and Power: Contemporary Jewish Jewry*. Lanham, Md.: University Press of America, 1990.

Greenawalt, Kent. *Conflict of Law and Morality*. New York: Oxford University Press, 1987.

_____. *Religious Convictions and Political Choice*. New York: Oxford University Press, 1987.

Harding, Arthur Leon, ed. *Religion, Morality, and Law*. Dallas, Tex.: Southern Methodist University Press, 1956.

Hart, H.L.A. *The Concept of Law*. Oxford: Clarendon Press, 1961.

_____. *Law, Liberty, and Morality*. Stanford, Calif.: Stanford University Press, 1963, rpt. 1965, 1969.

Hauerwas, Stanley. *Suffering Presence: Theological Reflections on Medicine, the Mentally Handicapped and the Church*. Notre Dame, Ind.: University of Notre Dame Press, 1986.

_____. *Naming the Silences: God, Medicine and the Problem of Suffering*. Grand Rapids, Mich.: William B. Eerdmans Publishing Co., 1990.

Itzin, Catherine, ed. *Pornography, Women, Violence, and Civil Liberties*. Oxford: Oxford University Press, 1992.

Jaggar, Alison M. *Feminist Politics and Human Nature*. Totowa, N.J.: Rowman and Allenheld, 1983.

Meyer, Michael and William Parent, eds. *The Constitution of Rights: Human Dignity and American Values*. Ithaca, N.Y.: Cornell University Press, 1992.

Mitchell, Basil. *Law, Morality, and Religion in a Secular Society*. London: Oxford University Press, 1967.

Monti, Joseph. *Ethics and Public Policy: The Conditions of Public Moral Discourse*. Washington, D.C.: University Press of America, Inc., 1982.

Outka, Gene and John Reeder, Jr., eds. *Religion and Morality: A Collection of Essays*. Garden City, N.Y.: Anchor Books, 1973.

Peerenboom, Randall P. *Law and Morality in Ancient China: The Silk Manuscripts of Huang-Lao*. Albany, N.Y.: State University of New York Press, 1993.

Pennock, J. Roland and John W. Chapman. *Religion, Morality, and the Law*. New York: New York University Press, 1988.

Perry, Michael J. *Morality, Politics, and Law: A Bicentennial Essay*. New York: Oxford University Press, 1988.

_____. *Love and Power: The Role of Religion and Morality in American Politics*. New York: Oxford University Press, 1991.

Reeder, John P. *Religion and Morality in Judaic and Christian Traditions*. Englewood Cliffs, N.J.: Prentice-Hall, 1988.

Santurri, Edmund and William Werpehowski, eds. *The Love Commandments: Essays in Christian Ethics and Moral Philosophy*. Washington, D.C.: Georgetown University Press, 1989.

Tong, Rosemarie. *Women, Sex and the Law*. Totowa, N.J.: Rowman and Allenheld, 1987.

_____. *Reproductive and Genetic Technology: The Ethical, Legal and Social Implications*. Cambridge, Mass.: MIT Press, forthcoming.

Welch, D. Don, ed. *Law and Morality*. Philadelphia: Fortress Press, 1987.

Westermarck, Edward A. *The Origin and Development of the Moral Ideas*. 2 vols., 2nd ed. London: Macmillan Co., 1924.

Zillmann, Dolf and J. Bryant., eds. *Pornography: Research Advances and Policy Considerations*. Hillsdale, N.J.: Erlbaum, 1989.

CONTRIBUTORS

KATHLEEN M. BOOZANG is Assistant Professor of Law, Seton Hall University School of Law. Prior to joining the faculty at Seton Hall, she was a legal practitioner in the health-care field, representing numerous hospitals and health care organizations in relation to a broad range of isssues including AIDS, withdrawal of treatment, organ transplantation, child abuse, quality assurance, and consent to treatment. She is an active member of the American Academy of Hospital Attorneys and the Catholic Health Association.

DEREK DAVIS is Associate Director of the J.M. Dawson Institute of Church-State Studies and Associate Professor of Political Science, Baylor University. He is also the Editor of *Journal of Church and State*. An attorney, his articles have been published in law reviews and other journals. He is the author of *Original Intent: Chief Justice Rehnquist and the Course of American Church-State Relations* and is coeditor of the revised version of *A Legal Deskbook for Administrators of Independent Colleges and Universities*.

STANLEY HAUERWAS is Professor of Theological Studies at the Divinity School, Duke University. His work has focused on Christian ethics, political theory, medical ethics, the care of the mentally handicapped, and questions of war and peace. His many publications include *Visions and Virtue: Essays in Christian Ethical Reflection; Against the Nations: War and Survival in a Liberal Society; Suffering Presence: Theological Reflections on Medicine, the Mentally Handicapped and the Church; Resident Aliens: Life in the Christian Colony* and *After Christendom*.

MICHAEL J. PERRY holds the Trienens Chair in Law, Northwestern University School of Law. In addition to numerous articles in many well known journals, he has authored several books, including *The Constitution in the Courts: The Judicial Protection of Constitutional Rights; Love and Power: The Role of Religion and Morality in American Politics;* and *Morality, Politics, and Law*. He is a frequent lecturer in the fields of constitutional theory, jurisprudence, church-state relations, and human rights. He is a member of the Editorial Board of the *Journal of Law and Religion* and the Academic Advisory Board of the Center for Church/State Studies, DePaul University College of Law.

ROSEMARIE TONG is the Thatcher Professor in Medical Humanities and Philosophy, Davidson College. She is the author or coauthor of six books including *Women, Sex, and the Law; Feminist Thought: A Comprehensive Introduction; Reproductive and Genetic Technology: The Ethical, Legal and Social Implications* and *Feminine and Feminist Ethics*. She is a frequent consultant to various private and governmental agencies on medical ethics, health care policy, and women's studies. Her numerous articles have appeared in a wide variety of journals including *Academe, Journal of Social Philosophy, Healthcare,* and *Journal of Medicine and Philosophy*.

WILLIAM W. VAN ALSTYNE is the William R. and Thomas C. Perkins Professor of Law, Duke University School of Law. His professional publications appear in virtually all of the major law reviews in the United States and address virtually every major subject in constitutional law. He has appeared both as counsel and as *amicus curiae* in litigation before the United States Supreme Court, and in numerous hearings before various congressional committees on proposed constitutional amendments, on questions on separation of powers, on war powers, on civil rights and civil liberties, and on nominations to the Supreme Court.

JAMES E. WOOD, JR. is Director of the J.M. Dawson Institute of Church-State Studies and is the Simon and Ethel Bunn Professor of Church-State Studies, Baylor University. His publications include *Church and State in Scripture, History, and Constitutional Law* (coauthor); *Nationhood and the Kingdom; Religion and Politics; Religion, the State, and Education; Religion and the State; Readings on Church and State;* and *The First Freedom: Religion and the Bill of Rights*. Founding editor of *Journal of Church and State*, he is the author of more than three hundred essays in a variety of books and scholarly journals.

CALVIN WOODARD is the Henry and Grace Doherty Professor of Law, University of Virginia School of Law. His areas of special interest include legal history, Anglo-American jurisprudence, political theory and economics, legal education, and the moral dimensions of law. In addition to numerous law schools in the United States, he has taught at law schools in Germany, Taiwan, China, and England. His articles have appeared in a wide variety of scholarly journals and law reviews, including *Yale Law Journal, Notre Dame Law Review, Journal of Legal Education,* and *Social Work.*

DOLF ZILLMANN is Professor of Communication and Psychology and Senior Associate Dean for Graduate Studies and Research, University of Alabama. He has authored or coauthored six books, including *Pornography: Research Advances and Policy Considerations* and *Connections Between Sex and Agression,* and his numerous articles have appeared in a wide variety of journals, including *Journal of Experimental Social Psychology, Communication Research, Journal of Applied Social Psychology, and Journal of Sex Research.* He has been a frequent consultant to prominent commissions on pornography and public health.

INDEX

Abortion, 17, 152, 153-54, 155, 168, 178, 179, 223, 225

Ackerman, Bruce A., 72q., 98n.41q., 104n.62

Aeschylus, 101n.50

African Charter on Human and Peoples' Rights (1986), 57, 58

American Civil Liberties Union (ACLU), 118

American Convention on Human Rights (1978), 57, 58, 159n.2q.

American Declaration of the Rights and Duties of Man (1948), 57, 58

American Jewish Congress, 3q.

Analects of Confucius, 24n.12, 25n.20q., 25n.28

Andrews, Lori B., 178q., 187n.35, n.36

Anencephalic infants, 195, 202, 211n.37

Annas, George J., 183, 188n.54

Anthropocentrism, 72, 75

Anti-Semitism, 8, 81

Aquinas, Thomas, 9, 14, 22n.1, 25n.26q., 68, 101n.50, 243

Aristotle, 9, 11, 249-50

Atwood, Margaret, 181, 187n.45, n.46

Austin, John, 35, 40, 53n.11

Bacon, Francis, 250q., 252; scientific ideas of, 252

Balkin, J.M., 218, 231q., 232q., 239n.14, 240n.46, n.49, 241n.56

Barker, Ernest, 12q., 25n.31

Barron v. Baltimore, 160n.8

Bartels v. Iowa, 162n.13

Bayle, Pierre, 86

Beiner, Ronald, 258n.8-9

Bennett, William J., 20, 26n.50

Bentham, Jeremy, 35, 37, 38, 40, 43-5, 53n.11; Benthamites (English), 36

Berger, Raoul, 217, 239n.8

Berman, Harold J., 14q., 22q., 25n.31, 27n.49

Betts v. Brady, 240n.29

Bible, importance to Christians and Jews, 234

Book of Acts, 25n.29

Book of Amos, 24n.11q.

Book of Deuteronomy, 24n.8

Book of James, 24n.11q.

Book of John, 25n.30

Book of Leviticus, 24n.9

Book of Matthew, 24n.8-n.10

Book of Micah, 23-4n.7q.

Book of Romans, 25n.30

Bickel, Alexander, 222-23q., 239n.26

Bilder, Richard, 113n.102-104q.

Bill of Rights (United States Constitution), 13, 149, 150, 156

Boddie v. Connecticut, 161n.10

Bokser, Baruch M., 63q.-64, 96n.34

Bokser, Ben Zion, 63q.-64, 96n.34

Borgia, Cesare, 64